The Inheriting

Of the Call

Soli Deo Gloria

To the glory of God and the advancement of His kingdom. May He use this work as He sees fit, for without Him it would not exist.
To God be all the glory and power forever. Amen

Steven.

Thanks!

I'd like to thank all those that have helped me prepare this work, the friends and family that have put up with my overly-enthusiastic recounts of my thoughts and ideas and have laboriously read each chapter and rewrite without too much complaint.

I'd like to specifically thank my editors, Dad, Grandma, Grandpa, my brother Matthew, and Michael Wallace, (the self-proclaimed "Grammar-Nazi") for reviewing and analyzing the content and structure of this book.

And lastly, I'd like to give a special thanks to my original readers, the students in my Bible study, for their continual interest in this story.

Steven.

Cast of Characters

Heroes

Aaron White (aka Clay) – Eldest of the six children born to the White family who was given the ability to stretch and form his body into various shapes like clay.

Adam Holmes (aka Atomizer) – The younger biological brother of Jessica Holmes. Is equipped with an Osrian based suit that allows him to shrink, absorb impacts, move at nearly the speed of light, and possess superhuman strength.

Bethany 'Beth' Arable (aka NightOwl) – Younger sister of Mark Arable, and close friend of Mary White and Jessica Holmes who was given a set of removable Mygan wings and a GRID connection allowing her to phase through objects as well as enhance her hearing and night vision.

Charlie Maxwell – Assisted Rick Stevens in establishing the SOS Corps and the developing of the Earthian Defender Corps. Recruiter and training supervisor for Silas Harrison, Marcus Williams, and Titus Martinez. Coiner of the term 'GRID' to describe the mindvoice phenomenon.

Grace Sevecian (aka Grandma) – wife of Rykard Sevecian, grandmother of Timothy. Joseph, Jacob, and Samuel Stevens. Native to Kalmar and original owner of the *mal'ak* bow now used by Timothy.

Kara Green (aka Plasma) – youngest granddaughter of Damien and Dina Kyul who inherited his ability to produce and ionize specific elements.

Kevin 'KT' Harrison (aka Swift) – Younger brother of Silas Harrison and friend of Joseph Stevens. Received enhanced sight, hearing, and smell via the GRID and wears fingerless gloves equipped with Sangátian claws located above each of his knuckles.

Jacob Stevens (aka Arcade) – Younger brother of Timothy and Joseph

Stevens. Has been equipped with an armored suit than can transform into different 'modes' with unique abilities for each setting.

Jennifer Green (aka Jade Green) – Older sister of Kara Green. Inherited her grandmother's ability to regulate the production and formation of the element giadan.

Jessica Holmes (aka Safeguard) – The older biological sister to Adam Holmes. Is equipped with the *lahat* shield *Natsar* that can render her invisible as well as produce Cainium-strength energy fields.

Joann West (aka Catamount) – A close friend of Mary White with no siblings. A Sangátian based GRID Connection has been given to her that has enhanced her hearing, sight, smell, and balance. She also has retractable Sangátian claws within the fingertips of her gloves.

Joel Porter (aka Carpenter) – The eldest child of the Porters and close friend of Jacob and Joseph Stevens. Joel has been given the ability to mold and shape wooden objects and direct the growth process of living trees. Is also armed with a piece of Cainium-Wood, which is also malleable in his hands.

Joseph Stevens (aka Reverb) – Younger brother of Timothy Stevens; he and Timothy are responsible for gathering much of the interdimensional technology for the SOS Corps, the Defender Corps, and the Defender Discipleship Program. Possesses the ability to absorb impacts and disperse the force as vibrations and is a skilled hand-to-hand combatant. He also is able to produce various sound blasts of different frequencies and can mimic a mindsong.

Marcus Williams (aka Alkali) – Friend of Timothy Stevens and Silas Harrison and is a SOS Corps officer in charge of training the new recruits. Is capable of flight, firing unstable energy blasts, and of using that energy to move objects.

Mark Arable (aka Maestro) – Older brother of Bethany Arable, and friend of Aaron White and Joseph Stevens. Is capable of using a mindsong to orchestrate inanimate objects of any size and density within sight.

Mary White (aka SongBird) – Younger sister of Aaron White who was given a set of removable Mygan wings and a GRID connection allowing her to sing a variety of mindsongs that affect her hearers and stimulate emotions as well as produce a sonic-scream to disorient or deafen her adversaries.

Marie Daniels (aka Oceanica) – The foster sister of Jessica and Adam Holmes who has received the ability to produce water with various volume and pressure levels as long as she remains hydrated.

Rykard Sevecian (aka Grandpa) – Grandfather of Timothy, Joseph, Jacob, and Samuel Stevens. Native of Kalmar with his wife, Grace. Immigrated to Earth and established the SOS Corps with the assistance of Charlie Maxwell and was the inspiration for the Earthian Defender Corps. Originally possessed the *mal 'ak* sword that Timothy now wields.

Sandra Stevens (aka Restorer aka Iaomai) – the promised wife of Timothy Stevens and mother of his twin sons is trained as a nurse and capable of healing various ailments or injuries with her medical training as well as with the GRID.

Silas Harrison (aka Chopper) – Close friend of Timothy Stevens and older brother of KT Harrison; currently enlisted in the US Army. Possesses increased stamina and improved healing along with excellent combat, mechanical, and military skills. Is equipped with a jetpack, which is armed with various firearms and explosives, and technologically enhanced aviator glasses. Due to a combination of Osrian and Myathian tech the pack can transform and shrink down to a ring worn on a chain along with his dog tags.

Timothy Stevens (aka Pentecost) – Eldest of four brothers, the original Earthian Defender, and the leader of the Defender Discipleship Program. His most valuable ability is the way in which he trains and equips others, though Is also capable of speaking and understanding multiple languages, can produce and manipulate fire while being immune to the flames himself, can generate winds of various speeds and directions, and can change the air pressure and density of a given air parcel. Can also render himself and others invisible as well pass through solid objects under particular circumstances. Is skilled in the use of his mal'ak sword and bow as well as in hand-to-hand combat.

Titus Martinez (aka Firecracker) – Friend of Marcus Williams and Silas Harrison and is also an SOS Corps officer in charge of training the new recruits. Is currently based in Logan, Utah and capable of moving at superhuman speeds and can produce controlled explosions of various sizes and intensities.

Villains

Azzata Feli (aka Panther) – Former head of the Tekoa tribe of Sangáti. Is outraged at his past defeat at the hands of Reverb and the subsequent conversion of his family to Christianity. Possesses catlike reflexes and senses and wields retractable claws hidden in the fingertips of his gloves.

Gerard Fitzwillyam (aka Abafando) – An Arenean governor that is angered by Reverb's interference in his suppression and restriction of the Church. Is capable of suppressing or muting the GRID Connections of an individual and can render a person's joints and muscles immobile for a time.

Jaxson 'Jack' Harper (aka Switchblade) – Australian mercenary recruited by respected 'friend' Will Zalinsky. A skilled swordsman and marksman, with whom any sharp blade is a lethal weapon. Throwing knives, sharpened boomerangs, metal discs, and throwing stars are part of his arsenal of ranged weapons that he carries along with his melee blades.

Luna Coterel (aka Lunulata) – The younger sister of Mygan born Emmi Coterel. Has become embittered against Timothy Stevens due to his encouraging Emmi to join the Mygan Defender Corps which ultimately resulted in Emmi's death. Like her sister, Luna is capable of breathing underwater, changing her appearance to that of another individual, appearing nearly invisible, and can produce a smoke screen in which she can disappear, all via her mindvoice. Unlike her sister, Luna can also produce a deadly poison that is absorbed through the skin.

Zilvia Krezel (aka The Widow) – Originally an Osrian assassin hired to track down and execute Church leaders, she now seeks to put an end to the Christian Church throughout the realms; beginning with Earth. A well trained combatant, equipped with INSECT shrinking tech, and is capable of shooting spider webbing from her gloves and wields two daggers laced with a highly toxic venom.

Rodger Jones (aka Virus) – Simon Vaughan's secret contact within the SOS Corps. Possesses an extreme understanding of technology and the mindvoice ability to telepathically command various electronic devices and is the main designer of the Earthian Komplo's weapons and tech.

Simon Vaughan (aka The Sorcerer) – Once a Myathian Defender under the alias the "Illusionist" and a friend of Timothy Stevens, but is now a devout member of the Occult. The Sorcerer is capable of producing a variety of illusions as well as sorcery with the aid of his demonic 'guides'. Is the leader of Earth's Komplo.

Athaliah Shirazi (aka Acedia) – Was a major influence in pacifying the Myathian Church prior to the arrival of Pentecost. Has since joined Simon Vaughan in his attempt to rid the realms of the Church. Is able to poison the minds of those nearby with apathy and weakens their will, resulting in the eventual coma of those that concede to her mental suggestions.

William 'Will' Zalinsky (aka Catch.22) – An arrogant marksman, mercenary-assassin, and a lady's man; Will Zalinsky will do nearly anything for a price. Armed with his custom made .22 and .223 caliber firearms, he was recruited into the Komplo by Simon Vaughan.

Heed the Call

The voice of Yahweh goes forth into all the realms. Those that we know – science, ethics, history, economics, geography, language – and those that are unknown and mysterious to us – the realms of Mygas, Arenea, Kalmar, Myathis, Osria and Sangáti. Some call the former unreal, and perhaps they truly exist only in one's imagination. Others claim that their existence is required in order to fully explain the realm of Earth.

But Yahweh is not limited by human expectancies, understandings, or experiences. Yahweh's truth goes out unto all men, in all realms everywhere. And all men everywhere can hear His voice of truth, regardless of what they claim.

The question for us all is this: what will we do when we hear His voice? Will we ignore it and claim it is unreal? Will we passively listen and expect blessings because we admit His existence? Or will we hear His calling on our lives and passionately cling to His every word, not resting until we have fully fulfilled everything He asks of us?

This is the story of one who heard the call from Yahweh, chose to follow it, and inspired others to do the same. You may look upon this and dismiss it as merely an example of an overactive imagination. You may read this tale of mine and find it strikingly similar to your own. Whatever you may think of it, I pray that these writings will inspire you to heed the call of Yahweh on your life.

No two stories are the same, no two people live the same lives, and no two lives have the same call. There are many crossing paths and many similarities, but Yahweh personally authors every life that is submitted unto Him.

Will you heed the call?

Prologue

Six years ago I had walked briskly through the hallways of the SOS Corps Underground Base of Operations located just a few blocks away from where I lived. Carlos Ortega, the director of local adolescent SOS Corps members, had requested a meeting with me.

The SOS Corps is still the largest, most advanced, 'nonexistent' interdimensional information gathering agency. We've been able to maintain that level of excellence thanks to the efforts of the Defender Corps and the Interdimensional Alliance formed during the first stages of that project; a project that my brother, Joseph, and I helped get started since the first day of our recruitment into the SOS Corps.

I typed in the passcode needed to enter the conference room that Carlos 'Carl' Ortega had arranged to meet me in. As expected, Carl was nowhere to be seen. He was usually operating at unhealthy speeds and chaotically moved from one task to another. With all that high energy he often struggled to keep on task or arrive on time.

I took a seat at the table and waited, reflecting on what had brought me this far. I had joined the Corps at the age of fifteen – which was three years prior to this meeting and eleven years removed from today – and had gone through extensive combat and tactical training. The main objective of the SOS Corps was to take spiritual leaders and train them in order to form a combative force that would be able to spiritually and physically defend the Church during times of persecution. Spiritual maturity, not physical ability, had always been the primary requirement for joining the SOS Corps or pursuing the Defender Corps. For if the individual wasn't spiritually growing on their own already, then there was little hope that they would be able to endure the struggles of SOS or Defender Corps work.

My brother and I were the first trained Defenders sent out by the SOS Corps. Our first objective was to travel throughout the realms and establish reliable interdimensional communication and transit.

God had divinely called the two of us on our own unique journey. We both were delivered from the Negative Zone, though we still struggle with what we saw there. Joseph traveled to the realms of Osria, Sangáti, and Arenea, while I journeyed to the remaining three realms, Myathis, Kalmar, and Mygas.

God had used circumstances and friends to train us in how to use our GRID Connections to glorify Him as we established alliances with various Defender Corps Units and helped each of them establish an interdimensional SOS Corps base, acquired memory orbs that taught us how to create, use, reproduce, and protect the equipment that we discovered throughout the realms, and brought back with us technology and science that allowed the SOS Corps to increase its defenses as well as equip and train more Defenders.

That first team of Defenders was an oddball mashup of personalities and abilities, much like the Church is in general. My brother and I worked alongside three friends of mine, Silas Harrison, Marcus Williams, and Titus Martinez, and together we formed Earth's first Defender Unit.

While the Lord had used the original Defender Corps to stop a threat that would have been destructive to the entire world and gone against the Biblical prophecy concerning Earth, the group suffered greatly its first year and has never fully recovered. Joseph, Silas, and I always remained close, even after Silas enlisted and joined the army.

I didn't have much opportunity for deep personal interaction with Titus, but what little I saw I respected. At least, in his non-chaotic moments, which wasn't often, I was able to see that he had a genuine heart for the kids under his influence and important truths to share with them.

There once was a time when Marcus, Silas, and I were close; however an unexpected conflict between Marcus and myself had caused us to part ways. While Silas maintained somewhat healthy friendship I continued to have uneasy interactions with Marcus for a while after that encounter, despite the restorative measures that we had both taken.

After that first mission together, the Lord called each of us in different directions. As I said, Silas joined the army, where he still maintained an undercover Defender role at his assigned military base and over the years advanced to the position of army ranger. Titus was effectively involved in training the young men recruited into the SOS Corps locally until he moved to Logan, Utah years later and continued his work there, and Marcus pursued a more traditional 'superhero' role in order to save the world around him while also training with the young SOS Corps members alongside Titus, while my brother Joseph and I continued to follow God's call for us to disciple and train young people outside of the SOS to first spiritually, then physically, defend the faith.

To say that local SOS Corps had drifted from that same original goal in recent years would be to understate. I believe it had a bit to do with the change in local management.

Charlie Maxwell, my original overseer and trainer while in the SOS Corps, was transferred out and Carl Ortega took his place over the adolescent recruits while my grandpa, Rick Stevens, had assumed a support role in the adult branch.

Speaking of Carl, I said to myself as the door opened and a frazzled Carlos Ortega walked into the room.

"*¿Como estas amigo?*" he said reaching out his hand.

"I'm doing well, Carl. How are you?" I answered, standing to take his hand in a firm grip.

"Great, great. Sit down. I have something to talk to you about."

Which is why you requested a meeting. I would have to work hard to keep such cynicism from leaking out into my voice.

"It's about this Bible study that you've been leading," he continued, taking his seat across from me.

"What about it?" I had started the discipleship group nearly two years prior to this meeting in the nearby home of a family friend. That was back before my first mission as a Defender.

"I understand that you have gotten ahold of some tech and have begun to train these students of yours for combat."

"Yes," I answered cautiously, "the same tech that I helped supply the SOS Corps with. God equipped me with these things to equip others; the SOS Corps as well as these students."

"I fully support that, Timothy. But if the students don't fully join the SOS Corps then the combat training will have to stop. Several of the parents have refused to allow the SOS Corps to take part in their child's training."

Lord give me wisdom.

Though several of my students were currently participating in the teenage contingent of the SOS Corps – some of them even served as positive leaders for the other adolescents – I knew that a few of the other parents didn't trust any kind of corporation to train their kids, spiritually or physically, and I fully understood their position and had strove to earn and maintain their trust. Also there had been enough incidents under Carl for me to distrust the quality of training for those under him.

"I'm sorry sir, but this study has been, and always will be, under the direction of the Lord God. I see no Scriptural basis for requiring the parents and students to consent to this organization or any other; we can't simply demand parents to raise their kids according to our own opinions. We are part of God's Church, and as such, these kids can be trained to spiritually and physically defend themselves and those around them."

Carl put up his hands, "I'm fine with that, but if that's

the way you want it, then SOS will stop funding and promoting your study and training program."

No big deal.

Every student that I had taught these past two years had come to the study because of a personal invitation. The SOS referrals hadn't contributed a single individual to the Bible Study, and I had never received a cent from SOS for anything. All the tech and memory orbs that I would need God had given to my brother and me.

"All right," I said simply.

Carl sighed heavily, "Timothy, do you even want to be in the SOS Corps?"

I was taken aback by that question. Was Carlos actually asking me to leave?

"For a while you've been distant from me and have been walking in and out of the training sessions without paying attention to what's going on," Carl continued, "It's like you're not even here."

I didn't feel it necessary to defend myself to Carlos. I didn't bother explaining to him that I had been praying for the kids and instructors as I moved in and out of the training rooms and that I wasn't paying attention to the lessons because the elementary principles were being explained by him in such a chaotic way that had I listened I would have gone insane and left long ago. The only way I could stay was to ignore what was being 'taught' and pray that the kids could somehow grow from it.

Instead I swallowed and answered calmly, "I have felt God leading me in a different direction for most of this past year Carl, even before there was a conflict between us. And to be honest, I've disobeyed God's leading by staying this long." I stood and extended my hand to Carl. "God bless you and the SOS Corps, Carl." I added when he took my hand, "May God guide and direct you as you seek Him."

As I walked out of the door, I knew that I was walking away from a very large part of my life in favor of something even greater. Not only would my brother and I be fulfilling God's call for our lives, but we would be equipping others to do the same.

God had blessed us with open doors to affect the lives of twelve students, a privilege that I vowed never to undervalue.

I messaged those closest to me that I trusted with this information: my father, brother, and grandfather. I knew that they would only share what was going on with those that we all trusted, and I would need their prayers and counsel in the days to come.

"Pray for me. We're on our own now."

My Grandpa was the first to respond. *"Grandma and I are praying for you. Continue to follow the Lord. I love you, my grandson."*

"I love you too, Grandpa," I replied, as I continued to navigate my way up the stairs of the original SOS Base. *"Lord, let me never lose sight of what you've called me to. Please show me how to help You teach these young men and women to do the same."* I prayed as I exited the SOS Corps facility, ready for the Lord to establish a new one. I couldn't wait to play a small part in that work.

Chapter One

This had been one of the highlights of my week for the past six years, over that time the study had gone through many changes; we did eventually move from Mondays to Thursdays in order to make it easier for the kids to come, those original four students grew within the first two months into twelve regular students, which eventually grew to be a small church when my wife and I purchased a house near the university where many of the students attended and began to hold regular services there every Sunday morning along with the Thursday night Bible study and the Friday night Alternative – where we provided food, music, and space for the outcasts to find acceptance and God's love.

All of these events were followed by a training session with the students that I had invited into the Defender Discipleship Program, which used the underground facility beneath my home – which I had constructed to mirror the original SOS Corps Facility – and any students who didn't know about the Defender Discipleship Program would arrive safely at home before the others went down into the base below ground.

Tonight I reflected on that first night four years ago when I had first revealed to the students the new 'toys' that Joseph and I had been working on for them.

For the first year and a half Joseph and I had prayed over which students to invite into this program, and as we brainstormed on how to use the talents, interests, and personalities of the students as a springboard for our GRID programs and memory orbs, we prayed earnestly as we went over each decision and program. Many fanciful thoughts were rejected, and other ideas were revealed on the basis of our prayer life with the Lord.

Because there were times were one-on-one conversations or counseling would be needed – and as a safeguard against the students wondering off somewhere – I had made sure that each room and hallway had security and accountability cameras installed to ensure the protection of everyone using the facility.

During our exploration of the realms, my brother and I had been given the GRID programing for a variety of technologies and abilities and we were able to construct our own underground base of operations.

I can still remember the first time I saw a pair of biotech-wings that were completely controlled by the GRID in Mygas, and when I learned how to attach a GRID code to stabilized stone or piece of metal in Kalmar.

Joseph had received memory orbs that could use the GRID to increase the senses and reflexes of a person while he was in Sangáti, and in Arenea, he learned how to use the GRID to produce vibrations and even songs that could be used combatively.

Technology blueprints were converted into these memory orbs to allow us to program and create our own Myathian Automated Production Tech. Once a device is 'MAPTed' it could then be programed with the GRID memory orbs. This had allowed us to produce and combine any dimension's technology with relative ease.

Which meant that the Osrian INSECT suits could be combined with Sangáti enhancements to produce micro-sized super-soldiers or Mygan wings can be safely combined with advanced Myathian technology and programming, making them entirely safe and removable. The large *lahat* weapons of Kalmar can be resized into a keychain and back to its original size via Osrian Tech.

"God has granted us a unique position, Joseph," I had told my brother when we first returned to Earth. "He has allowed us to see and use the best of all that His children have created throughout the realms."

"Yeah, and we're going to need all that tech and know-how to keep those interdimensional bullies in line," he had replied, reminding me of how greed and revenge had stirred various men to pursue us across the realms.

One man, in his own realm, would be a limited threat if there were trained individuals who could recognize the threat and were capable of subduing it. However, in a realm without those same filters or defenses, a single man could decimate the globe. Without any Biblical prophecy the realms are in a place of much greater danger of destruction than Earth.

Whether the Disciples would primarily defend the Church, the Earth, or the realms would be up to the direction of the Lord for each individual. God didn't plainly reveal to me exactly what each of these students would do with their abilities, but the Lord had been clear with me on one thing: I needed to be sure that I continue to teach them His Word plainly, and show them clearly how to stay close with Him without allowing their gifts to eclipse the Giver.

That's why I had spent the two years spiritually teaching them before I considered giving them their 'toys'. I wanted to be faithful with what God had put before me. Actually, I wanted to spend more time training them before sending them out, but the world stage wasn't waiting for my schedule to come to pass.

I also made it my goal to ensure that the Defender Discipleship Program didn't end up disbanded like the original Defender Corps. To avoid repeating the errors of my past I strove to remind everyone that they were disciples first and warriors second; something that the original five of us forgot as Defenders. Submission unto God would be the only thing that would keep our gifts from becoming curses, our strengths into shortcomings, and our godly desires from turning evil.

Tonight was much like that night when the Defender Discipleship Program officially began; everything was set, I only needed to wait and see which students showed up.

While I knew the students preferred the time spent underground participating in an epic version of dodgeball – or as time elapse a more intense training simulation – my favorite part of the evening was spent before and during the Bible study portion of our night. Getting to know the kids and exercising my primary spiritual gift – teaching –made me feel more alive than anything else in life, because it was then that I was closest to the heart of God. A movie quote sums up my reasoning, "There is no better place to be than in the center of God's will, unless it's in His presence."

Tonight was actually Mark's turn to lead the study; we began a book-by-book study through the New Testament this past year, and I had asked Joseph and a few of the other guys to take turns leading parts of the study once or twice a month; tonight we would be in the book of John chapter 6.

Each of the students had grown considerably in those first years, and I grew right along with them. Each night I taught them, I learned something new about myself and my relationship with the Lord. Each one had their own strengths and struggles, and each revealed something in me. Tonight – as the kids fellowshipped in the kitchen over goodies my wife had prepared – my mind flashed back to the night when the Defender Discipleship Program had first started.

Chapter Two

After study that night, Joseph and I had taken the twelve down into the facility. "Now, before you guys play with the 'dodgeball' equipment I want to give you something."

"Presents? Really?" Mary White jumped up and down excitedly.

"Mary, settle down," Joann West chided.

I grinned at their exchange, "Now I'm sure that all of you have heard or seen reports of the two local 'superheroes,' Alkali and Firecracker."

Mark Arable interjected, "Oh man, I saw this video of Alkali stopping a gang heist."

"And Firecracker raced in and saved that kid from getting run down by a bus yesterday," Marie Daniels recounted.

"Yeah, and my dad was talking about how there might be a secret military project taking place in Colorado with another hero," Joel Porter added.

Beth Arable made the comment, "Man, those guys just showed up out of nowhere."

"Yeah, where do you think they came from anyway, Tim?" Aaron White asked.

Joseph grinned, *"Now what Brainiac?"*

"Now we let the cat out of the bag," I messaged back.

"Actually, I know exactly where they came from," I told the group before briefly recounting Joseph and I had been part of Earth's original Defender Corps.

"So you and Joseph used to be part of a secret team of superheroes with Alkali and Firecracker?" Aaron clarified after I briefly recounted the part that Joseph and I had in the Defender Project.

I nodded, "Yes."

"And that's how you got this cool underground base set up under your house?" Mary inquired.

"Yes," replied with a nod. "Part of the gifts that God gave me is to see exactly what abilities He wants to give others and provide ways for them to be equipped and trained accordingly."

"So what does that have to do with us?" Mark asked.

"God has shown me that He wants you twelve to train as Disciples: students and warriors to defend His Church."

That had produced the expected level of child-like wonder. No one said anything. Some weren't sure if they understood correctly, others struggled with the sort of internal battles that I started fighting years ago.

"It isn't because you are amazing dodgeball players that God made this decision; it's not even because we're 'super-Christians'. None of us are invincible and all of us need God for anything good to come out of our hearts. God has grown me in amazing ways as a Defender and as the leader of this group. God has used you kids to teach me a great deal about myself in these two years we've been together."

I had looked around the room that night, I can still recall sensing those feelings of self-doubt and insecurity still roaming the room.

Good. That'll keep them humble for the first few months at least.

"God has shown me small glimpses of the warriors, spiritual and physical, that he wants to awaken in this group. He's given Joseph and I the ability to equip and train you in that calling. The choice is yours…do you want to be His Disciples?"

Bernie loved his job; most of the time. Being a Las Vegas bartender had its difficulties, to be sure. I mean, there never did seem to be enough cash flowing for all the luxuries the city had to offer, but there was always enough to get by and have some fun along the way. He enjoyed being able to watch people mill about, and being an observant and helpful bartender had its perks too. Staying alive while earning some extra cash were at the top of his list.

Bernie looked around the room. It was close to empty at the moment, but the night hadn't even started yet. He was merely enjoying the calm before the storm, as there would soon be enough demanding and ill-tempered people to go around. Serving the well-to-do, high-society didn't guarantee better treatment, but knowing how to take their ill-treatment well is another reason why Bernie was still alive.

Here we go, Bernie thought as a tall man walked into the room. The man was wearing a very expensive three-piece suit and held his head high as he approached the bar. His jet black hair was slicked back and contrasted with his olive skin as his fiery red eyes combed the room.

Another stuck up out-of-towner. Wonder which mob family he's related to, Bernie wondered as he looked the man over for weapons. He couldn't pinpoint the telltale bulge of a firearm anywhere on the man, but that didn't mean that the man wasn't carrying or dangerous in other ways.

"What can I get for you, sir?" Bernie asked politely as

the man reached the bar.

The man sat on a stool at the bar and inhaled deeply, "I'm here primarily for information. Which is extremely fortuitous considering as unlikely as it is that this establishment has anything to offer that could compare to what I am used to. However, I will accept whatever you consider to be the best drink in the house."

Bernie was a bit taken back at the man's eloquence and his unidentifiable accent. It almost sounded German, but Bernie hadn't heard anything that matched it perfectly before.

"What kind of information?" Bernie asked, as he began to serve the man.

"I'm looking for a man," the man answered simply as he watched the bartender.

"I'm pretty good at knowing people, if they come through here that is. You got a name for me?" Bernie placed the glass down on the bar in front of the man.

"I was hoping that you would give me his name," the stranger answered, swirling the drink gently in the glass.

Bernie couldn't help but smile, "And how am I supposed to do that? I don't know anything about this guy you're looking for."

The man inhaled the aroma of the liquor before answering, "I'm looking for a man unlike any other, the kind of person that is only questioned by those who are eager to die, the kind of man that you cannot escape and you dare not anger," and with a warning glare that seemed to pierce Bernie's soul he added threating, "a man very much like myself, Bernie."

Bernie swallowed deeply. "Why are you looking for someone like that?" he asked mainly because he didn't want to get killed for flippantly giving that kind of information out.

"I am not a member of your dimension's police force, nor am I a man that desires to hunt down and eliminate this man. I care not what race or age the man may be; I only seek to align myself with such an individual for our mutual benefit. And I am willing to pay whatever amount of your currency that you request." The man answered before taking his first drink.

That got Bernie's attention. "I get to set the price?"

"Agreed," the man answered as he brought the glass down from his mouth, content but not impressed with the drink Bernie had served him. "I believe you have a saying here; I've written the blank check, Bernie. All you have to do is fill it out and give me a name."

"I'm not greedy, sir," Bernie answered as he began wiping down the already clean bar with a towel, "but times are tough."

"I've already told you, Mr. Quill, money is no object."

"Fair enough," Bernie answered, tossing the towel over his shoulder and putting his hands up. "The guy you're looking for goes by the name 'Catch.22'. He's an assassin for higher, and he's extremely pricey and full of himself, but he's the best there is."

"Can you arrange a meeting?"

"I'm pretty sure," Bernie nodded. "If you come back in two days I can let you know the details."

"All right, Mr. Quill," the stranger said, reaching into his coat pocket and pulling out a couple of bills and placing them on the bar. "You'll receive your five hundred million when the meeting is arranged and the rest after it has taken place. Have a good night," he said as he stood to leave.

"You too," Bernie picked up the money and then remembered something. "Oh wait! Who should I say is wanting this meeting?"

The stranger paused and glanced over his shoulder to answer, "Tell this 'Catch.22' that the 'Sorcerer' is looking for him."

Bernie squinted his eyes and held back a chuckle. "All right," he replied, as the Sorcerer turned to leave. It wasn't until then that he looked down and realized that the man had given him two hundred dollars for his drink.

"The guy tips well for information," Bernie said with a smile as he pocketed the money and cleaned the man's glass.

A thought occurred to him that wiped the smirk off of his face, "How'd he know my name? I never introduced myself to him."

Chills ran up his spine and his head continued to spin as he poured himself a drink. "And how'd he know the price I wanted for arranging the meeting? What in the world have I gotten myself into?"

Timothy Stevens

After Bible study we went down into the underground base for warm ups and training, just as we had done for the past four years since I had handed over the 'toys' to each Disciple and given each of them some basic instructions on how to use them during the future training sessions. Each student would go through a solo exercise with me each night along with participating in the group dodgeball game. I would usually have anywhere from fifteen to twenty ComBots carrying various firearms loaded with simulation rounds for the Disciples to defend against; sometimes in solo rounds and others as a team. We also occasionally enjoyed playing dodgeball with the guns mounted into the walls of the room.

Those ComBots were specially programmed combat robots made out of a silverish giadan alloy and clothed with a sleeveless shirt, running pants, and combat boots that were all silver in color, causing the ComBots to look like the ornament for the top of a second place track and field trophy. There was a danger to training with these things, because like animals, the ComBots were extremely intelligent and had their own limited personality; that was only the first of many similarities between our pets and these ComBots as both these ComBots and animals both desire to make their masters happy and can be trained to accomplish specific tasks. While the ComBots may be more versatile, easier to train, and much easier to communicate with than animals, they – like animals – are capable of becoming aggressive when mistreated. An abused dog will turn on its master, and so will a ComBot that is needlessly abused. Ultimately, we may have no other option but to 'put down' an aggressive ComBot.

I had designed the ComBots to be the sparring partners for the Defender Discipleship Program, which caused some confusion at first. "I thought you said that they don't like getting abused?" Mark had asked when I first explained the idea.

"They don't," I had replied, "but like a good natured dog they like to play rough every now and then. Just so long as we aren't ruthless or needlessly destructive." Which meant that as we trained we would only inflict as much damage as necessary. Like in a real life mission, the goal would always be to preserve as many lives as possible.

I had originally begun training with NightOwl and SongBird, the two girls that I had given Mygan wings to and I had wanted those that could fly to know how to do it safely without plummeting to the earth below. Because the wings were an additional challenge of coordination they understandably required more time for the girls to master; although Bethany's skill as a dancer had aided in her mastery of flight.

Beth Arable and her older brother, Mark, had always been very close friends with Aaron and Mary White and both Beth and Mark were active in the SOS Corps and had trained under and with Marcus Williams for a time and had grown very close to him as they had helped Marcus lead his sessions and also trained alongside the other SOS Corps adult members – myself included – over the years.

While the two siblings had much in common, Bethany was a much greater mystery than Mark when we first met as she had always been a bright and well educated young girl, with a genuine love for the Lord, and interacted joyfully with others, and yet her preferred style of clothing made her to appear untouchable and distant. Later, I would come to see her as a potential missionary to the cold and distant young women her age as she could pass through the emotional walls to those that wouldn't interact with the outside world and bring Christ to them. Though her dance classes had periodically prevented her from attending the study weekly she had always looked forward to breaks in her schedule when she could come and it was partially because of Beth that I was able to see my own hesitation in reaching out to others outside of my circle of 'acceptable'.

Four years ago I had taken Beth's personality and developed a physical manifestation out of it, coming up with the alias 'NightOwl'. I gave her a removable Mygan wing-pack and used a custom memory orb to stimulate a GRID connection that would allow her to phase through solid objects, as well as have enhanced hearing and night vision.

The wings that I had designed were large enough to carry Beth's slender frame and had a dark, charcoal gray color and were attached to a black leather breastplate that would strap onto Beth over a thin, yet shear-resistant, black, long-sleeved shirt while a black leather mask helped to protect her identity, and the charcoal-black, slip-resistant, leather boots would allow her to perch with greater ease.

The first ComBot fired its gun and Bethany phased herself to allow the round to pass harmlessly through her while she unfurled her wings and took to the air.

I reflected back to the first time that I had asked Beth to phase through a dodgeball as it came flying at her and the way she had sarcastically replied, "Yeah, because standing still while a dodgeball comes flying at your head is *SO* easy." While she maintained her knack for sarcasm, in the six years leading up to tonight she had learned to allow shot after shot to sail through her without worrying about being hit even as the room began to shift and blocks of the Cainium-lined walls began to mechanically move around the room.

I remembered the first time I had sprung that development on the kids. And the sarcastic way she had quipped, "You really like on-the-job training, don't you? A heads up would have been nice before you suddenly moved cement blocks into my way."

And when I had clarified that they were made of Cainium rather than cement she had sarcastically scoffed, "Oh, because that is *SO* much better."

Personally, I had always thought that I was being extremely generous compared to the way Charlie Maxwell had combat trained me; being thrown into the 'Rotating Gauntlet of Doom' was much more intense and sudden than anything I had planned for these kids.

Bethany flew about the room and would tackle a

ComBot into a wall before she phased harmlessly through it, or swipe one of their guns in order to hit one of them over the head with it and at this point in time she had grown past the initial sensory overload of the heightened senses and they had become a tremendous aid to her as she silently used them to avoid being hit by the guns.

She looked up and sarcastically called to me in the observation room where I and the other Disciples waited, "Can you make these ComBots any easier for me?" In case you were wondering, Bethany had greatly enjoyed sarcasm and had perfected it many years prior to tonight.

"I'm sure that can be arranged if these prove to be too difficult for you," I replied through the speakers. Since all the ComBots lay on the ground, I disengaged the simulation and added, "Nicely done NightOwl; go ahead and make your way up here and get some water."

As NightOwl flew up to the observation area where the rest of us were waiting I turned to Mary – the next student in line – and told her to head down into the warm up room as I reflected on the point that I had emphasized with Bethany and all the other Disciples that first night; that even if NightOwl never did anything extraordinary or amazing in life, she could still be a memorial stone to remind Bethany to reach out to those around her. It was a lesson that each of them took to heart and sought to live out as they trained and learned how to defend the weak and helpless.

"That was a pretty nice warm up," Bethany remarked as she took a seat on a stool with her wings folded tightly behind her and opened her bottle of water to take a drink.

"When are we going to start the mission simulations?"

"After everyone has had a solo session for me to evaluate," I replied with a nod. "We don't want anyone to strain themselves and pull a GRID muscle," I quipped referring to the possibility of overextending one's abilities too quickly and increasing the likelihood of a stroke. My wife was actually a key part in monitoring the health of all of us – myself along with the Disciples – as we would often get carried away and push ourselves too hard.

"You're doing great Bethany," my wife Sandra said looking up from her monitors and notes, "All your vitals are within a normal range and you seem to be adapting to your GRID Connection nicely. Did you have any questions before the others come back in?" We had established early on the routine of sending everyone else out after these solo sessions so that the Disciples wouldn't feel uncomfortable when Sandra shared their physical information with them or I talked with them about their spiritual or combat level. Another benefit was that there was some brief personal time with each Disciple so that they could ask questions privately if they needed to.

"Well yeah, actually I do," NightOwl answered reservedly. "I'm just not exactly sure if it's like completely a medical thing or if it's more of a GRID Connection thing."

"What seems to be the matter?" I asked rolling my chair closer.

"Well, I thought that the whole sensory overload thing was behind me – I mean, I haven't had an incident in years – but lately I've been hearing and seeing things that aren't really like what I'm used to. I mean…It's kind of hard to explain, but I've been like having visions and stuff and it's kind of weird; I thought at first that it might be some kind of increase to my eyesight and hearing, or something like that."

"Well there are some ways for us to figure out exactly what is going on," Sandra said softly, looking up from her notes.

"Do you have like a hearing test for me to take or something?" Bethany asked, wondering exactly what would be entailed.

"Yes," I replied with a nod, "And if it's okay with you I'd like to take a look at what you've experienced while Sandra runs those tests. All right?"

NightOwl nodded and took hold of my hand as I extended it. I had given each of the Disciples some basic training in the more internal and mental side of the GRID as far as telepathic communication and the sharing of memory orbs was concerned, but a few of the others needed some more advanced training because of their unique GRID Connections and I was beginning to think that NightOwl might be one of those students.

As Bethany shared her memories with me I knew exactly what she was going through as I had experienced similar dreams and moments as she was enduring.

Sandra had finished running the visual and auditory tests as Bethany had finished sharing her memories. "Your hearing and sight are obviously GRID enhanced Bethany as the range of the sound levels you can hear pushed my tester to its limit and the optical GRID cone count in your eyes is off the charts, but all of that is consistent with your last readings and the progress of your GRID Connection; I don't see anything medically responsible for what your describing Bethany."

"Is that a good thing?" Beth asked nervously.

"I believe it's a very good thing Bethany," I answered as I leaned back in my chair. "It means that God is growing you in a new way."

Bethany was worried that somehow her GRID Connection was going to become something that she feared and couldn't control and so she asked hesitantly, "What kind of a way?"

"First let me explain that I see two things going on inside of your memories, Beth. Number 1 is that you are having some visions from the Lord concerning what His will is in your life and in the lives of those around you. This is one of the 'normal' gifts of the Spirit that the Bible talks about and you can use it for His glory and the building up of the Church."

"Oh, yeah," Bethany remarked, "those are some completely 'normal' gifts talked about in the Bible."

Sandra chuckled, "Only when compared to flying through walls."

I had previously taught the group concerning the spiritual gifts unto the Church and that the GRID was one extension of the working of the Holy Spirit in our lives, and all of the Disciples understood that if the Church had as hard of a time accepting the 'normal' gifts of the Spirit as they did then it would be almost impossible for them to accept the

GRID which is part of why they were discouraged from sharing their knowledge of the GRID openly.

I then moved on to talk about the other thing that I saw in Bethany's memory. "The second thing that has been troubling you is the way that you can hear the thoughts and feelings of people and see their feelings. I believe that is a mental manifestation of your ability to see someone's hurt and hear their cries for help and you've literally been able to see and hear part of what's going on inside of the people around you; you're starting to develop the ability to sense their thoughts and emotions."

"So why don't I hear the two of you and what you're thinking?" Bethany asked in an attempt to solve the mystery of her GRID Connection. "Why has it been so inconsistent? I mean I've been like hearing bits and pieces of everyone's thoughts at random moments and it's all jumbled together, but right now with you two it's quiet."

Sandra took a seat and rubbed Bethany's shoulder, "I know that it's been very confusing and difficult for you the last few days and we will do all we can to help you sort this out."

I shifted in my seat and spoke to Bethany, "What you're experiencing is common among new mindvoicers and essentially you're picking up on the latent GRID Signal of the people around you as everyone has an innate knowledge of God and their thoughts can be detected by someone with the proper GRID Connection. Not everyone emits this signal and those that do are usually pretty inconsistent with it, and even those without a strong GRID Connection," I said motioning to my wife, "can learn to suppress this kind of random thought projection. I struggled with coping with this sort of thing for weeks myself until I learned to control it."

"So how do I control it?" Bethany asked a bit desperate. "I mean, can you just give me a memory that will show me how to control this? I can't keep going around and hearing everyone's thoughts and feelings or I'll go crazy."

I swallowed and nodded, "I can use my own memories to show you how I managed to find some control, but you'll have to figure some things out on your own." I formed a blue memory orb in my hand and extended it to her so she could view the memories. "Basically you'll have to learn to filter out the static noise of everyone's thoughts in order to hear only what you want; it'll get easier over time and you'll be able to pick out precise thoughts and conversations to listen in on."

After watching through the memories that I had shared with her and going through the steps to control her new abilities, Bethany rubbed the sides of her head and put her face in her hands. "Why does this have to be so hard?" she mumbled through her hands; she had thought that at the age of twenty that most of her growing was finished as she had begun to pursue a carrier as a dancer and was in a serious relationship in route to marriage. Now this new and unexpected growth spurt –and the growing pains that came along with it –had taken her by surprise and threatened to overwhelm her.

I smiled and patted her shoulder gently, "Not everything in life is easy Bethany, but the challenges that you've already overcome with the Lord can encourage you to carry on. Remember that first night when you asked me about your codename?"

Bethany chuckled, "Yeah, you said that it was a cool name that fit with my abilities and that the abilities were a reflection of who I was and what God could potentially use me for."

"Exactly," I nodded and looked intently into her eyes. "Your personality and preferences have always lent themselves to make you a missionary to the 'undesirable', 'untouchable', or 'inaccessible' people around you because of the way you could get past their protective barriers by looking like 'one of them'. I've seen you bring gifts, other people, and ultimately Christ with you through those emotional barriers as God gave you the eyes to see through the darkness and ears to hear the quiet hurt. None of that had been easy to learn or put into practice, but God has done amazing things through you Bethany. You can trust Him to keep doing what He does best as He takes care of you and guides you through life."

"Thanks Timothy; I'll keep working on controlling this new insight and see where God takes it."

Sandra hugged her from the side and encouraged, "That's all any of us can do as the Lord works in our lives, Bethany."

"Well, let's get this show on the road," Bethany perked up and looked down into the training room, "Mary's waiting for us to activate the ComBots."

Moments later Mary called up to us, "Are you guys

ever going to start up the ComBots?"

I chuckled and looked down into the training room and called through the speakers, "We'll get started now Mary; sorry to keep you waiting."

Sandra stood and went over to the door, "I'll let the other students in so they can watch."

"Thank you dear," I replied to her before turning back to Bethany, "Hang in there Beth, I'm sure that there can't be too many more surprises to go through."

"I sure hope not," Bethany chuckled and shook her head, "I don't think that I can handle any more weird developments."

"I think that you've officially entered the 'Land of Weird' so you better get used to it," I laughed as Sandra returned with the other students and the ComBots began to fire their guns at Mary below.

As the students cheered and enjoyed her performance, I couldn't help but feel the foreboding sense that things were about to get much more intense in the future.

Chapter Five

Surprise, AZ   Thursday, June 21, 2044

I parked alongside the curb outside of my grandparent's home at 3:00 pm Standard Grandpa Time, which means 2:30 pm local time.

"Hello, my grandson. How are you today?"

"I'm blessed Grandpa. How are you?" I replied as I had worked over the years to correct myself from responding with 'I'm doing well,' or 'I'm fine,' to remind myself that Christians are always doing better than just okay; we've moved from wrath to life, we are blessed beyond measure, and our faces and vocabulary should show it.

"I am doing fabulous. And how are my great-grandsons doing at home with my granddaughter?"

I smiled at the thought of the two twin boys that were at home with my wife Sandra and answered, "They're doing just fine, Grandpa. Thank you for asking. Is Grandma here today?"

Grandpa shook his head, "Grandma had some errands to run, so she won't be here for our 'G-time'." For a four years now we had been regularly meeting for some special time together, time that Grandpa called 'G-Time'. Sometimes I would bring one of my younger brothers over with me, but usually this was just some special private time with my grandparents whenever one or both of them were available.

"Grandma picked up some cantaloupe yesterday," Grandpa smirked and raised his eyebrows.

I grinned and moved towards the fridge, "I'll get out

the ice cream then." Grandpa had taught me to turn a cantaloupe into two perfect bowls for vanilla ice cream by cutting the melon in half and removing the seeds. If Grandpa happened to have a cantaloupe and enough ice cream for the both of us we would often enjoy this tasty treat; I still considered it to be his best food idea since we combined corn chips with cheesecake.

"So, how have things at the church been going?" Grandpa motioned to my usual seat on his couch and scooped a mouthful of ice cream and cantaloupe.

"Things are going well," I answered, carrying my cantaloupe bowl to my seat, "God's been blessing it and the kids seem to enjoy the study. I just don't know how well I'll be able to keep up with them physically; those football sessions with the guys this past week have been taking their toll."

Grandpa grinned, "Well maybe – and this is not to say that you're an old man or anything – but maybe you should let those young guys have their fun playing football and you just watch."

"We'll see," I chuckled, knowing that there was wisdom in those words but I also know that I won't be able to bring myself to say 'no' to these guys anytime soon. Besides, I do enjoy being able to tackle them every now and then.

"So how has that other situation been going? It seems a bit awkward to me."

He was asking about the situation with Carlos, who had been making some waves about the training with the students being an offshoot of his division of the SOS Corps and that he had authority over it. Grandpa was one of few people that we trusted with that kind of information and I knew that he was worried about us and that Carl's prominent position within the SOS Corps also concerned him.

"It is awkward. Carl has been fishing for information, but I have interacted with him enough to expect his current state of avoidance and information seeking."

"That's what I noticed. Have you talked with Pastor Juan about what has been going on?"

I shook my head, "You and Silas are the only two outside of my nuclear family that I've talked to about this."

"All right. I was just wondering. I haven't said anything to anyone, and I won't say anything to anyone. I'll leave that up to you, but now that I know, I can be praying for you. "

"I appreciate your concern and I value your prayers very much, Grandpa," I thanked him, taking a bite out of my ice cream and scraping off some cantaloupe from the edge.

"You're welcome, my grandson," he said taking a bite from his own bowl.

As we sat, we talked about different things. Grandpa used some of the things that he had gone through in Kalmar that were similar to my current situation as examples for me.

I started to think about all the things that the Lord had used him to teach me over the years.

Through him I saw the value of actively serving the Lord and being busy about His business. You would be hard pressed to find someone that worked harder or put in more hours at church than my Grandpa.

One thing that Grandpa and I are still learning together is the value in saying 'no' to good things so that we can have enough time and energy for God's things. Being available and sensitive to God's directing, even if that means handing over a good thing to someone else. That is still a hard lesson for both of us, but we're getting better at it.

Grandpa had been a source of comfort and joy in my life for a long time, and Grandma couldn't be forgotten either. She is obviously a very patient woman; just ask my Grandpa and he'll tell you what she has to put up with. Grandma's also a very insightful and diligent student of God's Word. I thank the Lord for both of them daily.

"So, back to your Bible study," Grandpa said bringing me back from my thanksgiving. "How is that other part going?"

"It's going well," I answered as I continued scrapping some fruit off of the edge of the bowl. "We just started the Defender training last night. The kids seem to be enjoying it, but at times I feel almost like the bad guy when I have to shatter their rosy picture of the future by telling them of the coming turmoil."

"Okay, I want you to remember something. You are not the bad guy, even though you may feel like it at times. You're actually the good guy. You know why? Because you are preparing them for when this nation – and even the whole world – goes to 'hell in a handbasket'. Because of what you're teaching them they will have a better chance of not only surviving that time, but also to help others along as well. Okay? And I'm not just talking about the physical combat training either. I'm talking about the way that you've spent these last two years or so pouring into them and helping them grow closer to the Lord."

He paused for a 'Grandpa Prayer moment' before he continued; whenever he was getting ready to say something important or somewhat controversial he would often pause and pray before speaking. Something that I tried to imitate when I could.

"And unfortunately, when I look at this day and age that we are living in now…and especially when I consider the times that we are going to be heading into…I don't believe that your disciples are going to have the luxury of simply using what you are teaching them as an insurance policy. I think it's very likely that they are going to need every bit of what you are teaching them. The fact is, I don't think that you will be able to prepare them enough for what is about to take place in this nation, and around the world for that matter."

Grandpa looked down into his bowl for a moment before turning back to me and putting his hand on my shoulder. "So no…you are not the bad guy here," he laughed.

I joined him in his laughter. "Thank you Grandpa."

"Well, you're welcome."

Grandpa helped to remind me why I started the combat portion of the Disciple Program, and why I first became a Defender in the first place. To be able to protect people in perilous times and to ensure that they would always be able to zealously follow the Lord in safety.

My only regret is that I didn't grow closer to Grandpa

and Grandma sooner. I thought as I got into my car about an hour later after we had finished and I was headed home. *Well, there's another lesson I learned because of Grandpa. Make the most of every opportunity and never take anything, or anyone, for granted.*

Chapter Six

The ComBots fired their weapons upward as Mary flew and rolled to avoid their shots and the aerial spectacle reminded me of the first night Mary learned to fly.

"I can't believe that I'm flying! This is amazing!" Mary had shouted gleefully as she had enjoyed her maiden flight around the ceiling of the training room.

Mary White had always been a bubbly little girl with enough joy and spunk for at least six people. And even all those years ago her voice was a beautiful gift from the Lord to praise Him in song. And she is quite comfortable using that gift to talk at great lengths about whatever happens to be on her mind. I had learned of the need for careful listening and strove to always display the joy that the Lord had given because of time spent with Mary during the group. Though she had now grown to the age of eighteen and her energy was more controlled, it was still a defining characteristic of the young woman as she began to study music and theater in college.

Mary's smaller size had made it very easy to construct the original set of chestnut wings for her that attached to a similarly-colored leather breastplate and were strapped over an aquamarine, shear-resistant, long-sleeved blouse. Mary's slip-resistant boots matched her breastplate, her fallow-brown pants were also shear-resistant, and an aquamarine mask would hide her identity from the world.

Once Mary had grown familiar with how to operate

her wings, I had worked with her to enhance her singing voice to new levels. Joseph and I had put together a memory orb 'songbook' of the different mindsongs and effects that Joseph had learned or experienced while studying with the Arenean mindvoicers. It had taken the past four years for Mary to learn and master how to use each of those mindsongs as 'Songbird' to directly stimulate specific emotions in people with different mindsongs; joy, excitement, sorrow, anger, exhaustion, remorse, confusion, peace, and frustration were all detailed mindsongs mentally but they all sounded as a single, emotionally stirring note that flowed out of her mouth. The mindsongs that trigger positive emotions had always been easiest as they fit better with Mary's cheerful attitude.

Tonight Mary was using those mindsongs to disable the ComBots while she avoided being hit by their attacks. Now robots do not exhibit emotions in the standard sense, however Joseph and I had programmed the ComBots with the ability to mimic human emotions and thoughts based on the GRID program they were running. Those that fired upon Mary were running programs that allowed them to pick up on her mindsongs and respond as an ordinary human would.

Several ComBots were staggering and struggled to remain upright as they were suddenly caught up in the soothing mindsong of slumber while others dropped their weapons and threw their hands over their heads and ran to the edges of the room as they began to cry and beg for mercy as they were overcome with a terrifying mindsong of fear.

Those that resisted Mary's mindsongs were subdued

as she flew around them and used the extra strength in her wings to throw the Bots around the room where they would land in a heap and seldom rose for a second round.

With a leap and a flap of her wings, Mary swung around in a roundhouse kick to take out a ComBot in front of her and two more standing behind her were also knocked to the side. However the final ComBot was also standing behind her and had avoided being swept up by her wings. Mary – who was under the impression that she had already finished her session – was quite startled when she turned and realized that there was still an armed ComBot standing not too far away from her.

There was a brief, high pitched screeching sound that filled the room and caused the ComBots to stagger backwards and Mary used its hesitation to leap forward, close the distance between them, flap and strike the ComBot in the jaw, lifting it up into the air as she flipped backwards.

When I picked up the sound I looked around the observation room and the pain etched on Bethany's face – along with a few of the other students, namely Joann West and Mark Arable who were more sensitive to sound — told me that I wasn't the only one had heard the sound. Even Joseph, who was nearly immune to sound waves, was rubbing his ears at the shrillness of the sound.

"What was that?" Mark asked, annoyed at the disruptive sound.

"What was what?" Aaron White asked, puzzled. "What are you guys talking about?"

"Your sister may be learning a new ability, Aaron," I

replied with a grin as I leaned forward to look down into the training room before messaging my wife about the sound waves that I had sensed as they disrupted the air molecules in the room below.

She moved over to a nearby monitor and answered, *"It seems like tonight is going to be a night of growth and change,"* she turned to look me in the eye, *"Mary just emitted a supersonic sound blast with her GRID Connection."*

I could feel my puzzlement spread across my face, *"Well, that's a surprising development, we'll have to talk to her about that tonight."*

Having finished with the training – and since she couldn't simply phase through the walls to get to us like Bethany had previously done – Mary headed up through the halls up to the observation room.

After the other Disciples had been ushered out of the room and Mary took a seat Sandra moved forward and asked, "How does your throat feel?"

Mary thought for a moment and shrugged her shoulder, which caused the wing behind it to move with the motion, "It's doing all right after the warm up; I haven't really had a trouble singing the mindsongs in training for a while now."

I thought back and remembered how singing through a single training session had caused Mary to come down with a bad case of laryngitis over the weekend, but the daily trainings and warm ups had strengthened her voice to the point where she could sing for hours without resting.

Sandra nodded and felt Mary's neck and into her mouth as she continued to perform her routine checkup. "Everything seems fine; no inflammation or redness that would cause any concern."

"All right then," I replied with a nod, "So how about we work on your voice then Mary?"

"Okay," she agreed happily before finding it necessary to inquire a bit more. "Wait, what about my voice?"

I smiled and did my best to explain to her what we had heard, "Your GRID voice emitted a high-frequency sound blast when the ComBot startled you that disoriented it and some of us were able to hear the sound up here; we'll need to see what kind of control you have over that supersonic scream for use in the future."

"Cool; so do you think it works?" Mary had asked, pulling a strand of her long blonde hair back behind her ear.

"I'm not really a sound expert Mary, but I've been given some pointers by some who are over the years," I had told her as Joseph sent over a memory orb of how he controls his different sound blasts.

I had touched her head and transferred those memories over to her and after reviewing the memory she concludes, "So more or less, what I need to do is mentally scream to produce the sound blast, and the longer and louder my scream the longer and more powerful the blast will be. Right?"

"That would seem to be the case based on what I know from Joseph," I replied with a nod.

"Okay," she had closed her eyes and prepared herself.

"Whoa, whoa, whoa! Wait a minute, Mary!" I had said, trying to save my wife and I from too extreme of an auditory beating.

"What?" She asked perplexed

"Because we're the only ones here you should probably go easy on the screaming so don't go as loud or as long as you can. Okay?" Sandra cautioned gently. "Just focus on control first because – like with your mindsongs – you'll want to focus your scream only on those you want to affect; you wouldn't want to deafen your teammates, now would you?"

"Right," she giggled.

I leaned forward and added, "Target a gentle scream at me – the same way you would a mindsong – while Sandra listens to see if she can hear anything."

"Okay," Mary replied, taking in a deep breath.

I nodded and braced myself – did I mention that she has a powerful voice? – my ears were ringing for the next several moments.

"Did you hear anything?" I asked my wife, once my ears recovered sufficiently from the assault. I could tell that I was probably shouting but couldn't do much about that

"No, darling," she chuckled; I could read her lips better than I could hear her at the moment. "I didn't hear a thing."

"One last thing before we call in the others," by now the volume of my voice had leveled out, even though my ears were still throbbing and ringing slightly.

"What's that?" Mary asked with a giggle.

"Well, Joseph says that you should be able to use your sound blasts to shatter objects," I explained. "Glass should be the easiest to practice on." I finished off what was left in my cup and set it on the table next to me. "Go ahead and focus your scream on the glass until it shatters."

Mary took another deep breath and opened her mouth in a seemingly silent scream, for although I couldn't hear any sound I could feel the disruption that her scream had upon the air molecules as they made a path from her mouth to the glass. A few moments later – after Mary intensified the strength of her scream – the glass shattered.

Mary put her hand to her throat and rubbed her neck, "Now that feels like the first night I learn how to sing the mindsongs."

Sandra rolled her chair closer and touched the sides of Mary's neck and asked to check her throat, "Your throat does seem to be a bit more agitated than when you first practiced the mindsongs – which is expected because the sound blasts are more intense – so I don't think that you should practice that much more tonight."

"Okay," Mary nodded, still massaging her neck.

"So when you're at home, Mary," I said in order to give her some homework assignments, "practice using your scream to shatter specific objects in the training rooms, or maybe even see if you can deflect a dodgeball; though I wouldn't recommend screaming at a person unless you're acting as their alarm clock," I added with a chuckle.

"Great; so you mean I can't scream at my parents?"

she asked playfully.

Sandra shook her head with a chuckle, "It's probably not a good idea."

"No, it's not," Mary answered, shaking her head emphatically.

"What is a good idea though, is to remember what I told you the first night you learn to sing the mindsongs: to worship the Lord whenever you sing, regardless as to what mindsong you're singing. As you sing, continue to think about the Lord; if you're joyful, remember where true joy comes from. If you're angry, let it be righteously instigated by sin instead of a wounded pride. If you're peaceful, remember the Prince of Peace is our God. If you're sorrowful, let it be a reflection of the heart of God for a dying world."

"Okay," Mary had nodded. "I've been working on that over the past four years and it really has helped me focus better."

"That's great Mary," I affirmed with a smile, "Now would you like to rest your throat for a bit and watch the others go through their warmups?"

"Sounds good to me," Mary answered, "I just have one question for you."

I smiled at her enthusiasm, "What's that Mary?"

"Will Amy and the others ever get these kinds of abilities and training? Can they become Disciples too?" Mary energetically asked about her friends that had also been attending the Bible study but had yet to be invited to join the Defender Discipleship Program.

I lowered my head for a moment and tried to explain, "Well Mary, some of them may be invited to join us one day, but I'm waiting for the Lord to reveal exactly who and when."

"We're not all called to have superpowers and fight in the war," Sandra added tenderly, "but we are all called to do whatever it is that the Lord calls us to. God has given me the ability to help bring healing to those that are hurting, but I'm not gifted as a warrior so I haven't forced myself into a role that God never meant for me to fill."

"I have been experimenting with different GRID Code possibilities for the students," I said to assure Mary that her friends weren't being ignored, "but for now I have been wanting to make sure that each of you are properly trained and ready before there are any more additions to the team and the GRID Codes have been coming a lot slower for some of the others at the Bible study."

"Okay, I understand; I was just wondering if you were planning on training others or not. I'll go let the others know that they can come in now," she concluded and rushed over to the door to let them all back in, picking up a glass of water to sooth her throat along the way. "Joel, hurry up and get down into the training room! It's your turn to get warmed up." Mary yelled teasingly as she opened the door and took a drink of water.

"That girl has no end to her energy," Sandra messaged me with a smile.

I shook my head and chuckled, *"No, she doesn't; hopefully it will be of good use to her in the future."*

Chapter Seven

"Hey, Joe?" I called for my brother down the hall of the Compound.

"Yeah, Timothy." My brother answered from the one of the training rooms. He was servicing one of the ComBots.

"I'm going to Connect with Silas. Can you just make sure I'm not disturbed or gone too long?"

"Got it. Make sure that no one kills you and that you don't have a stroke," he called back teasingly.

I smiled and rolled my eyes, "Right. Thanks Joseph."

"Anytime, bro."

I went back into the Conference Room and closed the door, and after sitting down in my chair and closing my eyes I pictured Silas in my mind as I mentally called out to him.

Silas was a close friend to me before he had joined the army and moved around the world as his assignments positioned him. He was currently an army ranger stationed in Colorado Springs for a few months.

"You have reached Silas Harrison. Please leave a message after the beep. BEEP. *How's it going man?"*

"I'm doing great," I chuckled. *"How are you, my brother?"*

"Can't complain. So how are things back home?"

Silas had enlisted into the army nearly six years ago. His father's training on engines had helped him in his job as a Chinook repairman, and surviving his two older brothers helped with just about everything else. He was a happy-go-lucky, redneck-cowboy. Before he enlisted he found a part-time job at a ranch and loved his job. He also enjoyed clowning around and making life 'entertaining' for everyone.

"Things are moving right along back here. The Bible study is growing and the kids are learning and being stretched. The Disciple Program started this past Thursday night."

"That's great man. How's Kevin doing?"

Kevin Tyler 'KT' Harrison is Silas' little brother. He is a rather scrawny fella, and he enjoys messing around with the SOS Tech. In a way, he was my undercover man inside of the organization.

"He seems to be doing all right," I answered. *"I've been trying to look out for him and everything. I think that the stress of maintaining the SOS equipment might be getting to him."*

"You mean that the fact that no one communicates with the tech-guys, that nothing ever gets put away, and that Carlos tries to intimidate you makes for a less than perfect working situation?" Silas joked.

"I guess you could say that," I chuckled.

"Go figure. So, has Keven joined you guys on Thursday yet?"

"KT hasn't stopped by yet," I answered soberly. *"He's still coming for our morning sessions when he can, but he says that Thursday nights are more complicated for him."*

Silas sighed, both of us understanding the difficulty he and his brothers shared at home, *"I worry about that kid sometimes."*

"Hey, it's a big brother's prerogative to worry, no matter how big our little brothers get, but God knows what He's doing. KT will come when he's ready and it'll be in God's perfect timing."

"I know. But that doesn't make it easier to do."

"Tell me about it. I didn't just say that for you, I was listening too."

Silas chuckled, *"So were you calling about something specific?"*

"Actually I did. My scanners have picked up the faint signal of several interdimensional doorways."

"So some folks from the dimensions are visiting Earth on their vacation? That's nice. Did they stop by the tourist booth or the gift shop for information?"

"I don't think they did. Whoever it is has put an incredible amount of resources into getting here as quietly as they can. I don't even think that I could open up an interdimensional doorway that would emit less GRID Signal."

"So these are sophisticated tourists." Even in his most serious moments Silas was still a comedian at heart. *"I wonder what their passports look like."*

"I wish I knew. That would make it a whole lot easier to track them down. An interdimensional traveler needs to be identified, either for their sake or for ours."

"Right. Some guy stranded in a strange realm with no clue how things work needs someone to show him the ropes. I mean, he might end up like you otherwise," Silas joked.

"Or maybe worse, he could end up like you," I teased

back. *"Or, these interdimensional tourists could be the power-hungry dictator type, seeking to establish a Komplo on Earth. Either way we need to find them."*

"Them? How many are we talking about here?" Silas was starting to get into business mode.

"I've been able to locate a doorway on each of the populated continents."

"And with the fact that they tried to hide their arrival hints to the fact that they might be the power-hungry dictator types.

"That's exactly what I'm worried about. You weren't supposed to say that I might be right." I whined jokingly.

"Sorry, but I think you might be right. Could this be a coordinated effort?"

"That's possible, Silas. It's also interesting to note that each of those doorways opened up to a different realm on the other side."

"So you mean that we've got immigrants from each of the six other realms wandering around on Earth? Do any of your contacts have any idea what's going on?"

I shook my head, even though Silas couldn't see me. *"They know that a doorway was opened, but they don't know by whom or for what purpose. They also detected some interdimensional chatter prior to the doorways being opened."*

"I think that there might be some moles within those Defender units," Silas said soberly.

"I think you may be right. That's the only way that they could get the technology needed for this level of

communication and travel. The question is, do we have moles on Earth?"

"Haven't you seen the little mounds of dirt in the lawn?" Playful mode was back. *"Seriously, Timothy, you need to be a little more observant. How have you survived this long without me?"*

"I've been doing just fine without you trying to get me killed, thank you very much. How is it that you've survived without me keeping you in line?" I teased back.

"All right," Silas chuckled, calling a temporary truce before getting back to business. *"So what do you want me to do?"*

"Keep your eyes and ears open. We need to try and find these guys and whoever their Earthian contact, or contacts, might be."

"Rodger that. Secret Agent Chopper is on the case," Silas said. I could almost picture him saluting as he said it.

"Just be careful out there, little brother," I replied; just before he deported I began to affectionately call Silas my 'little brother' and I tried to incorporate that into each conversation I had with him.

"Hey, don't worry about me," I could picture Silas spreading his arms out and smiling to blow off the danger he was in. *"I can heal from just about anything, remember?"*

While it was true that Silas did heal faster than the average person and could recover from other injuries that would kill almost anyone else, he was far from invincible; but at this point in time I had given up any serious thought of actually convincing him of that fact or that he should try and stay out of trouble.

I braced myself as I said, *"I'm going to have 'Swift' do some snooping around the different SOS databases."*

I could feel Silas' frustration; he didn't want KT put in danger any more than I wanted Joseph to be, but both of our little brothers had Defender aliases that would put them in danger.

I tried to reassure him, *"KT is the only one within the Corps with access to the computers and can get me the kind of information I need right now; he looks unassuming and nonthreatening, his job as a photographer takes him around the country to visit the different bases, and as 'Swift' he can take care of himself."*

"I know," Silas sighed heavily, *"but it doesn't make it any easier."*

"I understand," I nodded and heard footsteps coming down the hall. *"Joseph's coming. If we go much longer we're both going to have a stroke."*

"All right. I'll message you if I hear any chatter," Silas answered.

"Thanks. I'm praying for you, my friend."

"Same here."

"God bless."

"You too."

The connection was disconnected just as Joseph opened the door. "So how's Silas doing?" He asked as he walked in.

"Like the rest of us, he's worried," I said taking a deep breath to help prevent passing out. Considering that communicating in that way easier for me to accomplish, I could only imagine the GRID lag that Silas was dealing with right now.

"When are you going to tell the Disciples about the tourists?"

I shook my head, "Not until it becomes necessary. Hopefully, the tourists won't become an issue."

"Yeah, like that'll happen." Joseph scoffed.

I shrugged my shoulder. "In the meantime, how are those EMA Devices coming?"

"The shells have all been made, I just need for you to get the program from Antoine." Joseph answered. "You sure that you want to have that many bases in one city?"

I nodded, "The Disciples need to be able to go wherever God leads. That means that they'll need to be able to train and be self-sufficient. That way they can train more Disciples down the road. Plus, they may need to be able to get their families to a safe and defendable location quickly."

"Got it. Everything is ready mechanically," Joseph said reminding me that I needed to get the program for the machines to run.

I nodded my acknowledgment, "I'll have to contact Antoine later. I don't want to overdo it and have a stroke. I'll need the IDC up and running for that though."

"You got it, boss. Anything else?"

I grinned mischievously, "Well, I could use a cup of coffee right about now."

"Good, when you go to get yours can you get one for me too?" Joseph teased as he quickly left the room.

"Sure thing, bro," I said grinning and struggling to stand. I'd need to build up my strength for using the Inter-Dimensional Communications system later.

I guess Grandpa was right about the Disciples needing of bit of their training in the future. I thought, shaking my head as I thought about the potential threat the tourists posed.

Timothy Stevens

The Friday night Alternative had ended a few hours ago and the Disciples were warming up. The Alternative had started up when the Bible study group had spread the word that anyone at the university that didn't have anything to do on Friday night was welcome to come to our home for some food and fun; this was one of our outreaches into the college community that allowed the social outcasts and the unpopular to discover that the Lord did love and care for them and that we accepted them. That they –regardless of what others said – had value, meaning, and purpose, and each Friday night I made it a point to gain everyone's attention and remind them that God truly did accept them regardless of their social significance and that He considered them worthy of His love and of His very life. Many of the people that curiously checked out a Friday night gathering returned to hear more the following Sunday because they saw the love of God among the students and the way that it spilled over to them.

Tonight as training carried on Joel Porter was down in the training room and the ComBots began to fire their guns as soon as they entered the room.

Joel Porter was a perky young lad and is good friends with both Joseph and Jacob. His early life was filled with spiritual warfare. To me it seemed obvious that Satan wanted to prevent Joel from maturing in the faith; that made it all the more important to see to it that he did grow. It was at the Porter's house that the Bible study first took place before moving it for the combat training to take place.

That first of training I had grabbed a small 2x4 and tossed it to Joel; I can still remember the way that he had caught it and was surprised by its weight. In fact he barely managed to keep a hold on it because of the shock and had enthusiastically asked, "Dude, what is this stuff?"

I had smiled and explained to him that he held a sample of cainium-wood; named after the element cainium manufactured by Myathian chemists and is several times stronger than titanium and was the most dense and most durable element discovered thus far. The Cainium trees themselves were once present on Earth but when a particular species of dinosaur died out the trees also died out because of the symbiotic relationship they had; the sample that I gave to Joel was sent to me from a friend in Kalmar were the dinosaurs were still abundant.

I had explained to Joel the interesting way that no matter what the heritage of the plant is, if it is disconnected from its life-support it dies and grows weaker with every passing day.

"So what? My super-power is going to be attacking people with a Cainium-Wood brick?" Joel had laughed and pretended to charge someone with the brick that night.

I had laughed and shook my head as I retrieved the rest of his 'equipment' from a hidden shelf in the wall. The piece of Cainium-Wood that I had given him was his primary weapon, but his enjoyment in woodworking would be taken to a new level as any green enough piece of wood would be as moldable and pliable in his hands as playdough, allowing him to be able to shape and create anything he would want.

Along with the Cainium-Wood, I had given Joel some leather construction boots, shear-resistant blue-jeans, a red long-sleeve button-down shirt, – also shear-resistant – along with a construction mask, and special safety glasses. Joseph and I had designed the mask to filter out all kinds of hazardous chemicals from the air as well as be much more comfortable than the typical construction worker's mask and the glasses would help him to see the precise angles and distances of any particular object, analyze the grain and potential of a wooden substance, and highlight the weakness of an enemy's technique along with protecting his eyes from various rays and other potential hazards; I had designed Joel's alias to be the 'Carpenter' and tried to design the uniform to be fitting.

I had used the 'Carpenter' persona and abilities to teach Joel some lessons about the Christian life; one of which was the comparison of how the Cainium-Wood, being nearly rock-solid and almost unchangeable, still molds easily to Joel's direction is similar to the way we as Christians must remain resilient to the world around us while consenting to the molding of God.

In order to allow the students to grow in their abilities I would routinely command the cainium lined room to restructure itself and have different obstacles or tools for them to use. In Joel's case that restructured the training room to become a home that Joel would have to defend against the onslaught of ComBots; with trees planted up front for him to use as weapons.

Tonight's simulation began and Joel formed his Cainium-Wood into a shield in his left hand to block the different shots of the ComBots as he made his way over to the trees so that he could give them commands.

Joel threw his shield forward at the ComBots and it reformed and split in midair, becoming three small spears and diverted to three different ComBots. The tree nearest Joel – which was still beyond his reach – began to move and grow according to his mental commands and subdued the different ComBots with its branches before retrieving the Cainium-Wood shafts to be reformed in Joel's hands. When more attackers came from around the corner, Joel used a second tree nearby to break its roots up from the ground and tangle up the legs of the ComBots and disarm them.

Everyone in the observation room was impressed because up until this point Joel, who hadn't commanded the wood with that level of precision unless he was touching the base of the tree, now managed to manipulate wood at a distance with almost as much ease as he had when in physical contact with the wood.

"Well done Joel," I said through the speakers, "go ahead and make your way back up here."

"That was pretty cool," Marie Daniels commented as we waited for Joel. "I haven't seen him command the wood like that before."

"It was impressive to say the least," I replied with a nod and caught a look of concern in my wife's eyes as she continued to review the medical assessment of Joel's warmup.

When Joel made it up to the room and the other kids were ushered out, Sandra began to double check the computer's readings and took Joel's pulse and asked him if he felt okay.

"Yeah, I feel fine," Joel nodded a bit hesitantly, "I mean, I kinda felt a little tired but I'm doing okay now."

"The computers showed that you were experiencing some major stress when you were commanding the trees. Do you remember feeling anything unusual then?"

Joel thought for a moment before nodding, "Well, I remember that my head kind of hurt and I felt a little dizzy, but it was no big deal; I'm fine now and I just needed some water."

"Just remember to take things slow, Joel," I affirmed my wife's concern and cautioned the twenty year old from being too careless. "You've grown past taking baby steps, but if you over extend yourself you could suffer some major consequences; keep working on using gestures and mental commands to control the trees, but slow down if that feeling comes back. All right?"

Joel understood the danger and nodded his agreement, "All right."

I had nodded, "There are some important practical things to remember, Joel, many of which can remind you of spiritual things of even greater importance and will help you right now; things that I had taught you that first night of training."

"Like what?" he asked, eager to learn and grow stronger in his abilities.

"Remember how I warned you about how wood that is dried out will be brittle and will splinter or break more easily when you try to work with it?"

Joel nodded, "Yeah, that's why I 've had to diligently polish and seal that Cainium-Wood block to keep it fresh and green these past four years."

I nodded, thankful that he had been keeping up with that discipline. "In life we must diligently take time to spend with the Lord – treating our souls and soaking up His Word to seal our hearts – and it takes effort and hard work to keep at it. But if we neglect that spiritual 'treating' of our hearts then we can grow brittle and crack under the pressure from the world around us. A big part of the GRID is in staying close to God; if we become distanced from God our GRID Connections will be weak and won't be able to handle the pressures of what we are called to do."

Joel nodded his agreement, "That makes sense; I'll try to remember to keep working on that."

"It's something that we all have to work on," I said to make sure he knew that I wasn't just picking on him, but that we all had this same struggle. "And it's not just because we have these abilities that this is important; the more important reason for you to spend time with the Lord is so that Joel can experience a deep and meaningful relationship with Him rather than so Carpenter can be better at controlling wood."

I knew that Joel's studies in forensic science kept him pretty busy and that times would only get more chaotic in the future, but that was exactly why it was paramount that he form good habits now before it becomes nearly impossible for him to start.

"You're making tremendous progress – as both Joel and Carpenter – just be sure that you don't overdo it. Okay?" My wife said tenderly to the young man in order to both encourage and caution him.

"Okay," Joel gave a chipper nod and stood up to head to the door. "I'll go let the others know that it's Jacob's turn for the warmups."

Chapter Nine

Simon's plan was beginning to come together. Four of the five interdimensional members of his Komplo had managed to make it safely to the prearranged location in the Black Mountains where he had constructed an underground base; Acedia being the only member that had yet to arrive. So as long as his contact within the main Arizonan SOS Base, his 'Virus', was able to continue to supply them with reasonably reliable tech and intel, things should continue to go according to plan.

Now if only Simon's Earthian addition to the Komplo would stop badgering him and interrupting his séance preparations.

"Yo, Simon," William called walking through the doorway. Simon was sitting on the floor in the center of his darkened room with his back to the door; various crystals and beads were hanging and lining the selves along with some dimly lit candles and other objects that were completely foreign to Will. "How's a guy supposed to keep from going crazy down here? There's nothing to do down here man!"

William 'Will' Zalinsky – Bernie's 'Catch.22' – had proven to be every bit the sharpshooter that Bernie Quill had made him out to be, and every bit the braggart as well.

"William, the purpose of our presence here is to remain concealed until the proper moment for us to strike our adversary." Simon answered flatly and drew in a deep breath, effectively hiding his frustration at Will's whining.

"What are we supposed to do in the meantime, man?"

Simon drew in a deep breath and closed his eyes, "We remain in a constant state of readiness, William. How's your aim?"

Will crossed his arms and rolled his eyes, "My aim is doing fine, just like it always has been. I can't do anything to improve it, so why do I have to keep wasting time around here? There's a city not too far away where a guy could actually have some fun for a night."

"William, we cannot afford such frivolities if we desire to conquer our adversaries." Simon said, continuing his attempts in stabilizing his impulsive ally.

"Man, what is up with you, Simon?" Will asked in frustration. "You got some control issues dude. I mean, what's the harm in me going out for one night? It's not like I need these losers you gathered from the seven realms to make a living."

"These 'losers' are part of the key to our success, William." Simon answered, continuing to mentally prepare himself for his séance.

"Yeah, right. Look, I don't know what this big scheme of yours is all about, but I'm going crazy down here man."

"Deal with it in training, William. Surely mercenaries such as Jaxson and yourself can understand the importance of remaining focused."

Jaxson 'Jack' Harper is an Australian born mercenary recruited into Simon's Komplo by his respected 'friend' Will. Jack is a skilled marksman in his own right, and the only difference between the two was that while Will preferred his lightweight firearms Jack favored a well-balanced blade. Any razor sharp edge could be thrown with lethal accuracy or used in hand-to-hand combat with deadly proficiency, and Jack was never short on sharpened steel.

"Oh, sure. Jack knows how to stay sharp all right," Will chuckled at his own pun.

"So tell me this, William: is it truly boredom that is bothering you, or do you have a problem with Jaxson's presence here?" Simon smirked, as he knew the comment would needle Will.

Jack and Will had a mutual respect for each other's skills and had a healthy, unspoken agreement between each other; neither of them would attempt to kill the other. Not that both of the men hadn't considered breaking that arrangement – and by so doing declare once and for all which was truly the best marksman and assassin in the business – but they both also feared being in the other's sights too much to ever attempt such a feat.

Yet another thing that both Will and Jack had in common was their uneasiness with each other. While both men respected each other, they also feared and mistrusted each other.

Will crossed his arms and shuffled his feet. "Jack's got nothin' to do with this. I just can't stay pent up like this, man. I gotta move where the wind takes me."

Simon couldn't help but shake his head at that comment. *Oh, my naïve companion. If you allow the wind to direct your life you will most certainly lose this war.*

Will shook his head as Simon tried to refocus his mind. "What is it that you do down here anyway, man? You're sittin' on the floor in a dark, smoky room. I mean seriously, how's this improving the training of your little team here?"

"I am attempting to contact my guides for knowledge concerning the war we wage." Simon answered through gritted teeth. "If I am left alone I can strengthen and empower our allies as they train in the next room."

Will scoffed and shook his head while putting his fists on his hips, "Man are you somethin' else. I mean what kind of guy not only turns on his friends and teammates, but sells his soul to the devil to do it?"

Simon closed his eyes and exhaled deeply. Will had crossed a line and he knew it. Worse, he was enjoying it. He crossed his arms and smirked in triumph.

The smoke in the room began to swirl subtly as Will looked at Simon's face in the reflection of the mirror on the wall opposite him. Simon's brow was furrowed in concentration and his jaw was tight in anger.

Then the hair on Will's neck stood straight up when he heard Simon's voice coming from behind him. "Where exactly do you believe *your* soul is going, William?"

Will spun around and stood face to face with a much taller and stronger version of Simon. His eyes were completely dilated and seemed to pierce deeper into Will's mind and heart than anything else had done before.

Will turned and looked behind him. Simon still sat in the center of the room with his eyes closed, only now his expression in the mirror was much different. Simon's face was completely relaxed and a smirk of revenge spread across his mouth.

A strange chill overcame Will's body as he turned again to face the strange horror behind him. Something in those eyes chilled him to the core and paralyzed him from the inside out.

"Both of us are headed to the same place, my dear William," Simon said flatly, "unless we do something about it. I've made the decision to control the spirit world to my advantage, while you, my friend, are simply a pawn in this game. However, if you play well then you might be upgraded to something of higher worth in the future."

The smoke in the room began to swirl around Will's neck and seemed to constrict tighter as Simon spoke; to Will it was like his life was being choked out of him by the darkness that surrounded him.

"If you ever dare to degrade me in such a manner as this again," Simon threatened, "I promise you, William, that the images of your worst nightmare will pale in comparison to what I am capable of."

Will's eyes began to roll in his head his body started to go limp. Just then the icy grip that was tightening around his neck relaxed and he was able to breathe again and regain control of his limbs.

"Remember who is in command of this Komplo, William," Simon said from his place on the floor. "Fall in line, or fall before me; I truly do not care which you choose. Now go train with the other pawns and leave me to my séance."

Will nodded in silent submission and made his way through the compound to the training room after retrieving his firearms, staggering from the shock and lack of oxygen to his chilled muscles.

When Will was finally able to speak, the only thing he could bring himself to say was, "What have I gotten myself into?"

Timothy Stevens

Jacob is one of my younger brothers and as such I had more time to train with him, even after I moved out of our parents' house. He had always been a bit clumsy and impulsive at times and struggled to find a place of belonging in life. While he sometimes got ahead of himself he was usually headed in the right direction and I've often wondered if I would be as frustrated if his same personality were applied to anyone else or if I would somehow be more understanding. So, I decided to try and nurture that same understanding within myself towards him that I would show to someone else, and it worked with mixed results. Jacob has grown into a stronger man at the age of sixteen than he was two years prior and has found his place of belonging in the Lord, and I had learned to be more understanding to all people; including those that are at times 'too' close to me. Neither of us we perfect, but we had made progress.

Because Jacob had always been attracted to movies and video games Joseph had designed a heavily armored suit for Jacob that I had programmed to function somewhat like a video game. There were designated 'power-ups' for the suit that changed the way it worked and I gave him the codename 'Arcade' to match the suit.

The suit was designed to include a helmet with a glass

visor that would help Jacob pinpoint his targets and manage his flight trajectory. While the physical structure of the suits were all basically the same, they each had their own unique colors and abilities. I had originally designed four 'modes' between which the suit could transform though I didn't leave room for programmable data packs to be added later via the GRID; those first modes were the standard mode, fire, ice, and rock.

The standard suit had a healthy balance between its speed, mobility, shielding, and blasters and served as the template by which all the other modes functioned and the baseline that differentiated them. The standard mode used jet-repulsion on his boots and back to initiate flight and its coloration was a very dark blue with a lighter navy for his gloves, lime-green and yellow accents to the body, a little orange added a splash of color to his gloves and his red helmet with clear visor completed the suit.

The second mode was the fire power-up that I had developed to maintain a higher thermal level to protect Jacob from extreme temperature drops. While in fire-mode, Jacob could launch fireballs, have limited control of nearby flames, and use rocket-propulsion to fly around; the downside was that if the suit came in contact with water while in fire-mode it would malfunction. Changing to fire-mode would cause the suit to change in color, with a red base and red orange streaks and joints that contrasted with charcoal gray gloves and boots.

The polar opposite of the fire mode was the ice-mode which would also protect Jacob from extremely cold weather conditions while also offering improved traction to prevent him from slipping, and an ice-ray could super-freeze anything within range. While water was no longer a problem, warmer weather would be as the suit would lose power if in hotter climates. The ice-suit couldn't fly, however Jacob could use form sheets of ice upon which he could walk or skate as he desired. The ice-suit was colored with white as the primary body color and had some pale blue streaks while the gloves and boots had a sky blue color.

The strongest, heaviest, and most resilient of all the different modes I developed in concept or in reality was the rock mode. However, it was also the only current mode that completely grounded Jacob's suit along with having a total lack of blasters. So while it enhanced Jake's physical strength to rival Reverb's it would require actual combat training to make it effective in battle. The power-up altered the color to a light gray as the primary color, with dark brown accents and charcoal gray gloves, boots, and helmet.

The suit was designed to where the transition between power-ups would be fairly quick and could be done on the move, however the way it left Jacob vulnerable to attack for that brief moment couldn't be helped and another thing that I wasn't able to fully remove from the programming was the potential for glitches during the transformation between modes. A glitch could result in a half-transformation – combining two power-ups at once – which could either be somewhat beneficial or extremely detrimental and the suit was particularly prone to glitching if Jacob was attacked during the transition.

By this time Jacob already knew the ins and outs of his suit – how to safely transition between the different modes, and deal with the occasional glitch – which meant that there wasn't much need for training him anymore and the fact that the suit was doing most of the work for him meant that there was little risk to his health.

The one thing that I had seen could've become a problem for him was the way he used to choose a particular power-up based on who was present. It was a problem that ran deeper than just his suit and was something that I had seen in my brother for years; he would often change his mind or claim to enjoy something out of the ordinary depending on which friend was in the room. If Joel liked something then suddenly Jacob would be interested in it, but if Joann wasn't crazy about it then Jacob would find it less appealing.

"Changing your preferences to accommodate a situation or the task at hand is admirable and often required in life; being flexible is a good thing." I had tried time and again to explain the issue I saw in him and usually for a few days or weeks after a conversation like this one I would notice a little more consistency in Jake. However, after a while I would find him saying or doing something out of character for him when others were watching.

I had often tried to convey that if God, or maybe even a leader in life, were to ask him to do something differently than how he might normally do it – as long as it wasn't contrary to Scripture – then it is a good idea to comply. However, the way that had tried to change his personality, likes, dislikes, and hobbies based what others *might* be thinking or enjoy would lead him to live an extremely disappointed and dissatisfied life because I knew he would ultimately grow discouraged and depressed in trying to change himself to fit into another person's script.

I had frequently attempted to stress the difference between virtuous adapting and cowardly campaigning in that while being able to see a need and take care of it is good, but compromising or changing our story to tickle another person's ears is wrong; adapting to fill needs is a good thing because we are God's servants and we adapt to the calling that He gives us, no matter what that means; but politicians are performing for the public when they tell their audience whatever they think the crowds want to hear.

Over the years – whether due to or in spite of constant reminding – Jacob had learned the difference between pursuing good things and Godly things and that the difference between them is always about why we do things; if we are doing things simply because they need to be done or because others expect it then we are settling for the good while serving purely for the pleasure of God is when we begin to strive for the Godly. Because he had learned this lesson, Jaco;b had found his story and satisfaction in God and asked Him what life he should be living, even if that meant going completely against what everyone else is doing. Even if his friends and brothers thought of him as weird, he was determined to do what the *Lord* had put on his heart, and to be obedient to *God* as he considered what *He* thought about him to be more important than anyone else's opinion, and began living a life full of *Godly* activity and he found satisfaction and lasting joy in that life.

Perhaps it was because he was the closest one to me in the group that I had always felt a greater burden to teach him and make sure that he turned out okay and because I had almost always been with Jacob it had been harder for him than for the other kids to wear a mask and he wasn't able to get away with as much as they did. But now – as my little brother flew around the training room and blasted away the simulation rounds – I could see the growth that had occurred slowly throughout the years, in both Jacob and Arcade.

Jacob flew down to the ground and quickly transitioned his suit to the ice mode and formed an ice rink over the Cainium floors and caused several ComBots to slip and lose their footing. Several of them had lost their grip upon their weapons when they fell and the ice climbed up around the legs of a few that remained standing and held them fast. One ComBot fired at Jacob from behind, but just before the simulation round struck him in the back Jacob's entire form blurred and shifted as though his suit glitched and the round passed through him and struck another ComBot in front of him.

Seconds later, Jacob switched over to the fire mode and took to the skies again in order to melt the weapons held by the ComBots. While the rest of us in the observation room were left wondering what in the world happened.

"I didn't know that Jacob could do that with his glitches, Timinski." Mark Arable remarked. "What kind of power-up was that?"

I shook my head, a bit baffled at what I just saw, "I'm

not sure what exactly took place with his suit; I haven't altered the program in any way. It seems as though the Lord is working in some new ways through you Disciples lately." I chuckled at the thought of the new abilities that the other students had discovered in the month or so before my mood became shadowed with concern; could these newfound abilities be somehow connected with the tourists that had made their way to Earth? It felt as though God was producing some rapid growth and changes to take place in many of these Disciples; was He preparing them for something dire or was it simply coincidence? The thought momentarily brought some humor back to my mood and I chuckled at the impossibility of coincidences existing.

With the simulation ended and Jacob making his way up to the observation room, I had the other Disciples move into the next room and asked Sandra, "What kind of reading did the computers pick up when that happened?"

She had a puzzled expression as she looked over the health scanners and what they were telling her, "They all went flat because they couldn't find him; I get similar readings when Beth starts phasing because the signals pass right through her."

I moved over and consulted some of the other screens and the information they displayed. "It looks as though there was a significant electrical discharge at the same moment that all the other readings flat lined."

"Hey guys," Jacob said as he came through the door, "any idea what's going on with those glitches?"

"You knew about them?" I asked, annoyed that he

didn't tell us about them sooner. "How long have they been going on?"

He shrugged his shoulder, "I don't know; maybe a month or so."

"What can you tell us about them?" Sandra asked concerned for his safety. "What do you feel when it happens? Can you see or hear anything that might help us figure out what is going on with the suit?"

Jacob held up his hands, "All I know is that my visor fills up with static and that there's a buzzing in my headphones; every now and then when it happens I end up being warped someplace across the room."

"Is there any consistency to it?" I asked, hoping that there might be some way to pinpoint exactly what was going on and frustrated that a history major in college would have such a difficult time recounting such important information.

Jacob shrugged his shoulder, "Sometimes it happens when I'm about to get hit by an enemy – and I think that there were a few times when I was able to kind of control it – but most of the time it's pretty random."

Sandra perked up, "You said that you can control it sometimes; how?"

Jacob shrugged his shoulder again, "I don't know, I just kind of fiddle with the controls on my suit and I find something that works."

"Can you try it now?" she asked as she moved over to the computers. "Now that we have an idea of what to look for we can have the computers focus on the mental commands you give the suit and we can record exactly what it is that triggers the glitch."

Jacob drew in a deep breath and I held up a hand to slow him down, "Remember to set your suit to simulation mode so that you can use whatever mental inputs you need to trigger the glitch."

After a few moments Jacob began to scramble through several commands for his suit – the GRID equivalent to button mashing – and after several attempts was able to trigger the glitch that teleported him into the wall on the other side of the room.

"Jacob!" My wife and I hurried across the room and helped pick up my brother from where he fell after colliding with the wall.

"Are you all right?" I asked alarmed.

"Just fine," he groaned and took my hand to pull himself up.

We heard a knock on the door where the other students were waiting and Joseph called to ask if everything was okay.

Sandra walked over to the door and opened it, "Everything is just fine. Um…Aaron, why don't you head on down to the training room and get warmed up? We'll wait for you up here."

As Sandra opened the door for the other students to join us I whispered to Jacob, "Until Sandra and I sort through the data try to avoid activating the glitches, especially during the training with the others. Okay?"

Jacob nodded, "I don't exactly look forward to the next time I have to do something like that again."

I solemnly considered the possibility that all of these students would end up finding themselves in many dangerous positions in the near future that neither I nor they would ever want to be in. Something big was happening but I didn't know what or how to adequately prepare my students; I could only pray that somehow they would be ready for what the Lord was calling them to.

Chapter Eleven

Zilvia Krezel was finally nearing her destination after nearly three days of hard travel. Immediately, after Simon had finished his séance he had given her the assignment to infiltrate the SOS Corps headquarters while Virus did his best to hinder the security programs to help prevent her detection.

Zilvia was specially recruited by the government of her native country of Jazabad – in the realm of Osria – because of her skills as an assassin for hire. Her job as an agent was to use her INSECT suit and various skills to locate and eliminate various Christian leaders hiding within her jurisdiction in Jazabad.

Along with her INSECT suit enabling her to shrink to nearly the same size as her namesake – the black widow spider – Zilvia is a highly trained and formidable combatant armed with specially designed gloves and boots that could grip to nearly any surface with ease allowing her to climb almost any wall, bracelets that contained a synthesized compound that she called her 'webbing' with which she could tether herself to various objects in order to climb or swing from one place to another, bind or otherwise inhibit her opponent, along with any other countless uses, and finally she had two daggers that were coated with a concentrated latrotoxin every time she sheathed them; an individual cut with one of Zilvia's blades would experience symptoms similar to the actual bite of the black widow spider, only exponentially more intense and usually fatal.

Over the years Zilvia had grown used to the psychological discouragement associated with being nearly the same size as a spider, foremost of which was the fact that it took nearly two days of rapid travel to cover a distance that could be covered in two hours at a gentle stroll. However, in Zilvia's line of work, one couldn't be too careful in avoiding being spotted by the prey.

This time her target was being protected by the SOS Corps security programs – which was a compilation of the best that all the realms had to offer by way of security – which meant that Zilvia would have to travel under greater risk of being discovered than ever before.

"Piece of cake," Zilvia had said, using an Earthian saying she had learned from Will. It was rather applicable to the sweetness and ease she found as an assassin for hire, and her job had become much easier since meeting up with Simon. Though to be more accurate, it was the way that Simon's Earthian contact within the SOS Corps based in Arizona had acquired memory orbs that had made the difference in Zilvia's performance. Those memory orbs would have been used by the SOS Corps to advance their elite members to Defender status, but Simon, as usual, had much bigger plans for the memory orbs and now the entire Komplo, including Zilvia, had been upgraded to a much higher lethal level of success because of these orbs

Zilvia could already appreciate her own upgrades as she knew that it would have normally taken her at least thirty-six hours to cover the distance to reach the SOS Corps headquarters and she had just covered them twelve. The mindvoice enhancements had given her an almost unnatural level of strength, endurance, speed, balance, reflexes, and perception of air pressure changes, which allowed her to sense when objects were moving towards her to allow for avoiding being hit or crushed.

The SOS Corps had sensors and cameras spread out giving them a five block security radius, so Zilvia had shrunk down and was then teleported by Simon from southern New Mexico to the rooftop of a house near the SOS Corps base hidden within a small neighborhood in Logan, UT; a rooftop which was conveniently located a block outside of the SOS Corps security perimeter.

Zilvia shot a strand of her webbing down to the ground, secured the web, and zip lined down to the earth to begin making her way through the neighborhood to the SOS Corps headquarters, hitchhiking on a car or other such mode of transportation when available. She would often cover greater distances by shooting her webbing and swinging from a nearby tree branch, light pole, or whatever else she could attach to.

And so, at around 10:30 pm local time, Zilvia finally scaled the wall to the backyard of the ordinary home that concealed the presence of the local, state of the art, interdimensional, intelligence gathering agency headquarters known as the SOS Corps.

As she trekked through the forest of grass in front of her – it was apparent that it had been several weeks since the lawn was last mowed – Zilvia began to hear something rustling in the grass to her right. It was small enough to be concealed in the grass with her, but still larger than Zilvia herself.

Zilvia prepared herself for battle; this was another one of those hurdles of being nearly a centimeter tall that she had grown accustomed to. Actually, Zilvia thoroughly enjoyed combating the various lizards and insects that had attempted to eat her over the years – much as she assumed the Kalmarian knights enjoyed slaying the dragons – it was proof of her worth as an assassin to not only survive but conquer any foe that opposed her.

Suddenly, a scorpion broke through the blades of grass, its poisonously barbed tail lashed out at Zilvia as she dove to the side. Zilvia had fired three web blasts at the legs on that side of the beast as she came up and the webbing held fast causing the scorpion to pull and struggle in its attempts to reach Zilvia.

Zilvia always preferred to kill only after she had completely removed all sense of hope from her victim and every possible source of escape had been blocked; she wanted her prey to know that she was in complete control over their death, not some God that had abandoned them to her power.

Zilvia began to circle the creature, tying each of its legs down with shots of her webbing as she went; the scorpion lashed at her with its claws and continued its attempts to strike her with its tail. Zilvia then secured the tail and claws of the creature to several blades of grass with her webbing, cutting off any means it had to defend itself.

After the scorpion was completely immobilized and

defenseless, Zilvia walked over to its side and climbed atop of the beast. She stared into where she knew the creature's eyes were as she knelt down on its back. The scorpion struggled helplessly against the cords that held it fast.

"Shhh…" Zilvia whispered to the beast; she knew that it couldn't understand her, but still found sadistic satisfaction in taunting the poor creature. "There is no point fighting me. You were as good as dead the moment you challenged me, monster."

Zilvia then pulled out the two daggers that were sheathed at her sides and plunged them through the scorpion's armored exoskeleton.

After sheathing her blades and leaving the poor creature to suffer the effect of her venom, Zilvia continued her mission of infiltrating the base; she was almost disappointed at the ease of the kill due to her newly enhanced abilities.

Zilvia would get into the house and down into the compound the same way that any other insect would, by finding a crack small enough to fit through and then making her way down the stairs to the room where her target was located.

According to Virus' intel, the hardest part was already past; most of the internal security protocols were being remotely hindered by Virus so that Zilvia could get in and out while avoiding detection.

When Zilvia made it past the trapdoor into the base she froze. There were still lights on and she could sense someone moving around somewhere down there.

"Virus, you bloody idiot!" Zilvia hissed through clenched teeth. "You said no one would be down here this late."

Titus Martinez, one of the Komplo's eventual targets, was still down in the SOS Corps base cleaning up after the training session earlier.

Zilvia climbed along the ceiling of the compound and quietly lowered herself down along a line of webbing until she could gently rest on the collar of Titus' shirt. She then carefully made her way to Titus' neck and readied herself.

Before Zilvia left on this mission, Simon had sternly warned her not to kill any humans during this mission because he didn't want their presence on Earth to be noticeable. For Zilvia, however, a mission that didn't end with her killing someone wasn't worth taking and would be extremely out of character for her considering she was an assassin; the scorpion out front was the closest thing to a kill that she had experienced in nearly two months and hadn't fully sated her bloodlust.

In order to make everything appear as though she followed Simon's orders Zilvia decided to use her second killing routine: slow poisoning. Zilvia carried with her several extra vials of the latrotoxin that her daggers were laced with, so that she could apply the venom to an object or person and cause it to be slowly absorbed through the skin rather than immediately entering the bloodstream and killing the victim shortly after being 'bitten'.

Zilvia opened one of those vials and poured it out on Titus' neck; if the poison didn't kill him within the next few weeks, then it would at least hinder him when the Komplo attacks.

Titus felt a water drop hit his neck and went to wipe it, causing Zilvia to flip off of him and swing from a newly shot web-line down the hallway to find her primary objective: the SOS Corps storage room.

Zilvia finally made it to her targeted storage room, the room where much of the SOS Corps' extra interdimensional technology was stored. Zilvia crawled through the crack under the door and then grew to her normal size for the first time in over twelve hours and made her way to the storage shelves that Virus had described.

Simon wanted Virus to be able to use the MAPT device to further the equipment upgrades for the Komplo as well as to perform some specific reprogramming tasks. Several of the MAPT devices – which would normally take up and entire room of the underground compound if they weren't shrunk down to the same size as Virus' Rubix cube – were sitting lined up on the shelf. Next to the MAPT devices were several EMA devices that were used to construct the underground base for the SOS Corps; Simon had already used the model that Zilvia had brought with her from Osria to build his own base in the Black Mountains.

Zilvia grabbed a handful of the EMA cubes and stuffed them in a pouch on her utility belt and held two of the MAPT cubes, one in each hand. Simon only wanted one MAPT device because he would be able to make whatever he wanted after that, but he never said that Zilvia couldn't grab anything for herself while she was here.

After coating each MAPT device with a soft, powdery webbing, weaving a small pouch out of a different type of webbing to carry the two cubes in, and attaching the pouch to her utility belt, Zilvia then re-shrunk herself and made her way back out of the compound, content in the completion of her mission from Simon and her personal vendetta in assuring the death of Titus and exterminating the scorpion.

It would take longer for Zilvia to get beyond the SOS Corps security perimeter as there were almost no cars driving this late at night and she would have to cover the distance completely on foot. However, she was still confident that she would return to the Komplo's hideout within twenty-four hours of her original departure. All Zilvia had to do was make sure that she wasn't eaten by some hungry predator before the night was up.

She grinned as she thought of the various creatures that had tried and failed in the past, and when she thought of the most recent attempt by the scorpion outside she almost pitied the next poor creature that would try and kill her.

Chapter Twelve

"I've noticed over the years that it can be fairly easy for you at times to reach out to others, even if you don't know them." I said, as Aaron entered the observation room where I was waiting with Sandra.

"And reaching out has gotten even easier now with this suit," he joked as he stretched out his arm behind him to close the door.

Aaron White's orange-clay colored suit allowed him to stretch and mold his body to fit the need of a particular situation with tremendous ease, allowing him to stretch and swing from building to building, to avoid being hit while remaining in the same place, play 'Jell-O' to absorb a blow without pain, to punch or kick several targets that would normally be out of range, or to rescue individuals that would be out of reach. All this had warranted the eighteen year-old the codename 'Clay'.

Aaron's long-sleeved shirt and boots were a dark, almost-earthy, orange with clay-red pants and I had designed clay colored 'ski-mask' for Aaron so that his head would to be able to mold like the rest of the suit.

Aaron had always been easy to work with, as his personality was flexible and shapeable, just like playdough, making for an ideal student at times. Unfortunately, you can't just wad up a person and start over with their life if you make a mistake, like with playdough, which necessitated a focused teacher.

Aaron White – a happy-go-lucky and entertaining young man – and his sister Mary were the original worship team with my brother Joseph and within those first months he repeatedly asked to begin street evangelizing and demonstrated his desire to reach the lost. I had to gather enough trusted leaders to help me 'shepherd the cats' but eventually the trip to the local park became a weekly stretching for me; Although evangelism had always been somewhere outside of my comfort zone but within my desire, Aaron had made my comfort zone a non-issue.

On one of the first nights we went out evangelizing together the two of us had started a simple conversation with an older gentleman with relative ease. However, the moment we attempted to speak of spiritual matters everything changed – it was like a switch went off and neither of us were comfortable enough to speak – and on that night we both saw the reality of the unseen warfare going on around us, a reality that we can't see but is even more real than what we can see. The enemy didn't care if we talked about the weather or circumstances, but he fought against us speaking the name of Jesus. I had hoped that 'Clay' could serve as a reminder that when reaching out became difficult was when it becomes all the more important to show God's love; that when it's hardest to stand firm is when it is most critical to fight for truth.

That first night as a test I had asked him to stretch his hand from the center of the room where we had stood to the door that was a few yards away and Aaron had drawn in a breath and stretched out his hand, his face had become strained and reddened as his arm had slowly extended farther out until he had reached the doorway. I knew based on his effort that night that he would eventually be able to stretch with greater ease and even use the suit to disguise himself – if he worked consistently at it – and warned him that holding a firm position would probably be more difficult for him than stretching and remaining flexible. Tonight he had demonstrated his growth as he disarmed and subdued each of the ComBots within moments of the simulation starting and avoided every shot that came his way, but there was still something that went wrong.

"Aaron," my wife began with a concerned tone, "have you been keeping up with those strength building exercises?"

"Oh, you mean my stretchy-weightlifting?" Aaron asked to clarify before answering with a nod and a shoulder shrug. "Sure, I've been building up strength to stretch out and move around heavy objects. Why?"

Sandra shook her head and looked puzzled, "Because the data from your tests shows that your suit is having trouble resolidifying after each use."

"What do you mean?" Aaron asked, obviously concerned.

I looked over the information that Sandra was concerned over and understood the problem. "Well Aaron, the integrity of the suit and the character of your heart will both be tested tremendously in life," I paused to put my hand on his shoulder. "As I explained to you before, the spiritual discipline it takes to stand strong when someone comes against you – or being a man of character when no one is watching – will always be a challenge for us in the flesh because Godly character is something that we must diligently watch over and maintain. It seems as though your suit is beginning to display physical inconsistency and is having a hard time remaining steadfast, presumably because you hadn't been consistently working at the strength exercises."

I was hoping that this conversation would help correct a minor concern I had developed over the years as I observed Aaron's interactions with his parents, siblings, and friends. It wasn't something that I was eager to confront him on, but I had noticed certain ways that his speech and behaviors weren't completely in line with where he was in his relationship with God; it had grown harder to ignore and the GRID Connection in the suit was beginning to reflect this truth that I hoped he would learn.

"But I have been training and working at it," Aaron said in his defense, "and it's been really hard to find time for it with my job with the police department."

"I'm sure that you've been doing what you thought was enough," I affirmed with a nod, "but apparently your suit has reached a point where more effort is needed to keep growing. God calls us to have continuous spiritual growth and keep progressing in our journey of faith as we will never fully reach the end until we are in His presence, with spiritual compromise and weak convictions being the dangerous results of apathy in our walk."

Aaron was obviously confused and frustrated that he hadn't been doing enough. "But if we never make it to the finish line until heaven then what's the point of trying?"

Sandra spoke gently, "Life is filled with one mountain to climb after another and we can see the rewards as we reach each new peak, even though we haven't yet reached our true destination. And whether or not we climb the next peak or remain where we are is entirely up to us."

"That's right, Aaron," I added thoughtfully. "Right now God is showing you that there is something more, something greater, to a relationship with him that you haven't discovered yet. I can remember several instances where God tapped me on the shoulder and pointed out that there was still room for me to grow and improve, even though I thought I was doing all right; God won't force you to grow beyond what you are willing to give Him so the strength of your relationship with Him is up to you."

"So the only thing that is stopping me from getting even closer to God, is whether or not I'm willing to spend more time with Him?"

"Right," I nodded, "I have reached places where I thought I was content with my relationship with the Lord until He showed me that there was something greater. Sometimes I waited until I couldn't stand the thought of staying where I was before I finally asked Him to help me draw closer to Him; God has a way of persuading us to ask for exactly what He always knew was best for us."

"Yeah, that makes sense," Aaron nodded his understanding. "I'll have to see what new mountains God might want me to climb."

I had held up a finger, "One last thing that we can learn from tonight is that we as human beings are physically but dirt and water – which means that we are basically mud or clay – and there is nothing special about us nor is there any good in our flesh. What makes us valuable is that we bear within our earthen vessels the glory of Jesus Christ which means that if we rely on the Almighty One living inside of us we can accomplish all that He directs us to complete; but if we rely on our own strength or abilities we will utterly fail because we are nothing in and of ourselves."

Aaron had nodded, "I understand."

"Now are you ready to see how Adam does with his warmup?" I asked to conclude the conversation.

"You bet!" he had perked up and stretched his hand over to the door. "You guys can come on in now, it's Adam's turn in the training room," Aaron called out as he opened the door.

"Is it okay if we start a dodgeball game now while we wait for the others to warmup?" Mary asked, energetically and politely. "I can't stand sitting still for this long."

At some point each night for the past four years Mary would find it difficult to wait for everyone to have their warmups and would ask to start a dodgeball game while they waited; tonight she had waited a bit longer than most before asking to start the dodgeball game, but that was because she had taken her turn later in the evening than was normal.

I smiled and nodded before turning to my brother, "Joseph would you mind taking those that are ready down into one of the other training rooms and having a dodgeball round with them? I'll send the kids down to where you're at when they're ready."

"Sounds good," Joseph nodded and began to lead some of the Disciples down to the training room.

I prayed that God would continue to challenge and strengthen each of these Disciples, Aaron included, to be ready for the ministry that He was calling them to, a ministry that my dreams and visions had been casting ominous dark shadows upon for the last several nights; the dreams were still chaotic and hard to piece together with understanding, but something grim was about to happen that would destroy everything and everyone that I held dear and had worked for and I didn't know how to stop it. I prayed that somehow these Disciples would survive the carnage that my dreams foretold.

Joseph Stevens

Life was good. I mean, the dodgeballs were flying. The kids were laughing and cheering. Joel had just gotten hit in the face with a dodgeball. Then the guys started laughing harder. Life was *very* good.

"Are you okay, Joel?" Mary had asked as she landed next to him, her wings still open and ready to take off at a moments notice.

"He's fine," Aaron answered with a dismissive wave of the hand.

I knew he was fine too. I mean, the whole point of the dodgeball game was to get the kids ready for a real fight one step at a time so there had to be some risk and pain involved. But this was still the little league setting so no one would get seriously hurt before they were trained to defend themselves. But just wait until we start using the DNNSH enabled ComBots, 'cuz that's when the fun'll really start!

"Are you sure you're okay?" Mary asked Joel again.

"Yeah, I'm fine," Joel answered picking himself up off the ground.

"Are you sure?" Mary asked again.

"Are you guys gonna play or just sit there?" Jacob asked, flying over to Mary's side.

"We'll be right there," Joel answered as he went over

and picked up his Cainium-Wood sword, or his CW-Block as the group called it. "Yeah, Mary, I'm fine."

"All right, Joel!" Mary flapped her wings and she and Jacob rejoined the dodgeball game.

"Heads up Joel," I called to him to get his attention. I had been using my sound blasts to block the dodgeballs that were headed for him and Mary until now; it might have been kinda funny to see Joel get hit with a dodgeball once, but I didn't want to see him and Mary get pummeled by them and they both get hurt. I might be a jerk, but I'm a jerk with a heart.

I do have heart somewhere and I can't stand by and watch a girl get pummeled without doing something about it; Timothy had always called it chivalry, I just call it being a real man.

Joel turned and narrowly ducked as the ball passed. "Thanks, Joe."

"Don't mention it," I said dismissively.

Part of my job was to make sure no one died during the dodgeball game, a task easier said than done since all of these guys had some kind of GRID Connection that made them dangerous. I mean, we don't want someone accidentally skewered or blown to smithereens now, do we? Thankfully the four years of training had given these kids more control over their abilities and I didn't have to worry as much about that, but the fact that the Disciples would have their warmups in a different order each night meant that there was always a different combination in the dodgeball game and I had to stay on my toes every time we were down here.

My older brother Timothy had always been a bit nerdy at times; by 'a bit' I mean, 'A LOT' and by 'at times' I mean, 'all the time'. It had been difficult growing up in his shadow, I mean, everyone kept expecting me to be just like Tim. I guess that it must be similar to growing up as a preacher's kid.

Why do people always put that kind of pressure on others? 'Oh, your dad is a pastor,' or, 'your brother is a leader', so therefore I need to be a spiritual giant? What's with that?

What may have been worse was having to grow up after him, because it was almost as though Timothy was plowing the way for me to take over. I was nervous about that, but if Tim could manage to pull it off it couldn't be too hard. Right?

A dodgeball nearly beaned Marie Daniels in the head and I was about to blast it with some sound waves to keep anyone under my watch from getting hurt, but Joel had already thrown his CW-Block at it and molded the wood into a spear, pinning the now popped dodgeball to the wall.

"That's right, everyone," I called out to the group, "we need to play this game as a team; watch each other's backs."

I made my way over to Joel and teased with a whisper, "Well that was sure sweet of you, Joel."

Joel laughed nervously, "What do you mean?"

"You know what I mean," I answered with a smirk.

"Dude, I don't like her. Remember? We have to play this as a team."

I nodded teasingly, "Uh-huh. Are you sure that's all there is to it?"

Joel shoved my shoulder playfully, "Yeah, I'm sure."

I looked at my shoulder and then glared at him warningly. Timothy and I were about twice as big as any of the guys in the group, and we were all muscle. It was easy – and fun – to act tough and threatening, especially since most of the guys knew that it was just a joke. Part of the fun was that the guys knew that the joke could become real enough to behave themselves, and at times it had been necessary to show some 'tough-love' to some of the guys to correct their behavior. As far as the jokes went, Timothy and I only messed around in that way with Aaron, Joel, Mark, and our little brother Jacob; you know, the guys we were closest to that we knew understood and could take it and knew the difference between the joke and a real threat.

"Oh, sorry man," Joel pretended to brush off my shoulder.

I chuckled and added, "I'm just giving you a hard time Joel."

"Yeah man, I get it," Joel nodded and assured me that nothing was wrong just as a dodgeball bounced off the ground behind him and knocked him in the back of the head.

"Ow!" Joel shouted and began to rub the back of his head and turned around to narrowly avoid getting hit again.

"I love my job," I thought to myself as the game continued.

Chapter Fourteen

Timothy Stevens

Watching Adam appear and disappear around the training room reminded me of the first night he tried out his suit and his initial excitement.

"This is so cool! I can fly and shrink and run and fight at lightning speeds. Es ist unglaublich!" Adam had shouted as he bounced back and forth around the room and my GRID Connection had auto-translated Adam's excited German outburst for me. *"It's incredible!"*

From the beginning, Adam Holmes and Mary White always had at least two things in common…small size and high energy as both of them were tiny packets of joy and enthusiasm, the last four years hadn't tempered their enthusiasm much, but it did give them both a chance to grow a bit in size. Adam and Mary had both encouraged with the way they lived their lives to always put God's love on display for others. God's joy in our lives needs to be apparent and obvious to the world.

That first night I had encouraged both of them to thank the Lord for their energy and youth while they had it, because I knew full well that one day they might not have it anymore and Mary had challenged Adam to keep track of all the times that he thanked God for his energy in a week; last I had heard his record is over twenty times a day.

When we first began training Adam and Mary were both smaller in stature and the short jokes made about Adam and his code-name 'Atomizer' were abundant. "Did you shrink or is that your normal size?", "Hey Adam, where'd you go? Oh, there you are. I didn't see you and I thought you must've shrunk, but I guess not,", "Are you *sure* that's your normal size?". If either Mary or Adam became seriously embittered by the teasing they never showed any signs of it, but as a leader I often worried about them and did my best to keep everyone from getting carried away.

To counteract the teasing I had encouraged the two of them often to use whatever people said to energize them and drive them closer to the Lord, because they would never have to respond insult for insult. I had learned that it is possible to live out the verse: "when someone slaps you on the right cheek, turn to him the other as well". All that was needed was for us to entrust ourselves unto God, because He judges justly and He will defend us against cruel remarks or accusations.

As far as their height was concerned I told them to always remember that their spiritual stature was something that they can grow in and strengthen, and is infinitely more important than how tall they may or may not be. I encouraged them to thank God every day for every inch that He had given them and not to waste their time wishing that He would change His mind and make them different. Because even though them praying to be tall one day was perfectly fine, their understanding that His will for their lives is perfect was of greater value than being six feet tall one day.

Just for the record, both of them have grown quite a bit taller at this point, though neither made it to six feet.

As far as I could tell, Adam didn't really feel pain or have an end to his energy supply, or as Mark Arable put it one night, "Adam doesn't feel pain; he just converts it into energy." Hence, Joseph and I designed his metal-armored suit to absorb impacts and convert the kinetic energy into usable energy that would be stored on several Myathian based, rechargeable, promethium batteries. This stored energy could then be used to alter the Planck length of Adam's atoms and cause him – and whatever object he happened to be holding at the time – to shrink, while also granting him superhuman strength and allow him to fly at nearly the speed of light.

The charcoal colored gloves and boots had increased grip to help Adam hold fast to various materials while moving around at that small size and could transmit the Planck-altering energy to whatever object he happened to be holding. The rest of the armored suit was colored cardinal red and had dark blue accents and the motorcycle helmet he wore was the same shade of blue and the glass face plating in the helmet was designed to help Adam pinpoint his targets as he flew around the room

"Okay, Adam, slow down for a minute; I'd like to point out some things to you." I had called through the speakers, my head spinning from trying to track his movements around the training room.

"Klare Sache," Adam had called from somewhere near the ceiling and appeared a moment later on the ground below; my GRID continued to auto-translate for me: *"Sure thing."*

I continued to call to him through the speakers, "You seem to have figured out the basics of your suit and you should continue to grow in your understanding of it in years to come. There are some practical upgrades that you should know about."

"Okay," Adam had answered nodding his head.

I nodded to Sandra and she pushed a button that commanded two ComBots to walk into the room – one of which carried a new pair of gloves for Adam – before explaining the purpose of this upgrade. "These new gloves will allow you to take the same energy that allows your suit to shrink and spray that at a distant object, which will then affect the object just as if you were holding onto it."

Adam took off his first pair of gloves and gave them to the empty-handed ComBot before taking the new pair from the other robot. "So now I'll be able to shoot a shrink ray out of my hands? Erstaunlich!" he said as he gleefully pulled on the new gloves; then the translation came to me, *"Amazing!"*

"Go ahead and try them out," I called through the speakers.

"Okay," he called back and extended his right hand out toward the ComBot that had given him the gloves. A few moments later he found the mental switch to activate them and a stream of iridescent blue flashed out at the ComBot and it disappeared. Adam walked cautiously forward and searched the ground until he found the shrunken ComBot and held it up in the air.

"Very nice Adam," I encouraged through the speakers and nodded, "now to return the ComBot back to its original size you'll need to shrink down to its level to make sure that it is the only object effected by the ray."

"Ich verstehen," Adam had replied with a nod before shrinking out of sight. *"I understand."*

Moments later the ComBot – followed by Adam – reappeared in the training room. "How was that?" he asked, stretching out his arms and facing up at us.

"That was great Adam," Sandra replied. "There are still a few things that we need to go over though."

"Okay, I'll be right up," he called back, shrunk, and flew over to the door in order to open it while still in his shrunken state and make his way around the halls and stairs to make it to the observation room and the other Disciples excused themselves for a few moments.

Suddenly the door opened and Adam appeared in the doorway, "Hey, guys. Whatcha want to talk about?"

As Adam moved over to his chair I explained, "First you need to know that firing the shrink ray will require a great deal more energy than shrinking something by contact, and the greater the distance between you and the object will increase the energy needed."

Adam nodded," Yeah, I kinda noticed that the battery levels were a little low so I hit the walls extra hard on the way up to charge up."

"It's important that you keep you energy levels up high enough to keep the suit functioning properly," Sandra cautioned. "Obviously there is the risk of getting stuck two centimeters in height with dangerous carnivores out to eat you without super strength and speed to fight against them."

"So I just need to make sure I don't overuse the shrink ray and that I always have enough power to slam myself into something and start recharging my suit. Right?" Adam attempted to ensure that he knew the basics of what Sandra was saying.

"Exactly Adam," I nodded and continued, "and I'd also like to encourage you to keep serving the Lord with whatever it is that you have – regardless if anyone says it's not enough – because God doesn't make mistakes and He always supplies us with what it takes to follow him."

"Will do," he had answered with a thumbs-up.

Sandra and I smiled as we realized that he was beginning to get fidgety from staying still too long. "How'd you like to get out of here and go use some of that bottled-up energy in a dodgeball game?" My wife asked playfully.

"Ich dachte du würdest nie fragen!" he exclaimed as he shrunk and flew over to the door; *I thought you'd never ask!"* came the translation.

"Man, do these kids have a ton of energy," I chuckled before closing the door behind Adam with a gentle breeze and opening up the door where the other Disciples were waiting. "You want to head down to the training room Mark?" I asked the young man as the group entered the observation room.

"Sure thing," he called back and headed in that direction.

I let out a sigh as the students and Sandra were preoccupied in conversation and labored over when and how to increase the level of training that I had been giving to the Disciples. Up until this point few of them had used their abilities outside of these rooms or on anything other than the ComBots. While they possessed great skill and were physically ready for a real battle I wondered whether or not they were mentally prepared for what war would be like. An Idea suddenly came to mind of how to ease into that kind of a lesson with the students and I offered a prayer of thanksgiving unto the Lord.

Chapter Fifteen

Joseph Stevens

That night the dodgeball game just kept getting more interesting each time one of the gang came back from their solo training with Tim.

Beth – aka, 'NightOwl' – had been soaring through the air most of the night, phasing herself as the dodgeballs got close, and swooping down to help some of the others avoid getting beaned.

Mary – aka, 'SongBird' – had been flying around the room, using her songs to encourage and energize everyone to keep playing as she avoided getting hit.

Joel – aka, 'Carpenter' – had been turning his CW block into different wooden weapons – a sword, bat, and a shield were the easiest for him right now – and was deflecting the dodgeballs as they came at him.

Jacob – aka, 'Arcade', aka, 'my annoying little brother' – had been using his standard mode to fly around and blast the dodgeballs.

Adam – aka, 'Atomizer' – had arrived and quickly disappeared out of sight. The sound he made as he flew around the room kinda reminded me of a balloon with all the air coming out of it; that is, until one of the dodgeballs that had been flying towards me sharply changed directions. After that, Adam had appeared in a heap leaning against the wall behind me because the dodgeball had hit him and slammed him against the wall and he fell down to the floor but Adam hadn't seemed to notice, he just jumped back up, shrunk back down, and took off again and I could tell by the sound waves produced by his flight that he was moving even faster this time.

Aaron – aka, 'Clay' – was to my left, dodging all the shots taken at him as he molded his body to avoid getting hit.

I had been busy using my sound blasts to block any shots that were coming out of the guns too fast for the students to avoid, especially the shots aimed at the students that Tim hadn't trained yet.

Aaron had then moved closer and whispered, "What's up with KT?"

"What do you mean?" I asked, already knowing the answer. Aaron had asked similar questions enough for me to know where this conversation was headed.

"I mean he's our friend and you and Timothy gave him GRID abilities but he never shows up to train with us on Thursday. Aaron had said in frustration. "Doesn't he take this stuff seriously enough to show up every once in a while?"

I sighed to vent my own frustration, which was targeted more towards Aaron for bringing this up again than at KT. "KT works hard and travels a lot, so he can't make it to training on Thursdays."

"Hey, I get how work can get in the way sometimes," Aaron said as he arched backward to avoid having his head pounded by a dodgeball, "but I don't think that's an excuse to blow off training. He doesn't even come to Thursday night

Bible study, so how can he be part of the Defender Discipleship Program?"

I threw a sound blast from my fist in order to deflect a dodgeball; it was more to relief stress than to block the shot. "You can't possibly know whether or not KT ignores his training unless you've been spying on him. You've gotta cut him some slack and give him the benefit of the doubt. Besides, doesn't the fact that he does his best to show up for Sunday morning Bible study and training with us mean anything?"

I knew that on a given night each of the Disciples had struggled to stay focused or be involved with the rest of the group; even Aaron had difficulty paying attention recently and there wasn't really anything that could be done about short attention spans. I also knew that even though we all went through our ups and downs, we were doing our best to follow the Lord and grow closer to Him. I also knew KT well enough to know that he wasn't lazy or the kind of guy that would ignore his relationship with God or his combat training

"I guess," Aaron said as he ducked under a dodgeball, "I just don't understand why Timothy trains him as a Disciple if he isn't here."

"I've talked to Timothy about what's going on," I said, twisting my shoulders to avoid getting hit by a dodgeball. "He says that people don't have to fit with our mold in order for us to reach out to them and grow together; just because KT can't make it to Thursday or Friday nights doesn't mean that he can't be used by God one day as a Defender."

"But why doesn't Tim talk to him about it?" Aaron asked, stretching backward and flipping to dodge another dodgeball. "I mean, he could be getting more training time if he came.

"Because you can't force someone to sign up for every activity and Bible study." I answered shortly as I blasted a few dodgeballs to keep Joel and Jacob from getting hit.

"I know that you want KT to be here; Tim and I want the same thing," I said with a nod as I waited for the next round of dodgeballs to fly. "But KT doesn't need us to push him to do something that is beyond his ability, he needs us to be there as his friends and encourage him to follow the calling of the Lord."

Aaron had nodded his understanding and said, "I guess KT does what he can and his relationship with God is just between him and the Lord anyway."

Aaron had twisted and stretched to avoid the six dodgeballs that the guns had fired in his direction before saying, "I know why KT doesn't come to the study and I can reach out to him every now and then. But if he doesn't take this stuff seriously, then how are we going to be able to depend on him when what we're training for becomes real?"

I dove to my right to avoid a group of dodgeballs coming at me. "You want to know how we can be ready to fight with him since he doesn't train with us?"

"Exactly. Has Tim said anything about it?" Aaron asked, desperate for some direction.

I shrugged my shoulder and shook my head, "He said

that he didn't know for sure what the perfect solution is, but he doesn't expect us to be comfortable working with Swift or to depend on him too much if we have a problem with it."

I blasted a group of dodgeballs that were headed towards Bethany and scattered them around the room before adding, "Timothy also wanted to remind us that we should probably be relying on God more than each other anyway."

"I guess that makes sense," Aaron had said, avoiding a couple more dodgeballs. "We can't force anyone to be a disciple, but we can keep reaching out to them and try to help them grow."

"And whether or not they are growing is a matter for the Lord to decide," I added. "We have no right to look down on anyone based on how we think they should be living."

"Thanks for talking with me Joe," Aaron had said becoming slightly more serious during a break in the dodgeball attack. "It really does help when I have someone to talk to."

"Same here," I had answered putting my fist out.

Aaron had then stretched his arm across the room to give me a fist bump.

Aaron pulled his arm back and then got excited, "Hey do that again."

"Do what?" I asked, a bit confused at his excitement at the time.

"Fist bump," Aaron answered stretching out his arm again so that his fist was within my reach. "Only this time, send out some sound waves when our knuckles meet."

I pounded his fist with mine and shot out some sound

waves into his hand which made Aaron's Jell-O arm start to vibrate and pulse like a sine waveform signal; at least, that's what I remember Timothy saying it once he saw it, I just thought it was cool how Aaron's arm was doing the wave along with the pulse of my vibrations.

"That's cool," I said, changing the frequency and making the wave in his arm become more intense.

"Okay, now that just feels weird," Aaron stiffened his arm and pulled it back.

The two of us had then focused back on the dodgeball game because the guns began to target us more intently.

"Man, I guess Timothy must really want to wear us out before the real training even starts." Aaron joked as he narrowly dodged several shots from the guns.

"I guess so. So why don't we disappoint him and completely dominate this dodgeball game?" I replied to help him focus on the incoming attacks.

"Sounds good to me. I bet you that I'll be able to last longer than you without being hit," Aaron challenged in reply.
"You're on, Play-Dough," I replied, accepting the challenge and waiting for the victory party later.

Chapter Sixteen

Rodger Jones was staring into one of the many computer monitors that were residing in the spare bedroom of his apartment; a room that he has slowly transformed into his own personal computer laboratory over the years.

To say that Rodger was not your typical computer nerd would be to understate as he was far more advanced and far more orderly. His computer room was extremely neat and orderly with cables of various types and lengths all categorically labeled and stored in the properly labeled and organized shelf in the closet of the room alongside boxes and bins of various computer components were also systematically organized and in their proper place in the closet. The papers and other office supplies were neatly placed in practical locations and all the active computers were neatly arranged around the room; some of the computers finding their home atop of a desk or shelf while others were mounted to the walls. To put it simply, Rodger was an obsessively compulsive organizer and a clean freak, but he was okay with that because it improved his work quality.

Rodger had long ago determined that Earth's current computer programing languages and protocols were far below him and his intellect, being able to access the CIA computer database at the age of seven without detection was a major indicator of that fact. So Rodger created his own computer language – one that he would soon discover was very similar to the advanced Myathian codes – and he used that to create the computer network in his apartment laboratory.

The most difficult part was in creating a suitable user interface for this advanced computer network that could keep up with Rodger's mind. This difficulty was alleviated in part by the fact that Rodger had made a large sum of money over the years as a black ops computer hacker, at least that was his title for himself. Over the years Rodger developed a mindvoice interface that would allow him to telepathically give commands to his PANIC lab, though if he really wanted to he could also use verbal or bodily commands to interface with his PANIC lab; but why would he impede in his progress by using a lower level of communication? Rodger didn't need the personal satisfaction of verbally expressing himself, he just needed to complete his objective.

In many ways Rodger had almost become a computer as commands came in and results went out. Rodger wasn't afraid of socialization, he just didn't see a point to it, so if Rodger left his apartment it was to purchase supplies – tech or food mostly – or to fulfill some other obligatory function that couldn't be done online.

As Rodger stared up at the monitor in front of him – his current project was to further infiltrate the SOS Corps database for the digital copies of the memory orbs gathered by Agents Pentecost and Reverb – an alert went off stating that a foreign presence was detected within the PANIC lab.

"What new assignment does the Sorcerer have for me this time Widow?" Rodger asked without averting his gaze, knowing that only Zilvia or Simon could have infiltrated the lab without being detected at the front door and Simon himself would have only been discovered when he decided to whisper sinisterly into Rodger's ear.

Rodger spun around in his chair as Zilvia grew from her shrunken size in the center of the room.

"What is your explanation for your idiotic failure last night, Virus?" Zilvia demanded angrily. Rodger had noticed that her accent seemed French but was still distinct from the French sound bites that he had heard over the years.

"What failure would that be, Widow? I gave you the information you needed to complete your mission." Rodger answered, annoyed at her disturbance of his work, and her accusation of him only made things worse.

"The information you provided proved to be false." Zilvia said, crossing her arms.

"How so?" Rodger answered, confident that he would have some explanation to excuse himself.

"You informed us that no one would be within the SOS headquarters last night, yet when I made it inside I found Firecracker still active."

Rodger smiled at how she had ignored his previous warnings, "I cautioned you before that I could not guarantee that the HQ would be empty."

"Yes, but why didn't you inform me that he was still in there before I entered the base?"

"Because I was preoccupied with making sure that no one was made aware of your infiltration into the headquarters." Rodger smiled mischievously, "And because I was also distracted with how you decided to poison Titus after Simon had strictly forbidden you from killing anyone."

Zilvia's eye's narrowed, "You were watching?"

"Of course," Rodger nodded, "and you have me to thank for the fact that Simon knows nothing of your disobedience and insubordination."

Rodger's arrogant attitude was accentuated by his youthfulness; it irritated Zilvia to no end to be spoken to in such a way by a boy of a mere sixteen years.

"Now was there something worth my time that brought you here this afternoon or was that all you had to say?"

Zilvia hesitated a moment before stating, "The day you are no longer useful to the Komplo is the day I am free to kill you, Virus."

At that Rodger had to chuckle, "I very much doubt that there will ever be a time when your Komplo doesn't have a need for my expertise. So, was there anything that I could do for you, *La Veuve*?" Rodger only used the French translation of 'The Widow' to add a new layer to his insult.

Zilvia turned her gaze to a spot on the floor and said, "Grow."

At that moment, a ComBot obediently used its INSECT technology to appear next to Zilvia in its silver standby form.

Zilvia lowered her hands to her side and gave Rodger his assignment. "Simon wants you to attempt to access the programming on this ComBot for rewriting. Should you ever find a way to reprogram the ComBot Simon will contact you with the specific changes he wants made."

Rodger nodded, "Anything to increase my *usefulness* to the Komplo."

Zilvia again narrowed her gaze, "Fail again and it will cost you your life, Rodger Jones."

"Oh, and here I thought that this was to be a professional relationship; I'm surprised now to find that you care enough to know my name, Zilvia." Rodger answered mockingly.

Zilvia simply shrunk back down and made her way out of the apartment building and back to the point where Simon could teleport her back to the base.

Rodger knew that the stakes of working with the Komplo were high, or at least higher than any other client because they were not only willing to kill him but knew exactly who and where he was. It was also concerning because the SOS Corps had a much more sophisticated computer system than anything he had ever infiltrated before and it had been painfully slow going. Simon had already chastised Rodger on multiple occasions for his slow progress. But despite the difficulty he had already overcome, Rodger knew from the history of these ComBots – how the greatest programmers in all seven realms had installed their own method of security systems to ensure the safety of these robots – that the hardest task was yet before him. Wouldn't Zilvia jump at the opportunity to punish Rodger for his failure? If Simon didn't kill him first, that is.

"I guess failure isn't an option, Virus. You better get the job done," Rodger said to himself as he walked towards the ComBot.

"Let's just hope that Zilvia brought me an agreeable specimen," he didn't realize until then that he had started talking to himself and took measures to correct that character inconsistency as he examined the ComBot.

Chapter Seventeen

Timothy Stevens

"Okay 'Maestro', let's see what you can do," I told the young man as I prepared to activate the ComBots armed to attack him.

"Let's have some fun," he replied with mock sinisterness.

Mark Arable had always been a confident pianist and had a good understanding of the interworking of musical theory. At eighteen years of age, he had a good head on his shoulders and is very straightforward and he told it like it was without holding back what was on his mind.

Perhaps the biggest struggle that I saw him deal with early on was in how to exercise his gifts with a genuine love for the Lord and people; to balance the truth of God with the love of God. Like me, his head was active and in line with God, most of the time. This was a characteristic that, over the years, had proven to be truer than I originally realized for both of us, but we both also had a problem with keeping our hearts on track at times. One of the things I'd learned was that it takes continual growth to keep that sort of thing in check in my own life, and I prayed then that Mark would similarly outgrow his impersonal approach as he got closer to the Lord.

I had incorporated Mark's understanding of music

into the GRID connection that I helped him establish. Part of that meant that he could use a mindsong to 'orchestrate' nonliving objects of various size and density around him with the aid of his conductor's baton; an ability that he could use to move a small platform while he stood on it to hover, or pseudo-fly, around the room.

Along with his conductor's baton, Mark was dressed in full music-conductor's garb, with a shear-resistant three piece suit, a red bow tie, and leather dress shoes that completed Mark's alias as 'Maestro' along black mask was added to prevent the world from knowing who he really was.

Mark had quickly learned how to precisely control smaller objects, however denser objects were more of a struggle for him and I had also noticed that the movements of the objects were rather jerky and sharp, so I arranged a special exercise for him to correct that. I had placed a small amount of explosives with some confetti inside of some paper containers so that if the explosives were jostled around too much they would detonate and send the confetti flying.

Mark had always been great with technology and instruments and while he was never very harsh at times, his interactions with people had needed some additional understanding. I was thankful that I had accomplished what I had hoped that night when I talked with Mark after he worked with the explosives. Mark began to accept that people aren't things and when we use our gifts – and that went for our spiritual gifts and our talents, as well as for our 'powers' – we need to use those gifts with gentleness and love. I knew that without love, everything we do in life would be meaningless before God and unbearably harsh before man. I knew that sometimes teaching was just a matter of compassionately finding the right way to say something for someone to get it, and I had been able to make some progress in teaching Mark how to do just that.

The ComBots had a small amount of biotechnology within them, which was just enough to make it so that Mark couldn't control them directly, however he could still use objects within the room as weapons; including his own baton, the light fixtures, wall panels, doorways, and the ComBots' own firearms. Within moments one of the light panels had been removed and broken over a ComBot's head, a door hinge had lodged itself into another's chest, several others were crushed by a Cainium panel that fell from the wall, and the rest were taken out by the fallen robots' weapons that were now under Mark's control.

After the last Bot fell Mark looked up at the observation room with his arm stretched out, "Well…What y'all think about that?"

"Nicely done, Mark," Sandra called through the intercom. "Come on up and we'll go over your performance."

When Mark walked into the room I turned and asked him with a grin, "So did you enjoy your coffee this afternoon?"

"Yeah…I did," Mark answered hesitantly. "How did you know that I stopped for coffee?"

Sandra smiled with a knowing expression, "We told you early on that the scanners that the Defender Discipleship Program uses to detect interdimensional threats could also pick up your abilities."

Those scanners that Sandra mentioned had detected the GRID lag of Mark's abilities and pinpointed his location for us as he used those abilities to make his own coffee and left enough cash in the tips jar to pay for it before leaving. This was something that Mark had done on occasion in the past but hadn't made a habit out of yet.

"Yeah, I remember," Mark nodded, "I was just in a hurry this afternoon."

"Mark," I shook my head with a slight chuckle, "I know that virtually every one of you Disciples have used your abilities outside of the training sessions; sometimes to save someone's life and other were just for sport. I don't have any problem with you guys finding some real world application for your GRID Connections when you go out with Marcus, but carelessly drawing attention to yourself like that will come back to hurt you one day."

I had always been thankful for Mark's straightforward nature because it went both ways; not only did he shoot straight and tell it like it was but he was okay with people shooting straight with him and being blunt without needing to beat around the bush. I would be relying heavily on his ability to accept the truth regardless as to how pointedly it came at him.

Mark nodded and shrugged his shoulder, "Yeah, I was just trying to avoid the line and get home faster; it just seemed easier to make the coffee myself."

I shook my head, "We don't always have the option to do things the easy way in life, because most often our responses to the situation need to be dictated by circumstances we find ourselves in. And avoiding one problem doesn't make it go away, Mark; usually another will spring up in its place."

Mark nodded and ran a hand through his long hair, "Right, because by using my abilities to avoid the line I could've drawn attention to myself and put my family in danger; I could've but I didn't," he added with his characteristic sarcastic enthusiasm; sarcasm ran in his family, apparently.

"I know that patience is one of those things that no one really wants to sign up to learn, but you might want to consider getting the 'class' over with." I said with a smile as I was flooded with memories of the various 'classes' that the Lord had enrolled me in to teach me life's lessons. Things that I had tried to avoid became my everyday life. "Besides, God doesn't usually let us get away with avoiding things like that forever."

"Yeah, I know," Mark agreed with a nod.

"Just be more careful about when, where, how, and why you're using your abilities, Mark," Sandra brought a gentle edge to the otherwise straightforward, factual, conversation and I was grateful for her input.

"I get it," Mark nodded before a puzzled expression spread across his face. "Have you guys been surveilling us?"

I shook my head, "No."

"But you said that you knew that each of us had used our abilities before. How could you know that unless you were monitoring us?"

I motioned with my hands to try and calm him, "The scanners pick up the GRID Signal emitted and the computers can decipher the GRID Code and determine whether the signal was produced by a person or if a Doorway is opening, the computers will then begin scanning the code for DNA segments of the person emitting the signal so that an ID can be made eventually, and in the event of one of you Disciples needing an organ transplant or a blood transfusion we have a supply of your blood and records of your DNA so the computer will quickly identify your guys' GRID Signal."

"So how did you figure out that I used my abilities at the coffee shop?" Mark asked trying to fit all the pieces together.

Sandra sat forward in her seat, "Whenever the computers notify us that one of you is exercising your abilities outside of the training rooms we immediately make sure that none of you are in serious danger and that any video cameras that might be in the area are disabled."

"We trust each of you implicitly," I added, "or else you wouldn't be in the program at all. We just do our best to make sure that we've got your back and that your families are kept safe."

Mark nodded, "Thanks guys, it's good to know that someone is thinking of the little things for us."

"That's why we work as a team Mark," I smiled, "so we can take care of each other and fill in where someone needs it."

Another thought came to Mark suddenly. "Hey, Timinski, how come Beth not only gets away with but has your permission to use her abilities to hide out and scare the heck out of me while I have to work on being more controlled and not get carried away?" he complained playfully.

I chuckled. "She told you about that?"

"Don't avoid the question," he countered with a glare. "She's been driving me crazy for the past four years and I'd kinda like to know why."

"Okay," I said, putting my hands up in mock surrender, "Her abilities necessitate that she hide within the walls, I simply gave her permission to give you a hard time while she does it. Plus, I doubt that you need extra encouragement to get on Beth's nerves."

"Well, she doesn't need an excuse to get on my nerves either." Mark had argued.

"True," I had nodded in agreement and replied, "Though I must admit that it has been fun to hear about how she gets to freak you out every now and then."

Mark had glared at me. "Every now and then? She's done it nearly day."

"Well then you should be expecting it and it won't bother you as much," I had teased.

He had replied by glaring at me again, only more intently this time.

I had chuckled again, "Well, at least use the opportunity as a practical exercise in dealing with people who are…difficult."

Mark shook his head and asked, "So was there anything else that you wanted to talk about?"

Sandra shook her head, "Not unless you have something you'd like to ask."

Mark hesitated for a moment before asking, "You guys don't have a problem with Beth and I being a part of The Squad, do you?"

Marcus had gone on some late night crime fighting outings with some of the young adults he had grown closest to from the SOS Corps for some late night crime fighting. Mark and Bethany were a part of 'The Squad' and because Marcus had trained so often with them it was easy for him to recognize that they had developed some unique skills over the years and asked them about it; at which point they had told him about their training in the Defender Discipleship Program.

"You don't have to be exclusively trained with us in order to be used by God and accepted here," Sandra replied with a gentle shake of her head. "One day God may call you away from this Program in order to take part in another ministry and it's important to follow His leading above what people might think about it."

I nodded and added to what my wife had shared with him, "It's not about us, Mark; it's about the glory of God being declare throughout the world. The only reason why you shouldn't be a part of a ministry is if God is leading you away from it, even if He doesn't give you a reason why. So if God is okay with you being a part of The Squad, then we don't have a problem with it at all."

Mark nodded and shrugged his shoulder, "I figured that's what you guys would say, but Aaron was asking about it and got Beth a little freaked out that you guys were offended by it or something."

I smiled to show that there weren't any hurt feelings, "Well, when you head into the dodgeball game, be sure to let Beth know that everything is fine."

"Will do," Mark nodded and pointed as he walked towards the door.

After Mark left and the others came back in I started to think about how The Squad had been very beneficial in helping Bethany and Mark have some real world experience, but I was still concerned that they – along with the other Disciples – might not fully understand the gravity of what they were truly training for. In the future they wouldn't be fighting merely to stop some thrill seeking teenagers or the like from robbing a bank, they would be fighting for their very lives and the lives of their families against desperate people with no concern about whether or not they lived or died; radical Islamists, starving refugees, or dedicated soldiers wouldn't care who tried to stand in their way which meant that there would be greater risk with higher stakes for losing.

"Who's next in line for the warmup?" Joann West asked from the doorway.

"I believe that it is Kara's turn," I answered as I contemplated the best way to teach my lesson to the Disciples. Suddenly an idea came to mind; *Thank you Lord... that's a great idea. This Saturday then? Yeah, that should work.*

I continued my private conversation with the Lord as Kara

made her way down to the training room. The group that would come over Saturday would be in for a bit of a shock.

Chapter Eighteen

Colorado Springs, CO   Thursday, August 8, 2044

Silas Harrison

The bell above Leon's Bar & Grill gave its familiar 'hello' as I opened the door.

"I'll be right with you," the waitress called out as she served at the corner table where two men shared drinks with another woman. The woman's sandy-blonde hair was neatly braided and contrasted with her lavender dress. One of the men seated with her looked like he was in his late fifties while the other man appeared to be much younger and had his back to the door.

"All right ma'am," I answered walking past a dark skinned man sitting near the door and heading to my usual seat at the bar. I had been sharing coffee and dinner with Leon at his place every Friday night since I was assigned to Fort Carson nearby and I preferred this seat at the bar because I could easily see both the front and back doors without having to turn around much. The mirror at the bar allowed me to see everything and everyone behind me. There was a spider that had made its web in the corner above the back door, but other than that everything was normal at Leon's. Except there was no Leon.

"Where's Leon?" I asked the waitress as she came over to where I was waiting.

"Oh, he took the night off, but I'll be sure to take care of you, Soldier boy," the waitress flirted as she wiped down the already clean bar with a towel. Her British accent was smooth and sweet as she commented on my uniform; I always came over right after my shift and didn't have time to change.

I was suddenly thankful for the extra people in the room tonight and the trio in the corner and the man sitting near the door suddenly seemed like a blessing. Usually, it was just me and Leon, but I didn't trust myself alone with this gal. I looked over and thought that it seemed strange that the man near the door was still wearing his leather gloves inside.

"So what can I get you, soldier boy?" The waitress asked. Her name badge read 'Luna', her curly blonde hair bounced on her shoulders as she moved, and her uniform was snug; I'm sure that she probably earned bigger tips because of it.

I shook my head and blinked to clear my thoughts, "I'd appreciate a cup of strong, black, coffee and a cheeseburger, ma'am."

"Are you sure you don't want something more relaxing?" Luna asked, hinting towards an alcoholic drink.

When we first met I told Leon that if I ever asked for anything stronger than coffee to refuse, partly because I knew that it was assumed that a Christian shouldn't drink and I have been much more open with my faith since those meetings with Pastor Juan. I guess I wanted to set a good example, and I knew it would be harder if my mind was clouded by alcohol.

But it's also because I knew that it would be very easy for me to become an alcoholic since the desire and the taste was there for it. If I allowed myself to go down that road even one step, then it wouldn't be long before I'd be in the gutter. So for my own sake, along with everybody else's, I made the personal decision not to drink alcohol.

"Yes, I'm sure," I replied simply and nodded my head.

"All right, one cup of coffee coming right up," Luna answered as she turned to retrieve the pot of coffee and a mug.

"So, what is your occupation, soldier boy?" Luna asked, leaning forward on the bar as she poured my coffee.

"I'm an army ranger, ma'am," I answered and scanned the mirror. The conversation at the trio's table had died and I noticed that the woman was rubbing the side of her head with her eyes closed shut while the older man facing me was staring intently into his drink and the younger still had his back turned to me but he seemed quite relaxed as he enjoyed his drink. "I've been helping train chinook repairmen while stateside."

"What's a chinook," Luna asked, setting the pot down and pushing the mug over to me, leaning farther over the bar as she did.

"It's a helicopter, ma'am," I answered, accepting the mug from her. I was suddenly thankful for the way that girls in high school would flirt and follow me around because it gave me some training in remaining polite yet distant.

"Really, now? And you get to work on them? That

sounds intriguing," Luna put her elbows on the bar and leaned forward in interest. "Tell me about the army. What's it like?"

"What would you like to know?" I asked, glancing at the man near the door and saw him rubbing the table with his fingertips while watching me in the mirror; I was starting to get a bad feeling about these guys.

Luna straightened slowly and started wiping the bar again with her towel, "Well, I was just wondering how tough you soldier boys were. Do you think, for instance that you could measure up to Her Majesty's marines?" she said teasingly.

I smiled and look up at the different bottles and things behind her. "I'm sure we could give them a run for their money, ma'am."

My first year enlisted in the US Army hadn't been at all like I had thought. I mean, whose idea was it to give the fuzzies stress cards in case their drill sergeants yelled at them a little too much? A lot of what we did at basic was all for show. I mean, sure, the first few weeks were real hard to get used to and they kept us in shape after that, but over the long haul it seemed easier than I was expecting.

Thankfully, I had a few contacts in the SOS Corps that had connections with some of the Army supervisors. Because of those connections, I managed to find someone at each assigned base that would make life harder for me and push me to my limits, 'cuz I like pain; I know, I'm a strange child.

"I'm hoping to get transferred to the Middle East

sometime soon," *As soon as my SOS friends can fix it, that is.*
That location would make it easy for me to make a difference
in saving lives as Chopper.

"Oh, that's a shame," Luna brought her hand closer to
mine. "That means our friendship will have to end soon," she
said gently stroking my hand with her finger, "and we've
only just met."

I cleared my throat and brought the mug to my mouth,
"Afraid so, ma'am." I had moved more to get my hand away
from Luna than to take a drink, 'cuz the coffee was still
burning hot. I blew gently at the surface before setting the
mug back down, putting my hands on my lap afterwards.

Luna leaned forward on the bar and whispered gently,
"Well, why don't you and I take a bottle over to my place and
make some lasting memories? I was getting ready to lock up
anyway."

I looked down at my coffee for a moment as ideas
battled in my mind.

Why not? I mean, it's not like anyone would ever
know.

Because it's wrong, Silas. That's why not.

But why do I have to follow these rules? No one else
does.

Because this is what God has shown me to be true
and I need to be obedient to that.

Well maybe…maybe I don't have to fight so hard.
Maybe I can cool off a bit and have some fun along the way.
If I don't ask God for as much, then maybe He won't ask as
much of me.

That was the breaking point; it was like the ropes holding my mind hostage broke. I used to live the lukewarm, carnal Christian life and I hated it and was miserable. It wasn't until God used Pastor Juan and the Defender Corps to shake me out of that life that I realized what I was missing. There was absolutely no way that I was going back to that life, 'cuz there was no compromise worth it.

I slowly lifted my head and looked Luna in the eye. "I appreciate the offer ma'am, but I respect you as a woman – and Jesus as my Lord – too much to do what you are asking." I stood and turned to leave.

As I turned I caught the glint of metal in the mirror. Something shiny was on top of the building across the street and was reflecting light from the moon.

I dove to the side just as I heard the pop of a .223 caliber rifle. I rolled and stood just as the man from up front leaped to his feet and moved forward.

"Finally, I get some action around here," I said, preparing for a tussle.

I heard the metallic sound of several knives being unsheathed as the man started to slash and swipe at me.

As I looked to try and spot the knives I heard, I realized that each of the fingertips on the dark man's gloves came to a shiny, razor edged, point; the man apparently had cat's claws in his gloves or something.

Movement at the bar caught my eye. I turned and realized that Luna had completely transformed from the blonde waitress I had just met, her once curly hair was now perfectly straight and had more red streaks in it and now she looked more like a biker wearing white leather with yellow accents streaked across everything, and her gloves, boots, and shoulder pads also had bright blue rings painted on them. Luna had leapt over the bar and her gloves began to glow an eerie blue color.

She may be trying to kill me, but man is she a head turner.

I held up a finger and turned back from Luna to the Cat-in-Black, "You guys must be the tourists that Pentecost was telling me about." My voice took on a mockingly polite tone as I continued, "So tell me, how do you like our realm so far?"

The man in black answered by slashing at me again, his movements were designed to push me back into the booths along the wall.

I knew I had to move; I had to get away from the window so the sniper would stop taking shots at me.

At least the three at the table weren't putting up a fight, the woman held her face in her palms and was breathing heavy, the older man continued to stare at the table, and the younger man was still enjoying his drink.

I charged forward as I heard another gunshot, the bullet whistled by where my head used to be. I tackled the man with the claws and drove him back into another part of the bar. The windows weren't as large in this part of the building so I wouldn't have to worry about the sniper as much.

As we went down, I felt the claws dig into my back slightly and I arched backward. When the man hit the floor he pulled his claws out of my back and went to thrust them into my ribs, but I grabbed his wrists rolled over to the side. With a mighty heave I pushed him off of me and to the side as we rolled. The man landed on his feet and charged forward again as I hurried to my feet and worked to keep his claws from slicing me open.

I heard a gunshot and felt the bullet make contact in my left calf. I ignored it and moved forward as I realized that I was having trouble using mental commands to activate my hover-pack. I know that there was enough firepower in that thing to make a quick end of this fight if I could only get the stupid thing to open.

I suddenly got an eerie feeling about the others that were sitting together at the table earlier. *I wonder if maybe those three are putting up a fight after all.* I thought as I barely ducked under a slash to my face and drove forward with some quick punches to the cat's midsection.

"Have y'all had a chance to see some of the sights here?" I asked mockingly.

A moment later, Luna leapt on my shoulders and wrapped herself around my neck causing me to struggle for breath as she tightened her legs around my neck. Thankfully, I grabbed her wrists just before she could touch me with that strange glow.

The cat wasn't waiting idly, but was moving forward with those claws ready to cut me open.

I slammed myself to the ground and kicked my legs out, making the cat trip and skid forward on the floor as I felt Luna's death grip on my neck loosen 'cuz she had hit her head hard when we went down.

"Tim always misses out on all the fun. I can't wait to tell him about what happened while he was leading the Bible study." I thought as I grabbed the .45 pistol that I always kept on my hip.

The cat reached me before I could fire it at him and slashed at my midsection while I bashed the side of his head with the gun. He went down in a heap on the floor, and the front of my now torn shirt became stained with my own blood.

I staggered backward, the hole in my leg had been bleeding a lot more than I thought it had, so the bullet must have hit an artery or something. "I guess you guys are the power hungry dictator type," I said as I limped and turned to scan the bar, holding my pistol out and ready to fire at whoever would attack next. "Well, I hope that you've had a pleasant visit to our realm, and please be sure to cause much less trouble on your way home,"

I felt the sting of a bug biting the back of my neck and went to swat it, as I did I turned and saw a small spider crawling on one of the tables nearby. Though when I looked closer I realized that it wasn't a spider but a spider-sized woman, running toward me on the table top.

When she reached the end of the table she jumped, and made it much farther than I expected. I swung my hand to swat her away, but she grew to normal size, blocking my swing and jabbing her knee into my ribs; sending shots of pain into the tender and bleeding flesh.

In my hunched-over position I mentally yelled at my

pack to activate and turn on the thrusters; I heard the older man moan from the other room as my gear finally started up and I flew forward, pushing the spider-woman into the metal doorway to the kitchen.

The woman went limp on my shoulder and I could mentally control my pack again. I lowered down to the ground and rolled the woman off of me, her long black hair came down to her shoulders and she was wearing black leather armor with red color patterns, with small red hourglasses on her belt, gloves, and boots.

I turned my body and leaned against the wall, before seeing the young woman from the corner table standing there reminded me that there were still others to deal with here.

Why do these Tourists of Terror have to be so cute? I thought as I tried to stand to face her.

"Shhh…" the woman from the table put her hand out to try and calm me. "You've already done so much."

I slumped back down to the ground and it felt as though all my muscles had turned to lead.

"Why do you need to sacrifice more?" the woman pleaded. Her face was overcome with sympathy and her lavender blouse seemed to stir as though there was a breeze in the building.

The pistol in my hand grew heavier than I could bear, and she did have a point. I had already done so much, I had already struggled, and fought with so much passion. Did I really have to be so aggressive in life?

"Just rest now, there is no need for you to keep fighting this war."

Again the light broke through my foggy mind. I struggled and pushed my way to my feet, even if I fell flat on my face I was going to stand and fight. "I am a soldier of the Lord, and I do not fight without passion and purpose, ma'am. As long as there is breath within me I am going to serve Him with everything I got."

The woman clutched her head with both hands and crumpled to the floor whimpering and groaning.

"Bravo, Silas!" a sinister voice echoed in the room.

"Oh yeah, there's still one more of you tourists to welcome to Earth and send packing." I wheezed looking over to where the man was last sitting with his drink. To be honest, I wasn't so sure how well I would hold up in a fight against another tourist with unknown abilities.

The voice chuckled, "You never stood a chance, Chopper. Now, shall I put the final nail in your pathetic coffin?"

"I'm not dead yet," I said, looking around to try and locate the man.

"Poor child. So weak and frail, and yet so bold and confident. Tell me, how do you know that my sniper doesn't have you in his sights at this very moment?

The room began to blur and colors began to spin. I could feel the back of my neck swelling and it was getting harder to breathe.

"It seems that the Widow accomplished more than either of us thought. Speaking of which, how do you know that these warriors aren't merely feigning defeat?"

The blurry forms of the fallen tourists began to rise

and surround me until I blinked and shook my head; my vision cleared for a brief moment and all the tourists were still lying on the floor in their places.

"If you don't mind I'd kinda like to get this over with and get home," I struggled to make out the words, "I've got to get an early start tomorrow."

"Very well," the man replied, appearing in the center of the room. Now he was wearing a dark cloak over his shoulders with white gloves that stood in contrast to his otherwise dark and sinister appearance.

"Let's get this over with, shall we?" he asked as he motioned with his hands and a neon green cloud began to form and circle around them.

The man threw a large green blast at me I dove to the side and activated my jet pack to fly around the restaurant; as I looked back I saw the cloud slam into the wall and explode.

"Leon's going to have a heck of a time fixin' this place up," I said after flying through the glass window up front. I headed towards the sniper with his .22 rifle and fired a few rounds at him, which made him jump off of the short building and roll on the ground before taking cover around the corner.

I flew in the direction of the army base, praying that the last two tourists would follow and that I could get some medical treatment soon.

I looked back over my shoulder, I was beginning to feel really groggy and had to put my jet pack on autopilot.

I turned and looked ahead and saw the last tourist appear in front of me. I swerved to the left and fired a couple of shots at him; he only motioned with his hand and didn't get hit.

"Now, I know I'm a better shot than that," I mumbled in frustration.

"Yes, indeed you are. So why don't we allow those bullets find their mark?" The man waved with his hand and I immediately felt the bullets bury themselves deep in my lower back.

My vision went black and I felt myself plummeting to the ground as I heard the man chuckle, "One down. Four to go."

Chapter Nineteen

"All right Kara, let's see what else you can do with what your parents have taught you," I called through the intercom of the observation room down into the training room where Kara was at.

When we first met, Kara Green was a quiet but confident fifteen year-old friend of Mary's and she – along with her older sister, Jennifer – had both surprised me with their lack of initial timidity when they were first asked to participate in reading Scriptures for the study. Both of the Green sisters – now in their early twenties – had both known what to say when they needed to, but they didn't have to be the center of attention and neither of them were afraid to ask hard questions, even as strangers to the group; that humble confidence was something that I appreciated and tried to maintain in my own walk with the Lord.

Equally as surprising to me was the fact that I had met their great-grandparents in Myathis, and that night I learned that the GRID Connections of Damien and Dina Kyul had been passed on through the generations dormant until manifesting themselves in Kara and Jennifer.

What Kara had inherited from her great-grandfather was the ability to combine, ionize, and control various elements on the extended Myathian periodic table. These ionized elements had a variety of results, from xenon's gentle glow, to electrium's explosive reaction, to dechomain's energy absorption qualities. These were a few of the possibilities that Kara would eventually learn to master under the alias of 'Plasma' as her great-grandfather, Damien, had done before he died.

Her parents seem to have done a good job teaching her. I had thought as I considered how there must have been some knowledge passed on through the generations for Plasma to be demonstrating this level of control this early on and the suit that I had designed for Kara would help her to control which elements and effects she would produce. The appearance of the suit was a deep purple color to match the glow of her ionized elements, with violet gloves and boots to complete the outfit. Joseph had also designed a thin visor that would wrap around her head over her eyes, and the translucent, violet glass had a nano-thin computer screen that would help her plot the course of her ionized elements; this same screen was applied to most of the other eyewear that the other Disciples possessed.

When she asked for points on how to control when the electrium would react with the air and produce and explosion I was reminded that no matter how far we come along with the Lord there is always more for us to learn.

I had referenced the custom of ancient Israel that is recorded for us in the Old Testament of setting up memorial stones to remind us of the blessings that God gives us and applied that to the way that God could energize and empower her the same way that she ionized and empowered her various elements; those elements which are extremely small and seem insignificant because of their small size, until when the right person energizes them and directs their use so that they become extremely useful and dangerous tools. In the same way we in and of ourselves are weak and rather insignificant and incapable of doing anything of eternal value, until we are motivated, empowered, and guided by the Holy Spirit so that He can do amazing things through us.

That night, I had been reminded of Isaiah 40:28-31 and shared with Kara what the Lord had brought to my memory. "It's the one that waits upon the empowering of the Lord that is strong. Those that stay 'plugged into' a relationship with Him. When we are empowered by Him, we can then exercise the gifts that He has given us under the direction of the Holy Spirit."

Kara had continued to nod as the pieces fit into place; if she would've had her notebook with her I'm sure she would have been furiously taking notes like she normally did during the study.

That first night Kara revealed her ability to control the various elements in order to hit various targets, defend against electrical attacks, and light up the room. I was able to help her control the timing of her electrium blasts by explaining to her that night how her great-grandfather used to create an absorption field – similar to Kara's dechomain field – that would stabilize the reactive energy blasts until either the reactive energy overwhelmed the protective coating or if that shielding was broken by colliding with another object.

There had been some difficulty in explaining how I could have met someone that died several years before either of us would have been born, because the distortion that traveling through the portals had upon the timeline was still a bit of an enigma to me. Despite the advancements that have been made through the efforts of the SOS Corps scientists to utilize the technology that Joseph and I had retrieved to stabilize the portals there was still a bit of time distortion that could take place along the interdimensional transit.

Tonight, Kara was exhibiting a new ability as she began to surround herself in another ionized element – that we had yet to identify – and levitate in flight; which would make Plasma the last of the 'true fliers' in the group.

Sandra looked up from her monitors, "There doesn't appear to be any abnormalities as far as her personal health is concerned; her blood pressure, heart rate, and oxygen levels are all normal."

"Thank you dear," I replied and consulted the readings that were on the monitor in front of me, "there doesn't seem to be any radioactive decay detected, so whatever this new element she's using should be safe for both her and the other students."

Moments later the element that allowed Chloe to float around the room was identified: maglevium. That helped explain the antigravity tendencies and why the computers had such a hard time identifying it; maglevium was an extremely rare element because it took such great and expensive lengths to manufacture it and so the computers didn't have an available model to compare Chloe's ionized element to.

The bright glow of the ionized elements triggered a memory and I shook my head as my most recent dream replayed in my mind. Eight shadowy figures had recently entered my dreams as prominent figures – eight shadows that embodied my worst fear for my students –and I could sense that several of these figures were from realms other than Earth; I assumed them to be the tourists that had recently arrived. Somehow these people would greatly threaten the lives of my students and I had to figure out a way to prevent that from happening; somehow.

"It seems like everyone is learning something new these past two months," Joann West remarked.
"It does indeed, Joann," I replied cheerfully before adding under my breath, "but I can only imagine exactly what new dangers all this is for."

Chapter Twenty

Jaxson Harper sat in his personal training room in the Komplo's base in southern New Mexico, a room that he was beginning to identify as his prison cell. Jack hadn't been allowed to leave the base since he had arrived and he was beginning to go stir crazy.

The only comfort he had found was in honing his blades to absolute perfection before using them on the nearest target and repeating the process. Jack was currently running his eye down the sharp edge of his custom made arming sword. Of all Jack's weapons this one was his baby – with the blade perfectly balanced and the grip perfectly molded for his hand – and was considered priceless to Jack.

The light reflected off the blade and caused a strange flicker to appear in the doorway of the room. Jack pretended not to notice as he put the stone down and grabbed his cloth to polish the blade, all the while he kept an eye on how the light moved. The reflected light would momentarily flicker in the empty space – as though it was shining on something even though nothing was there – before shining back on the wall where it should be.

Jack deftly sheathed his precious arming sword and pulled out a small throwing knife, one that he had already honed to perfection, and pretended to examine it for flaws.

After a moment of this charade, Jack spoke up, intentionally moving the light reflection from the blade to keep his eye on the intruder he knew was there. "The only hope you have in getting out of here alive is if your name is Luna, and then only if you show yourself in the next two seconds."

Luna then appeared in the room, a step to the right of where Jack had expected her to be but still close enough for him to have seriously wounded her if he had thrown his dagger.

Jack pointed at her with the blade, "Sneaking up on an assassin is as good a way as I know for a Sheila to get herself killed." Jack said, intentionally making his accent more pronounced to hopefully get her attention. Luna was definitely worth his time and attention and had a much more agreeable personality than Zilvia.

"What do you want?" Just because he was interested didn't mean that Jack could just let her sneaking up on him slide.

Luna shrugged her shoulders, "Simon wanted me to check up on you and Will."

"Oh," Jack said, slightly disappointed that she hadn't come of her own accord, a touch threatened by the fact that she had stopped by to check on Will first, and extremely paranoid by the fact that Simon had sent her.

Luna took a step closer and continued, "Simon noticed that you Earthians have a problem sitting still, which is a behavioral trait he thought strange for two highly trained assassins."

"Well, it's true that part of the job is all about staying out of sight and waiting for the target to be exactly where you want. But there's another part that everyone seems to forget." Jack added, motioning with the dagger before once again returning it to its home in the scabbard. "The part where I'm allowed to roam free wherever and whenever I please and do whatever I want with nothing and no one to hold me back; I may as well be in prison here."

Luna shuffled on her feet during that moment of awkward silence after Jack's rant.

"So I hear you went out on the team's first strike," Jack said if for no other reason than to keep her in the room and conversing with him.

"It was our first step to accomplishing our goals." Luna said with a nod; it sounded more like she was trying to convince herself more than anything else. "So why didn't you join us?" Luna added with more conviction and her interest in Jack gave him hope that he might just be able to reel her in.

"Simon didn't want me to join the Komplo on a mission until Virus was finished with my upgrades." Jack shook his head, frustrated at the way this operation had been run so far. "I don't know what took the drongo so long to design the tech, or why Will has a higher priority rating than me, but at least now I'm ready for the next mission."

"So you're looking forward to our next attack?" Luna asked. Something about how she asked made Jack think that she might be disappointed at his eagerness to get to work.

"Heck yeah. I'm going crazy down here and it's been at least two months since my last job," Jack said, more for Simon's benefit than for hers. Jack wanted his new employer to know that he wasn't crazy about being cooped up since he arrived.

Luna looked down at the ground for a moment before turning back to Jack and asking, "Do you ever regret the choices you make?"

"Of course I regret some of the poor choices I've made." Jack shrugged off the question with a smile and joked, "Like last night, I knew then that I shouldn't have eaten that last slice jalapeño pizza and I regretted it this morning."

Luna shook her head and tried to clarify, "No, I mean, do you ever regret your decision to become an assassin? Have you ever finished a job and wished you had turned it down?"

Jack let out an irritated sigh as Luna was awakening his slumbering conscience; it didn't matter if Simon sent her to test him or if she was genuinely asking his opinion at this point because she had dug up something that he wanted buried deep.

Jack calmed himself by taking another knife out and rubbing the edge against his sharpening stone. "Luna, if you want to survive in the business you have to learn to accept the facts of life; people live, people die, and some people need to be forcefully removed from life because they're causing problems. I've learned how to profit from that reality by being the best security guard around," he glared at her and put away his knife and stone as he finished.

Thankfully, Luna got the hint and changed the subject. "So what kind of upgrades did Virus work out for you?"

Jack grinned as he took this opportunity to show off his skill. Virus had designed special metal armguards that covered Jack's forearms and could produce any kind of sharpened blade that he could think of; the device could be operated mentally as well as manually in case there was a mindvoice interference while operating completely concealed by the sleeves of Jack's shirt.

Jack pointed to the target along the wall to his right, bent his arm at the elbow to raise his hand up, and swung his arm down in the direction of the target; a moment later a small throwing knife was stabbed directly in the center of the target.

As Jack brought his arm down he had commanded the device to create the perfectly balanced blade and eject it into his grip so that he could then throw it at his target with a deadly flick of his wrist.

Jack turned back to face Luna with his arms held out, "Amazing right? Now I don't have to worry about smuggling half a dozen weapons across the world to do my jobs."

The two arm guards designed by Virus couldn't eject the blades they produced with enough force to fire them at Jack's target, but they could supply him with a virtually unlimited supply of sharpened steel.

"I'm sure that will save you a great deal of time indeed." Luna answered cordially, but there was a distance in her voice that Jack didn't care to notice.

"It will indeed, Sheila, and there's more," Jack said, motioning with his hand and triggering the device on his arm again, causing a uniquely designed magnet within it to pull the knife out of the target and back into Jack's hand where it could be reabsorbed by his armguards.

Jack smiled holding up the blade for Luna to see, "Now I don't have to worry about picking up after myself."

Luna smiled and then asked a question motioning to the sword at Jack's side, "So why bother with these other weapons if those can make anything you want and retrieve them to be reformed?"

"Well, let me put it this way, Sheila. I don't want to take the chance of completely relying on Virus only to find out in battle that the drongo botched the programming; I have the foresight to hold on to these 'old-school' methods," Jack said referring to the sword on his left hip, the throwing stars in his coat pockets, and the throwing knife sheathed at his right hip.

"Plus, I've grown quite attached to these beauties," Jack added, affectionately patting the sheathed sword at his side. "Call me sentimental, but I just couldn't bring myself to get rid of some of my old tools of the trade."

"Simon will be pleased to hear that you're enjoying the upgrades that he was able to provide for you," Luna said, closing off the conversation and preparing to leave. "I'll be checking in on you later," she said, slowly fading from sight; if Jack looked hard enough he could just barely make out her outline as she walked directly out the door and around the corner.

Jack was puzzled to say the least; he knew that Luna was a shapeshifter and very good at her job, but he wondered at how deeply he could trust what she said and did. She made a profession out of acting and deceiving people, which meant that the very reason that Simon recruited her for the Komplo was exactly why she couldn't be trusted.

Still even more puzzling was how Jack could actually trust any of these people; he knew for a fact that everyone was looking to take advantage of him because that was precisely what he was trying to do to them, and that knowledge is what kept everyone in line. Everyone was out to take advantage of all the others and the number one rule in this business was to look out for one's self. The Komplo was like a pack of ravenous wolves, and Simon was the Alpha male; with everyone else looking to take advantage of anyone that seemed weaker than one's self as long as they could get away with it while Simon kept a watchful eye on those under him.

But where did Luna fit in all of that? Why was she asking such probing questions? Was she really snooping around for Simon like she claimed, or was there something deeper going on? Should someone be watching Luna to make sure she stayed loyal, or would it only upset the delicate unity that held the Komplo together?

A string of profanity poured from Jack's mouth as he flung his arms at the target on the far wall, sending several throwing stars into it and creating a perfectly shaped X centered on the bullseye.
Jack recalled the steel stars and wondered if it was too late to recall his allegiance to Simon.

Timothy Stevens

"So how are the boys doing?" I asked Sandra as she returned from checking on them upstairs.

"Still fast asleep in their beds," she replied, gently closing the door as she entered the observation room. "How's Jennifer doing down there?"

"She seems to have perfected much of her grandmother's abilities," I replied, still looking over the computer's analysis of Jennifer's performance.

Jennifer Green is Kara's older sister and because of her schedule she had been the study's least-regular regular; by that I mean that she was there regularly about every other week or so. Jennifer and Kara were the two most dedicated note takers, with Joann and Mary coming third and fourth.

Like her sister, Jennifer had inherited certain GRID skills from their great-grandparents with Jennifer being able to use the very malleable metal giadan to create various objects, from actual statues, pots, weapons, and tools, to a physical shield. As an element, giadan would allow air and energy to pass through it and its physical strength is determined by its thickness. However with increased thickness and greater resilience came less malleability. The giadan Jennifer had had a unique chromium impurity to it, giving the otherwise clear metal a jade green appearance and that became the basis for her alter ego namesake.

The jade-green colored suit complemented Jennifer's chocolate-colored skin and her emerald-green gloves would help her control the formation of the giadan; the boots and mask that I gave Jennifer also matched the color of her gloves.

The higher level of instruction that had been passed down to Jennifer and Kara by their parents had put a greater level of accountability on them as they began to unwrap the gifts they had been given. Because with that knowledge comes accountability for their actions; when one knows that an action is dangerous, or that a certain comment is hurtful to someone, then one comes under greater judgement for doing or saying it.

Another thing that I had pointed out to the girls that was equally as important to consider is the way that their family had remembered how to control these GRID Connections and the way they have passed them down. Pastor Juan has recounted to me how his pastor used to tell him, "The first generation experiences a move of the Spirit, while the second enjoys the legacy of the first, and the third destroys it."; God doesn't have grandkids because we all have to establish our own relationship with Him. And the Green family had done well to pass down important knowledge in order to keep the legacy from being lost. A legacy that went beyond 'Jade Green' and 'Plasma' the superheroines; the Green sisters along with many of the other Disciples had been blessed with godly parents who had given each of them a beautiful inheritance in a righteous upbringing. Now, what they all did with that upbringing was as much up to them as the use of their abilities was. However, there is a greater measure of accountability for those of us with that kind of upbringing along with a greater sense of urgency to pass on that knowledge to the next generation; one of the reasons why Israel had such a hard time is that they didn't pass on their experiences with God to their children which is why the Scriptures state that, "another generation arose after them who did not know the Lord".

Jennifer understood that part of our job was to make sure that this generation didn't forget, or to make sure that they were reminded if they've already lost their legacy.

In tonight's training, Jennifer formed a long giadan staff and was using it to fight off the ComBots at close courters and spread it out to form a protective barrier when the more distant attackers began to shoot at her. I raised an eyebrow when small circular portions of the protective shield began to remove themselves and fling out at the remaining ComBots, arching and diverting themselves in order to subdue one ComBot after the next.

"It seems like Jennifer has grown beyond the need for physical contact too," I mused, thinking of Joel's earlier performance as 'Carpenter'.

"Yes, she certainly has," Sandra looked at the computers that monitored Jennifer's vital signs, "her readings are similar to Joel's which means that she'll need to increase her skill in this area very carefully so that she doesn't put herself into danger."

I nodded, "We'll need to avoid as much danger as

possible in order to leave room for what we can't change."

My wife turned to me and gave me a look and asked via the GRID, *"You're worried about more than just the graduation of our Disciples into Defenders, aren't you? Are you still having those dreams?"*

I nodded sadly, *"They've been getting clearer and more ominous each time I dream; God is warning me about something, but I don't know what to do about it."*

I looked down into the training room as the giadan pieces continued to reshape and fly around the room – following the motions of Jennifer's hands and her mental orders – and sighed, "We'll caution Jennifer to take it easy and go from there."

"And what about your dreams?" Sandra messaged, her voice still carrying concern.

"I'm still trying to come to terms with them." I answered. *"We'll trust in God and go from there."*

"Sounds like a plan," Sandra replied positively and I prayed that my fears would submit to the plan.

Timothy Stevens

Joann West had already made her way into the training room, Jennifer joined the dodgeball game for the night, and I was admiring the way that Joann was handling herself as the 'Catamount' below.

Her Catamount suit was a tan colored shear-resistant material with a matching mask while the gloves and boots, or her 'paws', were a cream color. There weren't any stripes or accents, but there was a simple beauty about the suit. The fact that the gloves contained razor sharp, Cainium-tipped claws that could be retracted into the fingertips meant that the suit could become dangerous if used improperly. Joann's abilities were wrapped up in a GRID Connection that heightened her senses of sight, hearing, and smell along with improving her balance and reflexes which needed little original explanation.

Joann West has been good friends with Mary White, however Mark and Aaron still to this day describe her as being 'anti-boy'. While Joann has always been a bit self-sufficient and strong willed, she has still maintained a healthy desire to learn and grow and I developed a greater appreciation and understanding towards her personality and corrected my own sense of being 'anti-girl' because of interacting with Joann over the years and I had chosen the alias 'Catamount' to both encourage and teach her. Encourage, because there had been many times where I saw her boldly speak to her friends and she wasn't afraid to ask questions these past four years; I wanted to encourage and draw out that lioness in her for the Lord. I had also hoped that the abilities she had would remind her to be sensitive to the feelings of others, because the enhanced physical sight, hearing, and reflexes mean precious little compared to spiritual tenderness and enthusiastic helpfulness toward another person and we all needed to be quick to react with love, regardless of our opinions of who we're helping. Her retractable claws could be used to hurt or to save in the same way that she had been both bold and distant, outgoing and avoiding, just like a cat that's friendly one minute and turns on you the next; I wanted her to let God's love flow from her continuously and without partiality because I understood that God is no distinguisher of persons, and that His children shouldn't be either.

I noticed a puzzled expression spread across my wife's face and asked her, "What's wrong?"

She shook her head and motioned to the monitor in front of her, "These readings…they don't make any sense."

I pushed my chair behind her and looked over her shoulder at the readings that had her baffled. "You're right… that doesn't make any sense at all. Have you checked the system performance for any malfunctions?"

Sandra nodded, "I've checked them twice and everything seems to be functioning normally."

"What's going on?" Marie Daniels asked a bit

worried.

I looked over the information a second time and asked my wife a question before I tried to answer Marie, "Have you ever come a crossed readings like this?"

Sandra thought for a moment before she recalled with a look of satisfied relief. "The only times I've seen results that were even close to this was when you and Joseph were in the training room, but this is even beyond the two of you."

"What exactly are you two talking about?" Rebecca Holmes asked worriedly. "Is something wrong with Joann?

Sandra shook her head and tried to gently calm their concerns, "No, nothing is wrong with Joann."

Mary was relieved but still concerned, "Well, what is it that you two have been talking about?"

I answered her gently, "I'm afraid that we'll have to talk with Joann about it first, but we'll let you know later. Okay?"

"Did you determine what exactly was producing these results?" I used the GRID to ask my wife.

Sandra replied with a shake of her head and a grin, *"I'm afraid that I'll have to talk with Joann about it first."*

I scowled at her, *"That's not nice."*

She only shook her head with a chuckle and turned back to watching Joann train against the ComBots and wouldn't say anymore until after Joann had joined us and the other Disciples had left.

"I heard you guys talking about how there was something strange about my health readings?" Joann asked, walking into the observation room with a concerned expression.

"Joann your heart rate, oxygen levels, and blood pressure are only half as elevated as I would expect after the warmup you just went through."

"So what does that mean?" Joann asked, still a bit alarmed.

I cleared my throat, "Well, considering what your levels should be after the warm up, it means that your body is outperforming any reasonable expectations."

Sandra motioned to the computer monitor, "The computers were also able to determine that that microtrauma that your muscles endeared has already healed."

"Microtrauma?" Joann asked with a confused shake of her head and a puzzled expression.

"It's a term for one of the ways that your body builds muscle" I answered with a nod. "When you strain you muscles the cells tear apart and mend back together stronger than before so you'll be better prepared for the next time you experience that same trauma."

Joann tilted her head thoughtfully, "That sounds like what you taught us earlier about how God uses the hard times in life to make us stronger and draw us closer to Him."

I smiled and nodded, "I'm glad to hear that you've been listening."

Sandra also smiled as she explained her medical findings. "I believe it is because God is giving you the ability to heal at a faster than normal rate."

"Is that why the microtrauma stuff has already been healed?" Joann asked.

I nodded as I began to understand my wife's theory. "Yes, and the normal soreness that you would normally feel days after working out would've occurred briefly as you made your way up here."

Joann nodded and recalled how her legs suddenly felt stiff for a moment heading up the stairs.

Sandra looked over her notes before adding, "From all my readings you should be able to heal even faster than Pentecost or Reverb."

"How fast is that exactly?" Joann asked.

I shrugged my shoulder, "It's not like in the movies where you get cut and it heals seconds later; more like minutes. Depending on the seriousness of the injury you could still be nursing a wound for a day or so instead of nearly a week at the normal rate of recovery."

Joann removed the glove from her left hand and extended a claw out of her right pointer finger, "So if I were to get a small cut it would heal in a few minutes?"

I nodded, "If we are correct in our assumptions."

Joann nodded and touched the sharpened tip of her claw to the palm of her hand. A small bead of blood quickly appeared after she retracted her claw and when she wiped away the drop the wound had already closed without leaving a scar.

"It's important to remember that this doesn't make you invincible," I cautioned. "Your body has limits as to what it can heal from, with the chief limitation being that you have to be alive in order to heal."

Joann nodded emphatically and pulled her glove back

over her hand as she stood to head to join the others in the dodgeball game. "I understand; and besides, healing fast doesn't take away the pain of the wound."

I nodded and could testify to the emotional and spiritual application of what she had said. Recovering from a failure or broken relationship was always hard and painful, regardless of the victory that came afterwards. As Pastor Juan had shared with me, "There's nothing like the school of 'Hard Knocks' because you will never forget your lessons if you can afford the tuition." Life's lessons were often painful and hard lived, but they were unavoidable and invaluable teachers.

After she left my wife stood to intercept me from gather the other students.

"What?" I asked, puzzled by her actions.

"You know what," she replied playfully. "You're letting these dreams affect you and your training of these Disciples; you passed up on several opportunities to pour into Joann just now."

I sighed heavily and said with a smile. "You know. It's at moments like these that I love you the most and that I am the most irritated at you for being my wife."

Sandra smiled and put her hand to my cheek, "I know that it's both a blessing and a curse, but you cannot allow fear to keep you from caring."

I held her hand in mine, "I know; it's just that these dreams have been reminding me of how special these kids are to me, how important they are to my life. I keep thinking of how easily you, Grandpa, Grandma, the boys, and these students could be taken away from my life and it scares me. I don't know if I can handle the feelings of loss again."

Sandra looked deeply into my eyes, "What was it that you were telling the students about life's painful lessons? Remember the way that microtrauma makes our bodies stronger? You can't allow the struggles of your past to make you become calloused or distant, Timothy. You have to trust God to use *all things* – bitter and sweet – to strengthen you and these students."

I took a deep breath and tried to allow what my head understood to overcome the turmoil in my heart.

Sandra wrapped her arms around me and continued, "I know that you feel the burden to protect all of us from everything, but you can't prevent God's will. And why would you want to? The Lord is good in all that He wills and He finishes all that He sets out to accomplish. We both know that this isn't something that you don't already understand."

I wrapped my arms tightly around my wife and breathed heavily, "I know; but the storms don't take place in my head, they happen in my heart and it takes some convincing to get things back in order."

I tilted my head downward, "I thank God that He gave you such a special place in my heart, my dear."

She turned her face upward and smiled, "I'm thankful that He gave us to each other."

Moments later the door opened up and some embarrassed Disciples interrupted our kiss.

"Are we interrupting something, Timinski?" Mark asked, playfully.

"Not at all, Mark," I replied and turned to the students as they walked into the room. "You're just in time for Marie to head down for her warmup."

"Are you sure that's all that's getting warmed up in here?" he quipped with a raised eyebrow.

"Get outta here," I chuckled with a dismissive wave and tried not to dwell on what would happen if anything endangered these students because of me.

"Are you ready Marie?" Sandra called down through the speakers.

"All set," Marie Daniels replied and the armed ComBots entered the room

As 'Oceanica' Marie was be able to regulate the flow, volume, and pressure of the water that her suit produces to accomplish anything from blasting a burning building or an adversary with a fire hose, to using a high pressured stream of water to cut through a steel wall, to being able to simply soak her friends. The suit that Joseph and I had given Marie was aqua blue in color, with light blue gloves and boots, while a pale blue was used to add a watery affect, and light blue protective goggles would help protect her eyes as well as her identity.

Marie had always been one of the more unpredictable Disciples, outgoing one minute and then withdrawn, which I believed to be in part because Marie grew up as a foster child living with the Holmes family. Marie, like her sister Jessica, was hesitant to interact with others in the study at first, but as friendships developed she began to enjoy the weekly studies and interacted more each night. For a while, Marie had seemed to be outgoing and playful with her foster-siblings or with some of her friends but was also very shy or distant from everyone else at the same time. Like water, she was bubbly yet reserved; understood, yet mysterious.

That first night I had arranged three targets for Marie

to practice controlling her suit; one for a gentle splashing, another for slicing with a waterjet, and the third was to be blasted by the blast of a firehose. The first time she used her suit to hit one of the targets the initial force surprised her and her arm was thrown back as she spun around, blasting the room with water as she went; I still remember the way that I was caught by the blast in the chest and thrown against the wall.

I had been hoping for a safer first training session but was rather disappointed as I felt for broken ribs and picked myself up from the floor making my way over to Marie; thankfully, she had shut off the water or the room would have flooded.

Marie had picked herself up from the floor and apologized, with a laugh as I walked closer. At the time I thought it was good to see that she found some humor in the situation, or at least in my soaked state, while still being sincerely apologetic about it. After that first attempt Marie was able to learn how to control the suit to hit each target appropriately.

After Marie went through a few more sets of fruit without incident I decided to establish a memorial stone for her as I had hoped that 'Oceanica' could become much more than a superheroine; the alias could be used to glorify God by reminding Marie as well as the world of who He is.

The practical manner in which the suit was limited by the nature of water – Marie would never be able to make water flow uphill because it's against the nature of water to do so – and that can remind her of the way that God is omnipotent and capable of doing all that He wills and yet His will never goes against His nature; God will never contradict Himself because He can't. God is truth and therefore cannot lie, so all the promises that God has made He is faithful to fulfill and His Word is unchanging.

Also, the suit could only pour out as much water as it took in, which reflected the way that we have to allow the Holy Spirit to pour into our lives in order for us to pour out His love unto others; the inflow and the outflow are equally important in our lives because we are to become a spring of water that can't be contained due to the Holy Spirit's presence in us. I wanted her to understand that we needed to allow God to soak us in His presence and wash us through His Word, and that we need to pour into those around us or we will become fruitless as Christians.

Tonight as I observed Marie's prowess I thanked the Lord for all that He had done in the lives of each of the Disciples over these past four years; both spiritually and physically. All of them had grown through different trials and had learned to overcome various obstacles in life as believers while learning new strengths and giftings in the Spirit. Similarly, they had all grown in their abilities through different tests and overcome several barriers and struggled to learn new techniques as they honed their GRID abilities. Both dimensions of growth were achieved through struggle and perseverance and God had produced some amazing fruit simply because these kids had trusted in God as they grew into adults.

As Marie finished with her warmup and made her

way up for her consultation, I admitted to myself that Sandra was right about my becoming paranoid that something was going to endanger these students. However, acknowledging that fact didn't make it any easier to deal with. I'm human just like the next Defender and I deal with my own hurdles in life. As I watched the ComBot pieces being gathered and reassembled by additional Bots I was finally able to surrender; and find victory.

"Oh, Father." I prayed silently. *"Please don't allow this to become something that I regret bringing these kids into. I know that I'm not the bad guy, but I don't want to feel responsible for what happens next. Please continue to remind me and these kids that You are always in control; I give them into Your care."*

Chapter Twenty-Four

"Sandra," I called through the house.

"Yes, dear?" I heard her answer from the front room and walked towards her voice; she was getting the boys ready to go visit Grandpa and Grandma.

I moved to tie little Ezekiel's shoes as Sandra finished up with firstborn Jeremiah. "Hey, I just wanted to thank you for helping me get all of that stuff together for when the Disciples come over later."

"You're welcome," she nodded. "I know that this is going to be a bit intense for some of them at first, but they're going to need everything that you can give them to prepare for what's coming."

I sighed as I started Ezekiel's second shoe. "I just wish I had some idea of what it is that we are getting ready for."

Sandra turned and answered thoughtfully, "Well, I'm sure that if the Lord *had* revealed that to you, you'd be wishing that He hadn't or that it was somehow avoidable."

"You're probably right," I nodded as I finished with Ezekiel's shoes. "I guess that's why He doesn't show us what's coming until it happens, because He knows how we'd fight against it and tell Him no."

"It's funny how He always seems to know best," my wife teased. "I guess that's why He's God, and we're not."

"Thank you for being there to help remind me of that, my dear." I took her hand in mine, "I'd be lost without you."

"I know you would," she answered with a chuckled. "I'll see you later."

"Okay," I chuckled, "Say hello to Grandpa and Grandma for me."

"I will; love you," she replied with a peck on my lips as she scooped up Ezekiel in her arms.

"I love you too, and you boys be good. Okay?" I said as Sandra reached for Jeremiah's hand and headed for the door.

"It looks like Joseph is here already," Sandra said as I helped her out.

"Yeah, he's going to help me go over some of the preparations to make sure that is everything ready for our surprise for the Disciples."

"All right, see you later," she replied with another kiss and together we loaded up the boys. Joseph and I waved them off before heading inside to go over the plan.

A little while later, Mark, Joel, and Aaron arrived and fished suiting up just as Mary and Bethany both arrived.

"Just so you know, I asked Joann and Kara to come by for this," I had paused for a moment as the guys groaned before adding, "and just for the record: this is going to be much more intense than any of our previous dodgeball games or even the training rounds."

"I can't wait," Aaron added enthusiastically.

A few moments later Kara and Joann both arrived and finished suiting up.

"So how is this training going to work?" Aaron asked, eager to get started.

"It's going to work a bit like capture the flag," I answered, "there will be a ComBot acting as a hostage and will be guarded by several armed ComBots. Our job will be to get in, rescue the prisoner, and get out without being 'eliminated'."

"What do you mean by 'eliminated'?" Jacob asked. Joseph knew how all this stuff worked but everyone else – including our younger brother, Jacob – were in the dark.

Joseph answered, "The ComBots have a super advanced weapons system from Myathis, the kind that makes you feel extreme pain without actually hurting you."

"How's it do that?" Mark inquired, hoping for a sci-fi technology explanation.

I spoke up in order to give Mark an answer with the level of nerdiness he wanted. "The Myathians have designed what they call 'Nervous System Stimulation for Hostile Suppression'; Basically, the NSSHS technology stimulates the nerves in such a way as to produce the programed sensation of pain without inflicting the bodily harm that is typically necessary for such a feeling to occur."

"What does that mean for the training rounds?" Joel asked, a bit unsure of this whole idea.

Joseph answered this question to give a more basic, easy to understand answer, "It means that every time a ComBot hits you, you're going to feel exactly what that injury would feel like in real life. A punch to the face, a kick to the ribs, or a bullet wound to the leg will all hurt just like the real deal; only without the actual bruising or bleeding that would happen in real life."

"That's right," I added once Joseph finished. "It's only a temporary sensation of pain without an actual wound to be treated, so there's no need for stitches or medication. All we need to take the pain away is for the simulation to be disengaged."

"So how do we get eliminated?" Aaron was asking for specifics so we could get started.

I stroked my chin and considered the most basic ground rules with which to proceed. "When the simulated wound is intense enough that it would either kill or render you unconscious in real life, you are completely eliminated. If you sustain that kind of an injury during the simulation you will black out until the training round is terminated, or the simulated pain lessens to the point of you regaining consciousness."

"So this is as real as training can get," Joseph said to help me get off of the nerdy track. "If you can handle the pain then you can keep on going until you drop; unlike with the simulation rounds where you're out if you get hit once."

"So when are we going to get this game started?" Joel asked, trying to seem pumped and ready to go.

"As soon as I explain the object. This is Mozart –" I said motioning to the ComBots that just entered the room, "and he is going to be playing the part of our hostage today. Isn't that right Mozart?" I asked, turning to the robot.

"Absolutely. I'm totally ready for this!" Mozart answered as its silver, OLED 'skin' recolored to the pinkish hue of real skin, blond hair began to grow from its previously bald head, and its silver-colored clothing morphed into the clothing of a typical college sophomore; in an instant Mozart had transformed from looking like the silver robot to a young college student.

"Whoa!" was all that any of the group could say.

"So Mozart is going to play the part of our hostage in need of rescue," I said, attempting to distract them from their amazement. "Our job is going to be to rescue him without any of us, or Mozart, getting eliminated."

"Just when you think you've seen it all," Mark whispered quietly.

I looked around at the still stunned expressions and asked, "So who's ready to get started?"

† † † † † † †

As soon as Timothy described the basic rules of the game the room around the Disciples shifted and transformed as machinery hidden behind the Cainium walls whirred to life and began to transform the empty room into the state penitentiary.

"Let's suppose that Mozart is a young member of a Bible smuggling ring and has been arrested and is awaiting his trial." Timothy said, explaining the scenario of the first training session.

"So why is he being held at an American prison?" Mary asked puzzled.

Timothy turned and answered Mary's question politely. "Because this is a situation that could very well take place in America in the years to come."

"So what do we do first, Timothy?" Joann asked, ready to get started.

Timothy held up a finger and replied, "Rule number one: from now on, whenever we are suited up always address each other by your codenames."

"You and Joseph never gave us your codenames, Timinski. So what are we supposed to call you?" Mark asked.

"Timothy goes by the name 'Pentecost' and my codename is 'Reverb'." Joseph answered.

"So when are we gonna get this show started?" Aaron asked excitedly.

"Right now," Timothy answered before he started to give directions to the team. "NightOwl, stick to the shadows and scan the grounds – I need to know how many guards there are and where they're located – and see if you can locate Mozart."

"Got it." NightOwl answered simply before she faded from sight and flew off on her reconnaissance mission.

"So why don't we just go in and rescue Mozart?" Carpenter asked with a puzzled tone. "I mean we're superheroes, right? So why don't we just go in and get the job done?"

"Because we need to plan out the best way to get Mozart out alive," Pentecost replied, "If we don't do this right then we could tip off the guards and Mozart could very well be killed before we even get to the front gate. We need to know all we can before we go in because we can't afford to be surprised by anything."

Just then NightOwl returned with her report, "There

are thirty-nine men stationed around the place."

"How are they grouped?" Pentecost asked her for more information.

"They're scattered around a bit," she answered, nodding her head and squinting her eyes in concentration. "There are twelve men posted on the outer wall of the prison, two men are in a room monitoring the surveillance videos, there are three men in each of the four guard towers at each of the corners of the prison, and the other thirteen are scattered throughout the building to keep an eye on things."

"What about the inmates?" Pentecost asked.

NightOwl shrugged her shoulder. "They're all over the place; a lot of them seem to be on free time right now."

"And how is Mozart doing?" Reverb asked.

NightOwl was obviously shaken up by that question, "He looks like he's been beat up; he's all bloody and bruised and they have him chained to a chair. He's calm and waiting for God's deliverance, but still afraid of what lies ahead for him."

"All right," Pentecost said, shifting into delegation mode. "SongBird, I need you to focus on controlling the other prisoners, we don't need to start a riot and let all the prisoners escape while we rescue Mozart."

"I can take care of that," SongBird answered energetically.

Pentecost turned to the student standing next to SongBird, "Catamount, can you creep up to the front gate and take out the guards posted there and then keep the gate secure?"

"I think I can handle that." She replied, making a fist and causing the claws in her gloves to activate when she stretched her fingers back out.

"Most of the prison has been constructed out of stone and concrete," Pentecost said as he continued to strategize the attack, "but the guard house and adjoining security room should have some wood studs in the walls to provide you some additional tools to work with, Carpenter. Think you can handle the five guards posted at that southeastern corner?"

"That shouldn't be a problem," Carpenter answered, semi-confidently.

Pentecost turned to his brother standing next to Carpenter, "Arcade, I need you to drop off Carpenter and Maestro at their guard towers before flying through the prison and taking out any straggling guards, starting with those stationed along the southern wall above the gate."

"Sure thing," Pentecost's little brother answered

Pentecost raised an eyebrow, "Maestro, you want to help Arcade route out the remaining guards after securing the southwest guard tower?"

"You got it," he pointed with his finger and nodded.

"Reverb, I need you to take the northwest guard tower and then move on to the western wall. Plasma, I'll keep you invisible until after I drop Clay off at the eastern wall so that you can take care of the northeast guard tower. I'll secure the northern wall and after that, the four of us can help Maestro and Arcade secure the rest of the prison grounds."

"Sounds good," Reverb said as the others nodded.

"NightOwl," Pentecost said turning to the last

Disciple, "I'd like for you to focus on getting to Mozart and getting him out of there."

"I don't think that I'd be able physically carry Mozart out of there myself." NightOwl answered, concerned. "I don't know how well I can carry someone his size."

"Don't worry," Pentecost assured her. "The rest of us will have the guards distracted enough for you to get in, phase Mozart through his chains and the cell door, and either fly or walk him out."

"Before we get going, I want to remind everyone to work as a team," Pentecost added before sending everyone out. "Watch each other's back and if someone is struggling cover them; especially if you're looking for something to do after finishing your objective. The rest of us will get in position and wait for Catamount to get close to the gate; I'll message everyone when it's time to strike and if all goes well, this warm up should be over in a few minutes."

With that everyone prepared themselves for the assault.

Catamount took a deep breath before crouching down behind the desert brush and making her way over to the front gate.

Once she made it over halfway to the gate, Pentecost extended his hands out to Plasma and Clay and asked if they were ready. They each reached for his hands and he grabbed their forearms for a better grip and molecularized the three of them before flying over the place where he would drop off Clay.

"Everyone get ready," Pentecost messaged the group.

Arcade responded by extending his hands for Maestro and Carpenter to take hold of, SongBird and NightOwl both unfolded their large wings and readied themselves while Reverb rolled his shoulders and cracked his neck.

Out of necessity, Clay had resorted to a two handed grip and Plasma began to levitate as they dangled below Pentecost's hovering position. "Clay, remember to go Jell-O just before you hit the ground to absorb the impact. Plasma, when we get close you'll need to blast a hole in the guard tower so I can drop you can get inside."

"Got it," Clay answered with a nod.

"Okay," Plasma replied as she readied herself.

"I'm ready," Catamount messaged from her position just a few feet away from one of the guards closest to the gate.

"All right, everyone; it's show time," Pentecost messaged, returning to normal form and dropping Clay down the wall below before flying off towards Plasma's guard tower.

Clay went Jell-O just as he hit the ground and flattened into an orange puddle before springing back up into the air slightly in full human form once again. He spun while in the air, stretching his arms out and catching two of the guards in the head with his fists while they least expected it, knocking one over the edge of the wall and the other hit his head on the wall as he went down; neither of them would be getting back up anytime soon.

Once Clay landed, he leapt back into the air, arching

backward and extending his right leg out to kick at one of the guards as he ran towards him from near the northeastern guard tower. Halfway through his flip, Clay saw two more guards standing behind him – near the southeastern tower – and a third guard standing next to the guy he just kicked; he figured his part in the battle would be over soon.

Having completed his flip, Clay launched one arm forward and grabbed the gun from one of the two guards, pulled it out of his hands and clubbed him with it. The last guard fired at Clay before he too was bludgeoned with his partner's weapon. Clay molded his body to avoid being shot by the guard's attacks and heard the remaining guard scream in pain. When Clay turned around he saw the final guard lying on the ground, a pool of blood flowing from his abdomen as his glassy eyes stared into the sky. Clay had been working and training with the local police depart prior to joining the Defender Discipleship Program and was currently an officer, so he had seen dead people and photos of crime scenes before, but this was strangely different somehow. Clay shrugged his shoulder and moved on, there was a mission to complete and the guards weren't going to just release Mozart without a fight.

While Clay was still performing his backflip, Plasma had blasted a hole in the guard tower and had dropped into it. She quickly threw three small electrium blasts at the guards inside; they were incinerated on impact and Plasma was suddenly overwhelmed by the stench of burned flesh. She quickly made her way to the staircase to go and look for anyone else and trying desperately not to vomit as she rushed by the charred and bloody arm of one of the guards.

As soon as Pentecost had given the order to strike, Arcade took off towards Carpenter's guard tower; both of them needed to use both hands to tightly hold on for dear life and when they got close, Arcade tossed Carpenter at the tower and banked hard to the left – aided by Maestro's weight on that side – and headed over to drop off his second package; firing at the guards atop of the southern wall as he went.

Upon being thrown at the building, Carpenter formed his Cainium Wood block into a large shield that he curled up behind and braced for impact. As he bashed through the wall and rolled to his feet, he heard shots coming from outside the room.

Instinctively, Carpenter threw his Cainium Shield straight ahead at one of the guards, reforming it into a pointed spear as it flew; the man was impaled and pined to the wall behind him.

Carpenter then caused the small, potted tree to his right to grow in such a way that it grabbed the weapon from the guard standing next to it and constricted his airways until he passed out while it pinned him to the wall.

Carpenter then used a wooden stool to pin the third man to the wall and strip his weapon away from him before moving to the security room where he was able to subdue the two guards there by restraining them with the wooden desk holding the computer monitors.

When Carpenter went back to retrieve his Cainium block, he too had to battle waves of nausea as he pulled the spear out from the guard and he crumpled to the floor. When he looked at the Cainium wood shaft in his hand and saw the blood clinging to it, he lost the battle and his lunch.

Reverb had used an intense sound blast to launch himself into the air so that he could drop down into the northwestern guard tower, drop through the roof, and land on the top floor of the tower; he needed to press his palms to the floor and focus on dispersing the accumulated vibrations of the impact through the building and into the ground to keep the structure from being too badly damaged; the resulting tremor jostled many of the guards and they had trouble standing.

As soon as he was sure the structure would remain standing, Reverb sprang to his feet, firing a sound blast with his right hand diagonally across the room to a guard standing to his left, followed by another diagonal shot from his left hand to the guard on his right, finished by a spin and a double handed blast to the guard standing behind him; all three men were thrown into the solid walls behind them and knocked unconscious.

Reverb then headed out the door leading to the western wall, crouching down to touch the ground again and triggered a localized tremor that moved back in a wave that threw most of the men to the ground and caused two of them to fall over the edge of the wall.

Reverb then ran to the closest pair of guards and met them just as they made it to their feet. One of them swung for Reverb's face, a swing which Reverb took and absorbed the vibrations to pack more power into his next punch. Reverb punched into the man's chest, crushing his sternum and sending him flying into the southeastern guard tower where Maestro was located. The second guard standing next to Reverb was hit with enough vibrations to rattle his skull and knock him unconscious; he'd wake up later with the kind of headache that'd make him wish he had remained unconscious.

The last two guards along the wall began to fire their guns at Reverb, so he produced a supersonic sound shield that shattered the bullets as they hit it and slowly moved forward until the guards were out of ammo and he was within range. Two well placed sound blasts to the head and they were unconscious, yet alive.

SongBird was busy flying overhead switching between singing songs of encouragement to her teammates and other songs of fear and slumber to the prisoners, causing several of them to pass out in the courtyard or their jail cells while some of the other thugs began to cower in the corner and cry for someone to protect them.

Catamount had sprung up from her hiding spot and sliced the closest guard's gun in two with her right hand and slashed at his face with her left. When she saw the slashed on the man's face she froze, she could smell his blood on her fingertips and began to wonder what she was doing just then the man backhanded her across the face and sent her sprawling to the ground.

From above her Arcade fired an energy blast down that vaporized the guard, giving Catamount enough time to get up and leap into the guardhouse at the gate to avoid being shot by the other guard from across the road. The guard manning the gate controls was stunned by her dramatic entrance through the glass window, and even more alarmed when she slashed at his throat to keep him from striking her.

She sensed the third guard had made his way behind her, so she dove out the open door to the guardhouse, ran up to the man, and stabbed her right hand into his side. The man grabbed at his wound and fell in a heap to the ground. Just then the overwhelming scent of burnt flesh hit her nostrils and Catamount also lost the battle to nausea.

Maestro had landed on the south wall – which was still being cleared by Arcade – and made a dramatic entrance into the guard tower while retrieving his conductor's baton from his coat pocket.

Maestro readied his baton and scanned the room to see what kind of objects were in the room for him to conduct.

"Well this is just great," he had said in disappointment as he looked around the room.

The guard tower was not intended to be inviting so there was very little furniture, however there were three chairs for each of the guards – all abandoned as the guards jumped to their feet when they first heard the sounds of the battle outside – a waste bin in the corner, and a small table that was currently covered in playing cards; apparently their game had been interrupted by the rescue attempt.

Maestro began to wave his right hand fluidly while motioning with his left and locking his gaze on the guard's weapons to instruct them that they were not to fire; a command that they followed much to the pleasure of Maestro, because at this point he still didn't have the focus to direct an object moving at the speed of a bullet.

Maestro quickly turned his attention to the chair positioned directly behind the guard closest to him. All three men – who had turned their attention to their jammed weapons – were surprised when the chair lurched forward, knocked the legs out from under one of the bewildered guards, and sent him crashing to the ground. The man was disoriented but still trying to regain his bearings and stand up, so Maestro commanded the chair to flip over the man and crash into his head; thankfully the man didn't attempt to get back up after that.

Maestro's hand then began to fly quickly and in a jumpy motion, which sent the playing cards flying up into the air as though they were being cast about by a whirlwind. The guards had to shield and turn their faces in an annoyed attempt to keep the cards from striking them.

Taking advantage of their distraction, Maestro disconnected the light fixture from the ceiling and threw it at the head of one of the guards, knocking him unconscious and causing him to drop his weapon. Maestro then leapt at the opportunity to conduct the weapon and fired a few shots into the midsection of the remaining guard.

Maestro's movements slowed and the cards fluttered down to the ground, but the rifle still gently hovered in the air. The sound of the gunshots had left his ears ringing, but Maestro was contemplating the thought of keeping the gun with him as he went through the prison looking for more guards. Suddenly, a hole was blown through the wall of the guard tower as the guard that Reverb had blasted flew in, crashing into the floating weapon and continuing out the other side of the tower with it.

"Gosh darn it, Reverb! Why?" Maestro yelled in mock frustration, after which he headed down the stairs to finish taking control of the prison.

After Pentecost dropped off his two students he flew over to the northern wall and since his hands were free he was able to retrieve his bow and an arrow from his quiver, firing it at one of the guards before they saw him coming.

Pentecost spiraled in order to dodge a stream of gunfire and threw a fireball down at the guard standing closest to the one he had already shot. Even with his evasive maneuvers, Pentecost had to molecularize a couple of times to avoid being hit by their gunfire before he was able to land.

Upon landing, Pentecost immediately swept the legs out from one guard, quickly rose to his feet and delivered a powerful roundhouse kick to the other guard's head, sending him careening over the edge of the wall, before drawing his sword and finishing off the fallen guard.

Pentecost then thrust his left hand forward and sent a

mighty torrent of wind at the remaining two guards that blew them up and over the wall's edge.

At this point Pentecost was able to sense from his connection with the kids that some of them were struggling. "SongBird, focus more on songs of hope and encouragement for the team."

"All right," SongBird replied and began to focus on a different tune.

"Arcade, Plasma," Pentecost said, beginning to try and give some practical pointers, "you two may want to consider using less intense blasts that won't completely incinerate the target but will severely wound them. Remember the goal is to preserve as many lives as possible. Arcade, your suit has an intensity meter that you can use to dial back your attacks. I hate to say this Plasma, but you'll have endure the putrid aroma as you figure out your attacks with trial and error."

"Okay," the two of them replied.

NightOwl flew through the prison buildings to the place where she had seen Mozart being held; the walls slapping past her face as she phased through them in her flight. She couldn't help but laugh at the huge, tatted up, thugs as they cowered in the corners of their cells with blankets over their heads and whimpered for their mothers; SongBird had some sense of humor.

When she reached Mozart she opened her wings like a canopy to slow down to a stop right in front of him before folding her wings behind her.

"Can you walk?" she asked him urgently as she phased the chains holding him secure off from around his wrists and ankles.

"I don't know how well I'll be able to stand," he replied weakly through swollen and bloody lips. "I think my leg might be broken," he moaned.

"Okay, just hold on," NightOwl paused for a moment to consider her options. While her wings could probably handle the weight she continued to doubt that she was physically strong enough to drag Mozart out of the building or mentally prepared enough to phase him through the obstacles to get him out.

"Hey guys, I need some backup," she messaged to the rest of the team.

"What's going on NightOwl?" Pentecost replied.

"Mozart can't walk and I can't carry him out of here," she reported in desperation.

"Okay," Pentecost said, assessing the situation and coming up with a solution. *"Arcade, are you available to carry Mozart out of there? Your rock mode will increase your physical strength so you can carry him without dropping or jostling him."*

"I'm sure I can handle that," Arcade replied, putting his thrusters into high gear and altering his course to take him to the room where NightOwl and Mozart were currently waiting.

After Arcade had launched Carpenter into his assigned guard tower and banked hard to the left with

Maestro still clutching his left hand, he had fired several blasts at the guards standing atop the southern wall as he flew to the southwest tower to drop off Maestro.

Several blasts were direct hits and the guards were immediately vaporized while others were standing far enough away to keep from being incinerated but were still thrown off the wall by the blast.

Arcade also saw the guard strike Catamount and fired at him to keep him from shooting her, though his high elevation saved him from having to endure the smell of the incinerated flesh below.

That was his first pass and a few guards still remained posted atop the wall. After dropping Maestro off at the doorway, Arcade turned around and focused on the surviving guards. That was when Pentecost messaged him about the intensity meter on his suit. Arcade also noticed that the energy levels of his suit had been drained much more than when he was using the stun blasts during the dodgeball rounds and decided that a lower intensity would also prolong his ability to keep firing his blasters and fly around.

Arcade lowered his blasters from level 5 down to 3; at this level the explosion produced would still knock the guards back a great distance, however only a direct hit would affect them because the blast radius was greatly reduced. Also, the three blasts fired previously at the more intense level would be equal to at least fifteen shots at level 3.

After he cleared the tower he began flying around the complex, firing warning shots at the guards and following through when they wouldn't behave themselves. He wasn't far from NightOwl's location when he got the message from Pentecost, so he flew down to the front door, blasted an opening, and continued on ahead to find Mozart; zipping around corners, blasting doorways, and either blasting or tackling the few guards that he came across.

When he reached the cell doors, Arcade switched his blasters to level 4 – a highly focused laser blast that used a lot of energy but had no explosive effect – however he decided against it because he didn't want to accidently hit NightOwl or Mozart with it nor did he have enough energy left to make the necessary cuts through the bars to make a doorway using the laser. So Arcade simply switched to his rock mode while NightOwl came, reached through the bars, grabbed his shoulders, and phased him through the bars.

"I was just going to bend the bars or rip the gate off but that works too," Arcade said afterwards.

Arcade went over to where Mozart was sitting and scooped him up with both arms before turning back around and letting NightOwl phase the three of them back out through the bars.

"Everyone get ready to leave, reinforcements are starting to show up," Catamount messaged the group.

"Everyone make your way to the front gate, and anyone that can fly needs to pick up someone that can't." Pentecost messaged everyone and encouraged them to get moving.

Arcade began to run down the halls in order to make it outside in time. Suddenly, an officer appeared as Arcade rounded a corner, holding a rifle and quickly pointing it in his direction. Arcade spun around and shielded Mozart with his body as the bullets began to ricochet off of the suit.

NightOwl phased through Arcade and the guard's gunfire, grabbed the gun, phased through him with it, and clubbed him with it as he turned around to face her.

"Let's keep going," she said, throwing the gun down and turning down the hallway. For the rest of the trip she was the bodyguard and took out two more guards that had stumbled out from their previous locations.

When they made it outside, everyone else was waiting for them.

"I'll take him," Pentecost said, reaching out to take Mozart from Arcade.

"NightOwl, do you think that you can carry Catamount?" Pentecost had asked her as the group arrived.

"Yeah," she answered with a nod, "she's smaller than Mozart so that should work."

"Good, then Arcade can carry Clay; Carpenter, can you form your Cainium Wood into a disk large enough for you and Maestro to stand on while he directs it to carry the two of you out?"

"Sure thing," Carpenter said as he spread out the dense wood into a think disk with a three foot diameter on which he and Maestro both stood. With a wave of his baton, Maestro began to conduct the flight of the disk and it levitated up off the ground.

"You keep this thing steady and we'll get along just fine, Maestro," Carpenter warned.

"All right, let's get moving everyone," Pentecost had

said, molecularizing out of sight with Mozart.

Reverb used another sound blast to launch himself away and Plasma was able to float off with the rest of the group away from the prison until everyone was miles away from the prison.

Then the simulation ended and everyone landed to regroup.

"That was more real than any video game and way cooler," Aaron said, taking his mask off for a moment to wipe some sweat off of his face.

"I'm not so sure that's a good thing," Joann replied, removing her mask with her left hand and watching the simulated blood disappear from her right. "Somehow I had a different idea of what it would be like to be a superhero."

"Superheroine," Mark corrected.

"Superheroine. Whatever, Mark," Joann answered sharply. "I'm just saying that I don't know if this is something that I can do in the future."

"Everyone listen," Timothy called to them, appearing in the room and setting Mozart down on the ground. "There is a reason why I wanted this to be as realistic as possible, other than simply letting you all see what a real battle was like."

"What would that be?" Mary asked, taking a seat on the floor with her wings stretched out behind her and her mask already removed.

"To teach you how to take the coming battles seriously," he answered as the others began to sit down in a circle around him. "Listen guys, it's important to remember our humanity and that we're not playing a game, we are dealing with real lives out there."

Timothy paused to catch his breath and let what he had said sink in before emphasizing his point with an example. "One day those guards won't be synthetic robots, but real people and it is an evil thing to needlessly end another person's life and send them to meet the Judge of the universe."

He swallowed and nodded at Mozart, "However, it's also important to remember why we are doing what we are doing, because someday Mozart won't be a synthetic robot either. In the coming days he could very well be an American brother or sister in the faith, or maybe even a blood relative."

At that statement, Mozart's appearance changed to that of Nona White, Aaron and Mary's mother, and then continued to scroll through the appearances of every parent and sibling of each student present before returning once again to the original appearance of the gangly teenager known as 'Mozart'. Each person that was mimicked by Mozart was bloodied and beaten just as Mozart had been and the effect on the group was sobering.

"One day," Timothy swallowed again to clear his throat and intently locked eyes with each student. "One day we might be fighting to save someone we love...one day we might really be the only thing that saves someone from a life of imprisonment and public execution. This is what we are fighting for: to make sure that the Lord's sheep are kept safe and alive to serve Him with courage."

He waited and locked eyes with each student before asking, "Who is willing to fight with me?"

Timothy Stevens

Jessica Holmes was down enjoying her routine warm up as I hadn't started the hardcore training regimen with all of the Disciples yet and I wanted tonight to at least start off a little closer to normal for them.

Adam's older sister, Jessica, had a reserved nature, much as I used to have – okay, so I still have a more reserved nature but I can at least talk to people now – and my understanding then was that she liked to know exactly what is going on and what to expect of someone before she exposed herself to anyone. Much like I was at that age, before the Lord shook my personality to the core.

I had named Jessica's four-point *lahat* shield '*Natsar*' and made it out of a lightweight metal alloy. *Natsar* had a pale blue leather covering in the center and Joseph had attached adjustable straps that would hold fast for a firm grip, yet stretch to allow Jessica to carry the shield on her back. The GRID program installed on *Natsar* allowed it to render itself, Jessica, or anything else around it invisible and create Cainium-strength energy fields; which meant that Jessica could create an impenetrable force field with *Natsar*.

In fact, there were unique qualities to each of the defensive fields made by the three Disciples capable of making such a field. Plasma could absorb energy attacks with her dechomain field, but physical attacks would fly through unhindered. Jade can construct physical shields, but her giadan couldn't stop energy from passing through and was weaker than Safeguard's force fields, however that weakness is what allowed Jade's to be so moldable and versatile as Jessica would only be able to make circular or semicircular force fields.

I had outfitted Jessica with a sky-blue, long sleeved shirt that was treated to be shear-resistant, a pair of brown leather boots, shear-resistant jeans, and a pale blue mask finished off Jessica's alias, 'Safeguard' a name that was used only after I decided to use '*Natsar*' for her shield instead of for her.

'*Natsar*' is Hebrew and it means to guard, or keep, from danger with fidelity and the word is used to describe the way that the Lord keeps us and holds us safely in His hands, no matter what takes place in life. It is also used in Scripture to speak of the way that He hides us in the shadow of His wings; as was poetically written.

Something that even I needed reminding of is that because of this knowledge of God's protection there is no need for insecurity; the righteous are intended to be as bold as a lion because "God has not given us a spirit of fear, but of power, love, and sound mind."

Like Jessica, I knew the safety in waiting until I was comfortable before exposing myself but I had also learned the danger of hiding from service by staying in the shadows. While I wanted to push her to unreservedly follow God's call, I didn't want to make her feel that she had to become as outgoing as Mary or any of the others, because God had uniquely designed her and He has hand-crafted her armor to fit her; none of us needed another's life, but we did need to live with bold obedience.

I knew that following the Lord would often take us to dangerous and unfamiliar places, and years ago I had rephrased a particular praise song into a personal life prayer; a prayer that had radically changed my life. A prayer that I again asked of the Lord in order to prepare me for whatever it was that lay ahead of me and my students.

"Holy Spirit, lead me where my trust has no limits, and take me to places where I can't take myself – where I'm totally relying on You – so that my faith can be made stronger. Help me follow Your voice wherever You call me, because I want to be where You are."

I had signed up to recklessly follow Jesus as His disciple and I had encouraged these students to do the same. To ask God to radically change us into who He wants us to be instead of who we want to be which was a very painful process of stretching and killing the flesh to be sure, but great gain was found in being strengthened in the Lord. No true disciple of Christ could live their lives while holding something back from the Lord as their own. All things must be given up to Him wherever He would lead. It was strange to still be learning the very thing that I had been teaching for so long, but I suppose that was part of the Christian walk of faith; nothing is ever truly completed this side of glory.

Over the years Jessica had learned to make different force fields of different sizes and in different locations in relation to herself. However, tonight she stumbled upon some new abilities; the ability to resize a force field and to throw one as a projectile.

Jessica had swung forward with *Natsar* and a force field flew forward out from it and collided with several ComBots before disappearing at her mental command. She then turned invisible and used *Natsar* to hit the ComBots over the head before she returned to the visible spectrum. A ComBot fired at her and she formed a force field to protect herself; a force field that rapidly expanded to crush many of the remaining ComBots against the walls. Those that remained shortly found themselves compressed within a constricting force field.

"That's rather impressive," I commented as Jessica finished and made her way up the stairs.

Sandra looked over the readings, "The GRID code on her *lahat* shield is responding appropriately, which means that the shield is doing most of the work; like your sword and bow."

I stroked my chin, "In theory, Jessica may keep growing until she doesn't even need the *Natsar* and can make force fields independently as her GRID Connection begins to take over. However, a *lahat* weapon always does most of the work and so *Natsar* will always make it easier for Jessica to activate her GRID Connection as my sword and bow do for me."

Joseph messaged me via the GRID and interrupted our conversation, *"So are you going to make the announcement to the rest of the group?"*

I nodded, *"Yes; just as soon as everyone finishes their warmups."*

I could sense his skepticism as he teased, *"Are you going to tell them everything?"*

I sighed and shook my head. *"Not all at once; I want to prepare them as gradually as I can."*

"All right," Joseph shrugged his shoulder and resumed a conversation with the other Disciples about Jessica's performance.

Chapter Twenty-Six

"All right ladies and gentlemen, please have a seat," I said as panels in the floor opened and chairs rose from underneath.

"This place never ceases to amaze me," Beth said taking her seat.

"Hey Timinski, does this place have a home theater system?" Mark joked as he made his way to a chair.

"Um, Mark, wouldn't that be a compound theater system or something?" Beth asked sarcastically.

"Yeah Mark. Get it right!" Aaron teased his friend from his place across the room.

"Whatever, guys," Mark answered shaking his head and shrugging his shoulder, "I was just wondering how much tech this place has tucked away."

I smiled and tried to steer the group where I wanted them, "In a way Mark, that's part of what I wanted to talk to everyone about."

I continued after the group settled down a bit more, "First off I wanted to let you guys know that Joseph and I have been able to construct an underground base at each of your homes."

"How in the world did you manage to do that?!" Joel asked in shock.

"Joseph has a friend, Dr. Eleazar Petric, who's father helped invent a device that will communicate with the local ants in order to complete various underground building projects," I answered. "He calls this device the 'Earth Moving Ants' device, or the 'EMA' device."

"So are those bases just like this one, Timothy?" Joann asked.

"Yes," I answered with a nod. "In fact, one thing that I would like to start doing is to take all of you through the areas of this base that you haven't explored yet and run through some of the other programs."

"No problem," Mark answered, "I've often wondered what all this place has to offer."

"Was there something else you wanted to tell us?" Kara asked.

"Well, on the practical side of things, you'll be able to use the system programs to train and improve your skills, but I don't want anyone to activate a new training program or mess with any of the machines until after I've taught you how to use them; we don't need the western half of the United States burned to cinders and leveled by a misused program."

"Yeah, that would be bad," Marie retorted.

I chuckled and continued. "Spiritually, I'd like to take this time to point out that each of you are as unique as your suits. None of you have the same personality, talents, or are at the same place in your walk with the Lord. Both practically and spiritually, we are not intended to measure up to another person. We are supposed to look to Christ as our blueprint for life, while using each other as partners to motivate us closer to Him."

I paused for a moment and looked around the room. It

has always been hard to gauge whether or not everyone or anyone understood what I was trying to impart to them, so I would usually try to hint at the same point in a few different ways.

"I also don't know where the Lord will be taking any of you in the future," I struggled to press on passed the thought that some of these students might have a danger filled life because of my actions. "Some of you may be led by the Lord to start another compound and raise up more Disciples. Some of you may be called to be part of the 'special forces' in the tumultuous times that are approaching. Some of you may be led to begin ministering to a dying world around you right away. I doubt that any of you will have the luxury to simply allow your abilities to remain as a private 'insurance policy' in the future. However, only the Lord knows where He is going to take each of you. Each of you need to follow His individual leading for yourselves."

I scanned the room with my eyes as I spoke, trying to keep myself from focusing on a particular student for too long and causing them to grow uncomfortable.

"I don't know if He'll have some of you go to college in the next couple years, or if He'll have you stay local. I don't know if you will always work as a united thirteen member team, if the team will grow, or if God will call some of you to work in smaller units. But I know that each of you need to follow Him."

I knew all too well that life has a way of radically changing in a very short amount of time. I wanted to be up-front with everyone that I had no clue what God had in mind for them.

"One thing that I would like for all of you to remember, is that the difference between the sacred and the secular isn't entirely about what you're doing or where you may work, though those are a part of determining our actions. You guys are smart enough to know that sin doesn't glorify God, right?" I asked half-jokingly.

Most of the room nodded and murmured their agreement.

Mark responded with, "Well, duh."

Aaron with a sarcastic "Of course."

I smirked and continued, "What makes something sacred is for *Whom* the action is performed. If you glorify God as you recycle aluminum cans, than that action is sacred. Wherever you are whatever you do, do it for the glory of God."

I paused long enough to swallow and then continued, "Always remember that God will stop using the tool that stops glorifying Him. This isn't an insignificant issue. 'God resists the proud, but gives grace to the humble.'"

I smiled as God reminded me of something that He had taught me, "The picture that – I thought – I came up with to illustrate our weakness was of a hammer boasting in how well it was driving in the nails, as though it were doing the work."

"That's a good way to put it," Joann added.

I smiled and nodded, "I thought so too. So much so that I started to take credit for it. That is, until I realized that God already had the copyright on it. In Isaiah 10 God is talking to one of the kings that He used to correct the nation of Israel. Apparently, this guy was developing an ego because the Lord tells him in verse 15, 'Shall the ax boast itself against him who chops with it? Or shall the saw exalt itself against him who saws with it? As if a rod could wield itself against those who lift it up, Or as if a staff could lift up, as if it were not wood!' God will not share His throne, or the credit for His work, with anyone. Always remember that these abilities are meant to glorify Him."

I looked at the watch on my wrist, more as a reminder of the times we lived in rather than the lateness of the evening. "I have one last thing to share before we start the dodgeball guns. What I'd like to have you all do is make sure that you have seriously considered what the price of living this kind of life is going to be, and you need to think about that before payment is due. Tonight's training will be much more intense and will provide you all with a better taste of the kind of events that we are training for and will be doing more often in the future. If there is anyone that isn't going to take training seriously, or if you don't think that this kind of life is for you, then I need to know tonight. You will still be welcome to participate in the dodgeball arena, but I need to know who is ready and willing to make a 'down payment'."

Those that had participated in rescuing Mozart were all ready to move forward with the training because they were intimately acquainted with why we were doing this and who we were doing it for and everyone else was on board for some more intense training.

"Thank you all for letting me know. It's important to

submissively obey those that God has placed over you and to know what you are willing to do. Don't ever feel pressured to disobey what God is calling you to do, or what an authority figure says, simply because your friends might expect it of you."

The guys that had previously trained with the ComBots were slightly disappointed that we weren't going to have as intense of a training session as last Saturday. I had told them then that Sandra and I wouldn't be able monitor sessions with this large of a group as effectively, but that we would be working on cohesive teamwork against real-life situations more often.

Everyone had started to quietly ensure that their equipment was all strapped on and ready for dodgeball. I don't really know how effective the dodgeball training would be against real world conflicts in the future, but I supposed it was a fun way to practice avoiding getting blown to bits by an energy blast or something like that. If nothing else, the kids got to spend some energy running around the room.

"The acronym 'GRID' stands for 'God Revealing Internal Dialect' for a reason. God will always be speaking to you and calling you to come closer to Him. He wants to reveal more of Himself to you. If you are willing to listen then you will grow stronger in your walk and closer to Him. Your GRID Connections are meant to be part of God revealing Himself to you."

I had looked around the room and I prayed for each of them. They all had such potential, for good and for ill, and the world they were growing into was not a place that I wanted to send them.

I had chuckled internally. *The place where the Church is most needed is where it's the hardest for us to stand.*

"I also want to point out that the Bible study and training don't have to end just because you guys can work at home. Everything will continue as they have been until the Lord changes things. Joseph will be leading the study next week, and tonight we will be starting a more advanced training program down here," I said, gearing up for the official unveiling of the new training rounds.

I had another Grandpa Prayer Moment and asked the Lord if there was anything that I was forgetting. I also asked again for His hand of blessing upon this group and that no one would get hurt tonight.

Thank You, Lord.

"Okay. What do you want to change?" Adam asked.

"Well, now that you all know how to operate your suits and are familiar with you GRID Connections, I'd like to begin establishing units and teams trained for future missions. We're not just here to have fun you know."

"Oh, you mean there *is* a point to all of this?" Aaron teased.

"Yes, Aaron," I smirked, "there is a point to all of this. If the Lord calls us to defensive work in the future we need to be prepared for it. I've programmed some mission simulations for us to accomplish."

I grinned, "Now we are not a peace-keeping or military force; we are not the aggressors. We, each one of us, are Defenders now; none of you are children anymore and it's time for the Disciples to become Defenders. You will always be students and keep learning, but now it is time for you to start leading and defending. As Defenders most of our missions will probably be rescue related; defending cities or villages, saving families, or rescuing hostages, that sort of thing."

"You mean we're not going to take over the world?" Beth joked.

I shook my head and moved on, "While we have not been delegated the authority to assassinate or arrest people, we have been given the God given right and mandate to do what is right, and both the government and Scripture approve of self-defense."

"You guys ready to fire up the dodgeballs?" I asked, already knowing the answer to that question.

The room burst into an excited flurry of activity as everyone spread out for the game.

"Just a head's up. I've made these training simulations bit more realistic than the previous dodgeball games have been."

"What do you mean?" Jennifer asked nervously.

"I mean that these training rounds with the ComBots will be as close to reality as training can get; the pain and injuries will be temporary but still feel just like the real thing."

"Can we train like this at home?" Jessica asked.

Joseph nodded, "There are a bunch of saved missions that we can complete here and at home with different settings depending on the size of the group."

"Everyone ready?" I asked, already anticipating the answer.

"You bet!" Aaron answered first.

"When are you going to start training them for Komplo situations?" Joseph asked via his GRID Connection. *"Soon. They need to be able to handle 'normal' situations first though."* I answered as the simulation began. Truth be told I was hoping that I could deal with the Komplo without involving the new Defenders so that they could escape whatever fate my dreams foretold.

KT Harrison

"Another day at home survived," I said to myself as I arrived for my training sessions at the SOS Corps base in town. "And another struggle at the SOS Corps," I added looking at the unassuming home that stood over the base.

I walked up to the front door and rang the bell, even the neighborhood surveillance cameras would have alerted anyone inside of my arrival long before now. Knocking was mostly for show because the SOS Corps didn't want the neighbors to think that the owners of the home just left their doors open for anyone to walk in.

"Hey KT. How's it going man?" Marcus opened the door and greeted me.

"It's goin'," I said and Marcus left to finish getting ready for the warm up session later. I was thankful to have gotten my work done sooner than expected and so I didn't have to worry about the photos my client had hired me to take for their creation magazine and got an earlier flight home.

I wasn't sure how many people would be showing up for the training, all I knew is that I had to be ready, both for training and for battle. With Silas in Colorado there was a lot more pressure on me at home; not like things were great when he was here, but the stress level has definitely gotten worse at least for me.

I started down the stairs of the secret passage leading to the underground base, since the aboveground portion served as the living space for Marcus there wasn't much point in hanging around up there.

I made it to the "Welcoming Room" of the SOS Base – this area was designed to be our last line of defense if everything went wrong. – and walked past the areas designed for cover from enemy fire, weapons, and ammunitions that were all strategically located throughout the room and headed to one of the hallways so that I could get the equipment I needed for recording the training session. The idea was that the trainers and students could review the videos and improve their strategy. Personally, I doubt anyone ever watches any of the videos, but hey, at least they have 'em. Right?

Before I made it to the door I heard Carl calling from the floors above me, "Hey KC! Or uh, CJ. Yo JD!"

It's KT, Carl. Usually, Timothy would have given the guy the right combination of letters, but he wasn't here today.

My GRID connection allowed me to hear Marcus say at a normal volume, "Hey Carl, I think he goes by KT."

"Oh, yeah, yeah, yeah. KT. KT." Carl said hastily to remind himself. "My bad. I guess I'll have to talk to him later."

"I'm sure you could go down and find him." Marcus answered. I could hear him moving around as he gathered whatever he needed from his office area.

"Yeah man, but I don't want to have to go all the way down there to turn around and come back. I got things up here I gotta do." Carl answered, semi-jokingly.

"Okay, whatever man," Marcus answered teasingly as

he finished what he had to do.

The GRID stuff was a lot of fun at times, even though I didn't have any amazing abilities. Timothy had established my GRID connection for me and showed me how to use my heightened senses to my advantage, and now I could see, smell, and hear almost as well as a swift fox; the hearing was very handy when it came to messing with my little brother, Isaac. In fact I could mess with just about anyone I wanted to.

Bringing in personal weapons was kind of concerning to the SOS leadership, but Joseph had figured out a way to get some Sangátian claws past the scanners for me. I had to wear fingerless gloves to prevent any suspicion, so Joseph placed a metal sheath on the back of each of my gloves with each sheath holding four claws that would extend to reach just past each of my fingers. The sheaths had mechanisms that were programed to regulate the length of the claws and keep them tucked away until I used a GRID command to activate them. The claws weren't retractable, so the sheaths would cut off the ends and I would have to wait for new ones to be made by the mechanisms stored inside the sheaths.

Per my request Timothy had programmed special GRID enhanced cameras into my glasses, which meant that in addition to being able to see farther and more clearly in the desert brush and having enhanced nocturnal vision I could take unbelievable pictures simply by looking at an object and activating the glasses; this had certain practical 'surveillance' purposes as well as helping me ace my classes and please my clients.

At this point I tuned out the noise that was coming from upstairs as it continued to fade with each step I took.

This was one more conversation that made me glad that I wasn't really involved with the teenage SOS Corps anymore; I hadn't trained with them since before Silas left for the army.

My ear twitched at the sound of someone talking with a GRID connection. *That's weird; Timothy and Silas said that the Defenders were the only ones around here with a GRID connection, and Timothy is the only one I know skilled at talking with the GRID like this.*

The sound was so muffled and hidden that I couldn't make out who was talking, but I could tell that at least one of the men was on one of the floors below me farther down the hall. So I moved in the direction of the voices as they got louder, but I still couldn't understand anything that was being said.

Eventually, I made my way to the farthest corner of the security storage area – now one of the voices seemed to be coming from directly below me – and looked around for anyone that might be watching. Then I laid down and pressed my ear to the ground and could finally make out what was being said.

"But sir, I've done everything that you've asked!" The voice from below pleaded defensively.

"How can you claim such a thing Virus? You have again proven your completely worthless and idiotic nature." I couldn't pinpoint a direction for the second voice. It was even more muffled than the first voice – the one belonging to Virus, I guess – and it seemed to echo from every direction.

"But sir, I gave you all the information I have access to; the only records of any of the Defenders are the personal notes of Carlos Ortega and he describes the training, codenames, abilities, and weakness of five individuals.

Agents Martinez and Williams, former Agent Stevens, Silas Harrison, and Joseph Stevens. There are some indications that the Professor has nearly finished upgrading some elite members of the SOS Corps to Defender status." Virus continued to defend his usefulness and diligent research.

"Enough. I did not journey from Kalmar to be bored by your excuses, nor will I be hindered by your incompetence."

The second voice must belong to one of the 'tourists' that Timothy had asked me to look out for, and Virus must be his mole.

"Are there any other new discoveries that you would care to inform me of?" The second, more sinister, voice asked derisively.

"Yes sir," Virus answered in a defeated tone. "I've discovered that the younger brother of Silas Harrison, Kevin Tyler Harrison, is training here in the SOS Corps and has had close interaction with Timothy Stevens."

"So there might be someone within the SOS Corps informing Stevens of our actions? Are you sure that you have a secure connection?" the second voice asked slightly alarmed.

"Of course, Sorcerer. I have taken no chances, and KT Harrison isn't due to arrive in the state for at least another hour." Virus obviously didn't know about my earlier flight that had allowed me to make it to the SOS Base already.

"Let's hope so. In addition to your failure to inform me of the growing number of Defenders you also failed to fully detail the extent of Chopper's spiritual training." My ears perked up at the mention of my brother; it was strange that I hadn't heard from him or even about him since early last week.

"Sir, I informed you of the danger in confronting Silas Harrison and I notified you of the spiritual training of each of the Defenders as you asked. Silas has been described as being a late starter, but the time he spent with Juan Martinez has awakened the warrior within him, so the failure of your team in killing him is not my fault."

"We may not have killed him, but he won't interfere with our plans in the future; no thanks to your incompetence."

"Sir, I have been doing everything I can to prove –"

"Quiet! What was that?" Sorcerer asked in a panic.

Someone was walking down the hallway towards the storage room below me.

"Someone's coming," Virus replied upon hearing the sound. *"We'll have to finish this later."*

"All right, do not disappoint me Virus."

When the connection was completely disconnected I exhaled deeply and sat up slowly; the GRID lag was intense and I had to steady myself to keep from falling over.

I'd have to contact Timothy about this, but any phone calls going out of the SOS Corps were recorded – if Virus could get a hold of Carl's personal files then he'd probably be able to see phone call transcripts – and whenever I used the GRID to communicate it set off a beacon to anyone within earshot; Timothy had said that I sounded like a coyote howling in the night whenever I had used the GRID to call him before.

"I guess I'll have to wait until I get home later," I said to myself and took a deep breath before struggling to my feet.

I tightened the strap on my gloves and rubbed the metal sheath concealing my claws.

"Nobody messes with my brother but me." I vowed as I left the storage room.

Chapter Twenty-Eight

Surprise, AZ   Thursday, September 5, 2044

Timothy Stevens

I knew when KT contacted me that things were about to get worse, and the fact that KT considered the matter urgent enough for him to use the GRID to talk to me instead of using normal communication channels led me to believe that he had found out some info on the tourists.

The moment I heard KT's GRID beacon go off I hurried to make a connection and quiet the GRID signal being emitted. He then shared a memory orb that recorded the conversation he had overheard.

"Have you heard from Silas at all lately?" I asked KT.

KT shook his head, "Not since early last week. What's is going on, Tim?"

I ran my hand through my hair, "There are a lot of things that we don't know right now. So what *do* we know?"

"Well we know that Silas is still alive and that he would contact us if he could," KT answered, remembering the fact that the tourists had failed to kill him.

"Right," I said with a nod. "We also know that these guys weren't interested in capturing him, so he's probably wounded, out of their reach, and unable to contact us for some reason."

"So what are you going to do?"

I sighed and answered with a shrug of my shoulder. "I'm going to fly to Colorado Springs and see what I can find out."

"Tim?" KT's tone and expression concerned me.

"Yeah?"

"When you find them, promise me you'll let me in on the take down." KT was out for blood, but his lack of information made him dependent on me to satisfy his desire for vengeance.

"KT, I have an idea how you must feel," I said, trying to reason with him, "but you can't take matters into your own hands."

"I'm not one of your Disciples, I'm not a Defender, and I'm not even an official SOS Agent, so I don't have to play by your rules, Timothy." I knew that it was KT's emotions talking right now and that he would cool off later, hopefully, but I didn't know how to talk right now with him being this upset.

Father give me wisdom.

"While you may be right about that, KT a Christian has to live by God's rules, and your conscience will be painfully scarred if you do this, so let God keep His promise to avenge us. I'd like to invite you again to come to Bible study on Thursday so we can learn together how to do this thing the right way; God's way."

KT glared at me, his eyes were burning with anger, hurt, and mistrust. "Where was God when your tourists attacked my brother?"

"God was fighting for your brother that night; why do you think they failed to kill Him? Our God has a sovereign plan for each of us that cannot be thwarted."

KT shook his head and crossed his arms. "Find out who did this and stop them. If you don't, then I will, and I won't need God to avenge me at that point."

As soon as I had finished talking with KT I turned myself invisible by taking on the physical properties of the air around me, and I flew at near-hurricane speed across the country to see what I could find out about Silas.

When I arrived at Colorado Springs, I found a secluded place atop of an apartment building to land and re-materialize. I nearly collapsed off of the building and had to lean on the short wall along the edge to steady myself. I always thought of the GRID lag as God's way of reminding me who was *really* doing the work; I was just the tool, and in my own strength none of these wondrous effects would occur.

Once I could stand up again without swooning, I again made myself invisible and made my way to the VA hospital. I had installed Silas' pack to check his vital signs, determine the best medical facility to treat his wounds, and automatically fly him there before deactivating and becoming concealed in the metal ring hanging on the chain with his dog tags. However, Military protocol would dictate that Silas would be medically stabilized and then transferred to the local Veteran's Association Hospital, I knew that I should start looking for him there.

When I found the VA, I gently flew in through the front door as someone walked out – that way those inside would mistake my flight for a breeze entering the building – and upon entering the building, I landed and walked around so that I wouldn't stir up as much wind as I would while flying.

I made my way over behind the receptionist's desk, noticing as I went that her name badge identified her as Betty Summers. I gently used the GRID to whisper to Betty, *"Silas*

Harrison."

Silas' name didn't register as being familiar to Betty; in fact she was puzzled by the fact that a random name would pop into her mind.

I whispered again, *"I wonder if there is a patient here with that name."*

Betty began using the computer in front of her to search the patient records for Silas.

"That's weird; He is a patient here," she whispered under her breath, before opening the record.

I began reading over her shoulder, a bit annoyed at the slow pace with which she scrolled down the screen.

According to the ER report, Silas had been found a block away from the ER in the northern portion of Colorado Springs and a very large blood transfusion was needed to help stabilize him due to the five minor stab wounds along his right side, four lacerations that went diagonally upward from his right side towards his throat, five additional stab wound located near his left scapula, a small bullet wound on his left calf that ruptured an artery, and two bullet wounds in his back; one in the lower right thoracic region and the other in the mid thoracic region just anterior to the spinal column. They also documented that Silas suffered from an unusually severe black widow bite on the back of his neck.

"It's a miracle that he's still alive," Betty whispered as she continued to read the report.

Betty pulled up the surgeon's note written by the doctor that had treated Silas; his liver was damaged by the bullet that entered through the right thoracic region of his back, and the bullet that had entered directly over the spinal column entered the spinal canal through the spinous process of one of his vertebra but stopped just short of entering the spinal canal.

When she finally got to the point that recorded what room Silas was currently staying in, I carefully made my way outside of the building as quickly as I could without creating too strong of a breeze inside before hurriedly making my way around the building to where Silas was. Silas' room was conveniently located on the outer perimeter of the hospital so I could phase through the window seams to get in.

When I finally found Silas, I was overcome by the wave of unexpected emotions that blindsided me. I'm normally a technically oriented, reserved, rationalistic individual, but my brother Joseph, Silas, and Marcus were three of the first tools that God had used to loosen that mechanical framework that coated my heart and protected me from this kind of emotional hurt.

I made my way to the chair beside his bed and sat down and all the practical reasons for being here were buried beneath a mountain of confusion and hurt. I wouldn't admit at that time, but the mistrust of God from my younger years threatened to return but I couldn't allow myself to question why, at least not yet. I had to stay focused on the task at hand until my reason returned, because stumbling over the why's in my current state of mind wouldn't help anyone.

I reached over and grabbed the chain that was around Silas' neck, hoping to find the circular ring that concealed the shrunken jetpack that he used; but the ring was nowhere to be found and since it wasn't on the chain, the pack must have failed to conceal itself before Silas was discovered by the paramedics. So whatever task force was investigating the matter would most likely have the pack in their possession, which meant that not only was one of my best friends almost killed by these tourists, but they had also caused his alias as Chopper – and the interdimensional technology hidden inside of his pack –to become compromised.

A strange wave of grief came over me, *"What have I done?"* My mind began to become bogged down and strained by guilt. *"I brought him into this, and if it wasn't for the fact that he was associated with me he wouldn't have been targeted. I encouraged him to become a Defender, and I caused this to happen."*

My mind then went to the Disciples that I had been training; I knew some of them almost as closely as I knew Silas. What was I bringing them into? And how many of them would suffer because of my decisions and actions?

"Maybe it would be better to stop fighting, because if I stop then no one else will have to get hurt. Is all of this exhaustion, pain, and loss worth it? Did God really call me to endanger those closest to me?"

I shook my head to try and clear away the lies that my own feelings had produced.

"There are some things that I don't understand, but I do know that God is in control. I know that He has called me to war against the spiritual forces of darkness and to train others to do the same; I have decided to follow Jesus, and there is no turning back now."

The guilt and grief didn't disappear, but they did decrease in their intensity. I had counted the cost of being a disciple of Jesus years ago; I knew what I was getting into and I didn't regret making the decision. I would have to make sure that the students back home knew what they were getting into as well.

I looked into the clean shaven, and peaceful 'baby-face' of my friend; just before he deported Silas had the fullest beard of anyone our age in church. It was strange to see him here, and without his beard, although it was even more strange to see him sleeping, something that he had to be coerced into doing back home.

"Don't you dare die on me Silas," I whispered via the GRID to my slumbering friend. *"How are we supposed to have that sparring rematch if you're dead?"* I asked with a chuckle. *"I've been looking forward to kicking your tail again, so you better pull through this little brother."*

My trust in the Lord was still strong, but my own understanding and emotions threatened to overwhelm me as I looked down at his resting form, and the closeness of the friendship I had with Silas only served to further anger me at that moment. Questions of why this happened and who was responsible began to cause my blood to boil. I knew the answers to those questions would be settled in my mind, however I couldn't afford the emotional battle to take place here in the hospital because the firestorm that could be produced would burn the entire building to an ash heap if I were to lose control of my temper.

I stood to leave, but first I placed my hand on my friend's head and prayed silently, *"Dear Lord, I ask You please, if it is in Your will, to extend Silas' time here on Earth and heal my friend. But if You have determined this to be his time to be promoted to being present with You, then free him from pain and comfort me in my grief. I ask these things in the name of my Savior and Lord, Jesus the Christ. Amen."*

I went over to the outer wall and phased outside of the building and looked around to see where I could go to rematerialize into the visible spectrum without being noticed.

I noticed a large man, with short, jet black curls atop of his head, and broad shoulders walking away from the front of the building; even from this distance I could tell that this was not a guy to be messed with.

The man hesitated for a moment before turning and looking back at the building. The man scanned the front of the building with his eyes before staring intently at where I was standing; it was almost as though he had locked eyes with me, even though I was completely invisible. As I looked at him I noticed a strange light that flickered in his eyes.

The man turned and walked away, and I felt strangely compelled to follow him. Being outside and invisible I was able to fly over to the man and stay just above him as he walked towards the end of the parking lot. The area around the VA clinic was still largely undeveloped, and the man simply walked north, out of the parking lot and towards the street beyond. There was a large incline between the road and the clinic in that direction.

The man began to descend down the other side of the hill, towards the road, and made his way to a clump of trees that were right by the road. The man then crouched down beside a tree and peered out towards the road.

The man suddenly spoke up, his eyes still scanning the road, "There's no one around to see you rematerialize now. Would you care to make this conversation less awkward for us both?" He asked turning and fixing his gaze on my invisible form.

"How did you know I was there?" I asked as I rematerialized and walked towards the man, my hand defensively holding the hilt of my sword.

"The same way that you were able to conceal yourself," he said matter-of-factly, "The Lord allowed for it to take place."

I looked at the man warily, "Who are you?"

He chuckled, "I was told that you would be able to distinguish between spirits. Did the light you saw mean nothing to you?"

I thought back to the light I saw flicker in his eyes, a light that still glimmered as his gaze locked with mine. It had looked more authentic then any of the counterfeits I had seen over my journeys through the realms. Of course, that only meant that this guy was an angel, but it didn't assure me of what side he was on.

"I've seen many manifestations of 'light' before," I replied, shrugging my shoulder, "some have been true reflections of the King of kings while others have been impressive counterfeits. A wise man carefully ensures that he knows which he is dealing with."

The man nodded and pondered at what I had said.

"Who are you?" I asked a second time.

"Who I say that I am matters little, something that I believe applies to your kind as well as mine. Yet another truth that I have learned through my studies of humanity is that, like with all of creation, our worth is determined by what our Creator says it is."

Now it was my turn to ponder at what was said. I then asked him a question, "Who do you say Jesus was?"

The man smiled, "I think you mean to ask, 'Who do I say Jesus *is*'. But to answer your question, I am fully convinced that Jesus is Lord of all creation, of all humanity and the angelic hosts, He is the I AM and will one day come again for His bride."

At this point I was confident that I was dealing with the real deal. "So why has the Creator sent you here?"

"I am the ministering spirit assigned to your friend, Silas; I believe that you humans often call us 'guardian angels'."

I couldn't help but smile as different conversations with Silas came flooding back. We had often joked about how Silas' adrenaline addiction must have over-worked his guardian angel to the point of exhaustion and rapid replacement.

The angel shook his head, obviously deep in thought. "I have learned many things as I've studied creation these few thousand years of its existence, but nothing compares to what I've learned while observing humanity. The ways of Elohim are truly remarkable, especially when it comes to you humans."

"What do you mean by that?"

"I speak of the greatness of God revealed by His interactions with your kind. Tell me…" the man hesitated and seemed unsure of how to say what was on his mind. "What is it like? To experience grace, I mean? To know that you are completely undeserving of even the smallest kindness, and yet be given a gift greater than any created being can fathom. What does it feel like to consider that truth?"

The truth spoken of in 1 Peter, that the angels long to look into the mystery of the Church partaking of both the sufferings and glories of Christ, suddenly became clearer to me. The obedient angels would have no need of grace and the rebellious angels were never granted any measure of grace or redemption, yet man receives not only a redeemed life but the promise of future glory with Christ.

I closed my eyes and tried to put into words the deep sense of gratitude and love that overwhelmed whenever I contemplated the engulfing grace of God. "I don't know how to describe it, but it is unlike any other feeling I know."

He nodded, and thought about my answer.

"Why are you here?" I asked him after a moment of waiting.

"My name is Tabansi, and as I said I am the ministering spirit assigned to your friend, Silas. I was there with him two nights ago when he was attacked."

Tabansi waited for a moment for the reality of what he had said to sink in. He was there? Why then did Silas go through such a defeat?

"I've seen God's power through an individual's few frail years on this earth, and although compulsiveness and recklessness of your friend has made keeping him alive a challenge these past years," Tabansi said with a chuckle as he shook his head, "and his decision to join the Defender Corps has made things even more challenging, you warriors are still privileged to take part in the work of guardians. Even still, the duties of your ministering spirits are much more complicated as a result of the Defender Corps." Tabansi shook his head with a sigh of exhaustion.

"Can you tell me what happened that night? Who is responsible?" I asked, a flickering thought of revenge tugged at the corner of my mind until I remembered my concern for KT and I pushed the idea aside until a more opportune time to apply some concrete truth to my mind.

There were so many thoughts and emotions vying for my attention that I would have to wait to deal with. *Oh*

Father in heaven, please keep me from doing anything I'll regret.

"I can do better than that," Tabansi said, calling me back to the present moment and stretching out his hand in front of him as a small blue cloud began to form above his upward-facing palm; slowly the cloud condensed and formed a memory orb.

"I can show you what happened," he said, extending the memory orb for me to take.

When I took the orb from him, I saw everything with even more clarity than I was used to seeing when I had viewed memories in the past. Tabansi had truly done everything within his power to assist Silas, even going so far as to prevent the bullets from penetrating Silas' spine or crucial internal organs.

I recognized three of the individuals and their abilities from Tabansi's memories.

The woman seated at the table goes was by the name 'Acedia' – though her real name is 'Athaliah Shirazi' – a Myathian witch responsible for poisoning the minds of countless Christians in Myathis while I journeyed there with the local Defender Corps.

The younger man sitting with her was Simon Vaughan who I had met in Kalmar when he went by the alias 'The Illusionist' and was part of the original Defender Corps of Kalmar. However, while the Kalmarian Defender Corps was still establishing itself, Simon turned on us and became the demonically empowered 'Sorcerer'.

The shapeshifter at the bar was Luna Coterel, a Mygan warrior and little sister to a trusted ally of mine, Emmi Coterel. Luna called herself 'Lunulata' and could produce a deadly blue poison from her hands, a poison to which there was no cure. I had a hard time imagining what could have motivated her to be associated with the likes of Acedia and The Sorcerer because she had been so close to Emmi when they both worked as Defenders.

I'd have to share the memory with Joseph to try and identify the man in black that fought with Silas, the older man that hindered Silas' GRID connection, and the shrinking woman that poisoned him.

"Silas has a soldier's heart, Timothy," Tabansi said after I had finished viewing the memory orb he gave me, "and that is one thing that I can relate to and understand about you humans. For we as the angelic host will fight with perfect submission the battle that our Lord commands us to fight, and no matter how hopeless the battle seems we know that He is greater than any foe and that victory is in His hands. What I don't understand is why you saints seem to give up so easily at times. Is not our Lord greater than any difficulty or cost you could pay?"

"Do you know if Silas will survive?" I asked, hoping that Tabansi had been informed about the earthly fate of my friend.

Tabansi smiled with understanding. I'm sure that he had witnessed many human beings suffer great loss over his existence and understood, in concept at least, what it was that I was going through.

"You know as well I do Timothy, Silas will live on into eternity should his body cease to function," he finally answered. "And while your friend has developed an accelerated healing ability to match his fighting spirit, I have not been told about whether or not this is Silas appointed time to be promoted to seeing our Lord face to face."

"Thank you, Tabansi." I said, with a nod of disappointed acceptance. "Is there anything else that you can tell me?"

He shook his head, "I am sorry but no, I have nothing else to share with you and I must return now to keep watch over Silas."

"All right, thank you for showing me what happened that night."

"You're welcome; stand fast Timothy, for the war is always waging around you. You Defenders have placed yourself at a critical place at a critical point in history, and so have your Disciples; make sure that you have truly counted the cost of choosing this path before it is required of you." Tabansi, said before vanishing from sight and returning to Silas' bedside.

"So Simon, you're trying to establish your own Komplo on Earth now." I said, after turning myself invisible again and beginning my return flight home through the sky above Colorado. I continued my struggle to push aside my emotions until I arrived back at the compound in my basement because I was concerned that I would begin to heat up in my anger and cause abnormal thermal changes in the air around me and I didn't want to cause any weather anomalies that could be used by the Komplo to trace my location, or Silas' for that matter.

I reviewed Tabansi's memory a few times as I flew home; As soon as Silas walked into the restaurant Acedia began her attempts to manipulate Silas' mind to keep him from fighting and the older gentleman caused a gray cloud to surround Silas' pack so that it couldn't receive any GRID commands while Simon quickly sensed Tabansi's presence and called for two demonic forces to hinder him from helping Silas.

When I watched the battle through an angel's eyes and ears I could see and hear all that God was doing to help Silas, for during Silas' struggle the Lord brought to his remembrance the things that he had learned from godly men like Pastor Juan and studying the Bible and that reminding is what kept Silas from being mentally poisoned by Acedia.

Despite the endeavors of the demonic forces summoned by Simon, Tabansi continued to warn Silas of shots from across the street and of other dangers from his other assailants in the restaurant throughout the battle. Silas was finally able to activate his pack after Tabansi had struck the mindvoice barrier that the older man had used to suppress Silas' GRID connection with his pack, and when Simon had caused the bullets to fire through the jetpack and into Silas' back Tabansi prevented any serious injury from taking place by placing his hand around Silas' spinal cord, so that as the bullet went through the spinous process it slammed to a stop before entering the spinal canal. Tabansi had also deflected the other bullet away from critical organs and into the self-repairing liver before catching Silas and carrying him to the earth below where he would be discovered by the paramedics. Finally, Tabansi concealed the jetpack so he could return it to me for repairs.

I made my way down through the secret tunnels into the compound underneath my parents' home and passed by Joseph on my way down the hallway.

"How did it go?" he asked, becoming concerned at the stern look on my face.

"I'll tell you after my first therapy session." I said, entering the nearest training room.

"So you mean I'm going to have to calm you down *and* repair our entire supply of ComBots?" Joseph asked with a groan.

"With the way I feel right now, I don't know if there will be anything left to repair," I said shaking my head and hesitating at the doorway of the training room. "You may want to be ready to have some new ComBots MAPTed."

"That bad, huh?" Joseph asked. He was trying to get me to talk through it like a normal human being, rather than create an inferno in the training room.

I created a memory orb of the events that took place that day in Colorado Springs. "Watch this," I said tossing the orb to my brother, "and see if you recognize any of the people attacking Silas. I need to do some personal wrestling and get some things sorted out and under control before I can talk about it."

I raised a hand to keep Joe from trying to talk me out of my decision. "If I'm going to start an inferno, I want to do it in a safe environment where no one gets hurt, and right now, talking about it may start something that I can't control." I reached into my pocket and pulled out the shrunken form of Silas' jetpack and tossed it to Joseph as well. "See if you can do anything to repair this."

God had given me some amazing abilities over the years – practical, spiritual, and GRID abilities that glorified Him when used properly but dangerous, destructive, and hard to control when subject to my flesh – and the last thing I wanted was to lose control of my GRID Connection and incinerate someone, especially Joseph.

"When I can talk about it without burning everything around me to a crisp, you'll be the first one I share it with, but right now I don't trust myself. Pray for me, Joseph." With a glance over my shoulder in his direction I added, "I haven't felt anything like this in years."

Joseph nodded without saying a word and I entered the training room and shut the door.

I walked into the center of the room and replayed the memory of the attack against my friend. The healing process would start with a fiery display of emotion, after my emotions are put out of the way I would be able to rationally deal with the situation in light of reality.

When I was young I had dealt with my emotions by yelling into my pillow as I lay in bed at night, later – when I began my training with the SOS Corps – I would push myself to my physical limits in a combat session, but now my GRID connection has made it so that either of these two methods of emotional venting would cause an uncontrollable firestorm.

So my new method of releasing my emotions was to walk into the Cainium-lined training room underneath my home and release my fury in a fiery windstorm, by causing the air around me to circulate in the room and I could feel my temperature begin to rise. The movement of the air around me continued to increase its speed until I was lifted strait up into the air by the rushing wind. I released the flame of fire with a yell of welled up emotion as bursts of ire were be carried by the wind and created a whirling inferno around me.

Once that initial burst of emotion was released I collapsed to the ground in a mentally exhausted and emotionally drained heap, after that I was able to come before the Lord broken and seeking so that I could yield to His will and listen to His voice.

For me, God spoke most often and most clearly by bringing to remembrance different lessons I had learned from His Word and from simply living life.

Outrage and confusion from my earlier childhood returned with a vengeance and surpassed the instances that occurred during my journeys through the realms.

For many years I had felt betrayed and used by God, as though I were His yo-yo and He enjoyed using my emotions for sport. Why would God give me a gift and then rip it away from me so abruptly when I had only just begun to value it? Was God playing with me? Was all of this pain the worthy price of love and friendship?

After the rage passed I was reminded of God's goodness and of the fact that in His sovereign wisdom He had always comforted me and accompanied me through the harshness of living in a fallen world, because He redeems the pain and suffering of this world to glorify Himself and to strengthen His children. Whether that pain is found in a close friend moving away or in the death of a loved one God has always used those experiences to grow my trust in Him.

Then I was reminded of that dangerous prayer that I had shared with Jessica and in my exhaustion I began to whisper my heart to God, "Father I'm broken and confused right now and I don't know why You would allow this to happen. But I know that everything You do is good, and You will be glorified in this. I know that there are lessons that can only be learned by living them, and that You desire to strengthen my trust in You through life. I ask You to comfort me now Father, and to help me trust You and Your plan for my life as You continue to teach me to follow wherever You call me to go. I ask for this in the name of my Savior and Lord, Jesus the Christ, Amen."

I managed to lift myself off from the ground and began to search for Joseph; we had some serious preparations to make, and if Simon was out to get me then everything that we had established by means of keeping our families safe was practically worthless since Simon knew who I was.

Chapter Twenty-Nine

Surprise, AZ   Thursday, September 5, 2044

"Well, I think that the world has finally started to fall apart," my wife, Sandra, remarked as I entered the living room, exhausted from my therapy session down below. Our sons were tucked away in bed and the two of us had gathered for a 'family meeting' in order to discuss the results of both our investigations that had occurred today.

"More than you know," I thought but didn't say just yet. At this point in time she only knew about the 'normal' chaos that was happening around the country but the fact that Simon had brought an interdimensional Komplo to Earth in order to wage his own mission of conquest made the situation all the more dire.

Sandra continued as we both found our seats, her stomach just beginning to reveal another growing life inside of her. "I've been monitoring the data coming in the INS downstairs, and I found several interesting developments are occurring as we speak."

"What kind of developments?" I asked, sinking down into the couch next to her.

"There was a recording taken by a high ranking government aid working in the white house; the aid is connected to the SOS Corps in D.C. the conversation he taped was concerning how the government should best present the public with the announcement of the collapse of the Supplemental Nutrition Assistance Program over the weekend."

"Well, I've gotta hear this," I mused stretching my feet out onto the ottoman we had been given. "How exactly do they propose to gently inform the public that their SNAP handouts have been cut off and still come out looking like the heroes of the nation?"

"I'm not entirely sure how they plan on lying to the nation this time," my bride replied, "but I believe that since over fifty-two million people in America are on welfare and aren't going to have any money handed to them for food this announcement could be the deathblow to our society that you, your father, and grandfather have been worried about and preparing for."

"When people are starving they are much more likely to take desperate measures," I replied soberly, "and I think that the expected riots will begin to start very shortly after the announcement; maybe early next week if we're lucky but it's more likely that it will be this weekend. The publicity of the announcement will be a large part in how soon we start having problems."

"Speaking of desperate measures: any guesses as to what the second most trending news is online?" She asked, putting a hand on my lap.

I shook my head; the base downstairs had all the information networking I would have needed to stay as up to date as my wife was, but with my trip to Colorado I didn't get the chance to use it as she had. "No, what?"

"The number of rallies taking place at colleges across the nation chanting for a socialistic revolution in America." My wife answered flatly.

I put my hand over my face, "You've got to be kidding me."

"I wish I was," Sandra replied, "but they're demanding that a revolt starts as soon as possible and that a new leader be put into power that will truly 'care for the people' and make college free and increase welfare handouts."

"The current administration is already more socialistic than democratic." I said, running my hands through my hair in frustration. "Who is it that they're wanting to put into place? Or do I not want to know?"

"Andy Bernard, the self-proclaimed socialist; although you've pointed out that he's likely be a communist at heart."

I shook my head and closed my eyes, "And the welfare crowd will be joining forces with the college students when they find out what is going on, no doubt."

She paused for a moment before stating, "Things can only get worse from here. Although, I also picked up some chatter from some militant Islamist leaders stating that they were going to capitalize on the current American weakness with a massive strike immediately following the announcement, so I don't see how things could get much worse after that."

"I'm afraid it can," I interjected and lowered my head, "and it's already much worse than you know."

"How so?" Sandra asked, concerned. "Did you find out something about Silas while you were away?"

I opened my eyes and nodded, fighting to control myself as I answered. "A team of trained fighters from across the seven realms have banded together and are now preparing for some kind of large scale attack; they've already taken out Silas and they seem to be moving in for the rest of the SOS Corps and the Defenders."

"I think that it's time for us to go underground then,"

my wife said, referring to the previously planned out escape route for my family in case someone ever found out about who I was.

I shook my head, "I'm afraid that may not be enough."

"Why not?"

"Because the leader of this group – of this Komplo – is a man named Simon; a man demonically inspired and empowered to try and destroy God by contradicting prophecy. He hates me and knows who I am and that I am from Earth; it's only a matter of time before he finds a way to locate me and those close to me," I replied, closing my eyes for a moment to bring some small relief to them.

"All the more reason for those close to you to get underground," she replied, not fully understanding my concern. "You've been preparing for this sort of thing for years now."

"All of which could be undone in moments," I countered, a bit more harshly than I had intended. "I'm sorry, but I don't know what Simon's capable of anymore and I can't handle losing anyone else."

The guilt and grief I had felt looking down at Silas returned to me as I remember the many close relationships that I had lost over the years and the way that God used four key people to break through the emotional Fort Knox I had built to keep control of my grief: Joseph Stevens, Silas Harrison, Marcus Williams, and Grandpa. And while those four people helped prepare me for the responsibilities of being a husband and father, they were also some of the ways that the enemy had tried to beat me back into the safety of solitude.

Silas was the first strike against my outer defenses, and I lost him once when he joined the army and moved away and now I might be losing him a second time because of this Komplo.

Marcus was still alive and well, but our relationship had been broken while we fought against Nimrod's Pantheon some years back; it was strange because all my other friendships had been stunted by distance, but my friendship with Marcus seemed broken by our closeness. I knew that the relationship had yet to be mended because of my fear in approaching him – I didn't want to make things worse – but I knew that the Lord was directing me to bring healing to that relationship; maybe one day I'll find that my friendship with Marcus is restored.

And perhaps my greatest fear in life was that something would happen to Grandpa, my wife, or our sons that would cause our relationships to become stunted. I had full assurance that if any of my family members were relocated somewhere within the seven realms, or if any of them were to be promoted to the presence of God, that he would always be my Grandpa and I would always be his Grandson, Sandra would always be my wife and I her husband, and Jeremiah, Ezekiel and unborn Daniel would always be my sons and I their father. However, I still feared the guilt that would arise should anything begin to threaten any of those relationships on account of me or my actions, and this kind of guilt and fear had already threatened to overwhelm me and remove my effectiveness when I saw Silas in the hospital, with the thought alone of my wife or children being hurt threatening to paralyze me.

"I know that I cannot live in fear of the unknown, that

God is in sovereign control, and that love cannot be without risk of hurt," I hesitated as an internal war raged between what I knew and what I feared, "but I'm going to need a lot of prayer in the next few days, even after you are all safe."

"So everyone that doesn't have SOS combat training is going to head down into our bunkers with our supplies and wait it out," Sandra brought the conversation back to what practical actions we needed to take to help keep my fears from coming true.

"Yes," I said nodding, "Only you can't just wait in the bunker."

"What do you mean?" she asked with a confused expression on her face.

"I mean, that each bunker has its own escape routes in place so that if the base becomes compromised, those inside can get out without detection." I explained.

"So our escape plan has an escape plan?" she asked to clarify.

"Yes," I nodded, "and a whole lot more. Tonight I'd like to show you how to locate those escape routes, hide there until Simon's Komplo is taken care of, and how to collapse the escape routes if you need to."

"But if those tunnels are collapsed," Sandra was worried and hesitant to ask, "how will you be able to get to us?"

"It won't be easy," I answered, "and that's the whole point; we don't want anyone being able to follow you deeper into the compounds and get to you." I didn't think it wise to tell her that I'd most likely be dead in the event that those tunnels would need to be collapsed.

"So you should try and meet with each of your

Disciples, both of our parents, and Grandpa in order to show them how to get their families to safety in preparation for this as well," Sandra added, rubbing her stomach where little Daniel was still being formed; we didn't know for sure that the baby was a boy, but I was still confident enough to have named him in my own mind.

I nodded, "The Disciples will be here tonight, so I can go over it with them then, and I'll be sure to meet with Grandpa and our parents before tomorrow night."

"I'll be interested to hear about how the parents of these different Disciples accept what is going on," she quipped. "I know that most of them are in their early twenties at this point, but the fact that you're leading their kids into a war that could endanger them all would be difficult for any parent to handle."

"I know; I'm worried about that as well," I answered with a nod and a new, but similarly discouraging, train of thought hit me. "Please pray that everything goes well, with the Disciples as well as with the SOS Corps."

"You're meeting with the Corps?" Sandra asked knowing very few people in power, which sadly included many Christians, were able to maintain a healthy relationship with God and the nature of espionage that permeated much of what the Corps did only added to the feeling of reservation that we both felt.

"Yes," I said with a nod. "They've asked for a meeting, a reunion of sorts, of all the highest level combatants, and they're expanding the Defenders to try and regain control of America and to ward off Simon."

"So they know that he's here?" She inquired.

"The SOS Corps now knows that someone has

opened up doorways into the reams because they're one of
the four organizations that I have equipped with various
pieces of interdimensional technology that would allow them
to detect doorways and abilities when they're activated. The
doorways that Simon opened up were so concealed it took
our more advanced equipment to detect them when they
opened; the SOS Corps was still able to pick up trace
amounts of residual GRID Signal it just took longer because
of their older systems."

"So who are the other organizations that you've given
this capability to?" my wife asked, curious.

"The Defender Corps and Israel." I answered simply;
I didn't need to disclose to her that I had given probably my
most advanced set of technology to a 'retired' Mossad agent
who had helped train me during my first years in the SOS
Corps.

"But as we both know," I continued, "meetings that I
attend involving the SOS Corps don't usually go well, and I
would greatly appreciate your prayers tomorrow."

"Always," she lovingly affirmed placing her hand
tenderly upon mine and, after giving me a kiss, went off to
check on the boys before finishing what she had to for the
Disciples training that night. As tired and fatigued as I was, I
couldn't bring myself to rest much that night before the
study; although sleep did overtake me while I was unawares
and visions of the coming battle continuously filled my
dreams until I awoke on the couch with a foreboding ache
gnawing at the pit of my stomach. This battle would mark the
beginning of the end.

✝   ✝   ✝   ✝   ✝   ✝   ✝

"So are you sure you're ready for this?" Joe asked as we set up the room for training later. Tonight was the scheduled night that the Bible study would take off, which meant that the Disciples could enjoy some extended training in the compound and we would have to be ready for it.

"Which part?" I asked in order to buy myself some time before answering as well as clarifying what I was answering. "Tonight's training or tomorrow's war?"

"Both," my brother answered simply.

I hesitated a moment to gather my thoughts. "Both will be challenging, especially knowing that tomorrow may end both the training and the Bible studies." I shook my head, "This may be the last night that I lead a training session, Joe."

"Nah," Joe tried to lighten the mood, "you're too ornery to die on me tomorrow."

I tried to conger up a smile, but my feeble attempt was short lived. "I need you to take over for me Joseph; in case I don't come back from tomorrow."

Joe shook his head, "Hey, what could happen in the battle tomorrow that would kill you but leave me alive?"

"Any number of things, Joe, especially since you won't be there."

"Hang on a minute," Joseph was understandably upset at the thought of being left behind. "What makes you think there is anything that can keep me from watching your back tomorrow?"

"That's exactly what I need you to be doing here, Joe," I answered with a nod and intently locking eyes with my brother. "I need to know that our work back here will continue on regardless of what happens on the battle field."

"So come back alive and everything will be fine," Joseph quipped.

"Neither of us can guarantee that'll happen, Joe and the rest of these Disciples need a leader. I've seen you lead them, and I know your skills as a combatant and your relationship with God as a disciple." I took a deep breath and prayed as I tried to steady my emotions. "You've been a trusted Barnabas to me over the years, little brother and I'd like to pass on my mantle to you as my Elisha."

"That's a tall order, Tim," Joe answered. "I don't know if I'm ready for that."

"I know that you aren't ready Joe." My answer visibly shocked him so I explained, "Neither of us will ever be ready for what God has in store for us, but God is completely capable of preparing and empowering us to do whatever He asks of us."

I continued arranging the training program on the room simulators as I continued, "I've been doing my best to prepare you for what God has for you by letting you teach every now and then and –"

"Letting me?" Joseph interjected to remind me about how I had practically coerced him into teaching that first time.

"Yes, letting you," I replied with my first genuine smile of the conversation. "I've been trying to let God show you that He is able to stretch you and take you to greater places if you let Him."

Joseph nodded, "I know you have, Bro, and I've seen God come through for me before," Joseph busied himself with a last minute repair on a ComBot before finishing the conversation simply with, "You can count on me Timothy."

We were interrupted by the doorbell ringing upstairs; it was a little early for any of the students to be arriving, but still close enough for that to be the most likely person at the door.

I quickly molecularized and flew through the door of the compound and went over to the front door, remolecularizing before I opened it, and was surprised to find KT standing outside with a backpack slung over his shoulder.

"I've come to learn how to do this the right way," he said with a smile."

"I'm so glad to hear that," I said, welcoming him inside with a brotherly hug and leading him down into the compound.

We waited a few minutes for the others to arrive – and then each of them taking a minute or two to get changed in one of the private prep rooms – before we got started with any serious discussion.

I looked around the room and reflected on the years that had passed since we first started training together and each of the students had grown from their adolescents and become a strong young man or woman for the Lord. All of them were now stronger than ever as they all had reached adulthood. Several of their younger siblings had joined the Bible study in the years past and a few had been laid upon my heart to train as Disciples once my other older generation of students graduated into Defenders.

"I need to let you all know tonight that things could get even more intense," I said in order to call the meeting to order.

"How so?" Beth asked.

I cringed internally and drew in a deep breath.

"Because there is a team of interdimensional supervillains seeking to establish itself as a Komplo here on Earth and they know who I am."

"Come again?" Mark was the first to respond.

"These people are taking steps to take out anyone that might stand in their way of dominating the Earth," I continued to explain the situation and affirm that they had heard correctly, "they know about the Defender Corps, that I'm a part of it, and that I have a habit of establishing these kinds of groups so it's only a matter of time before they begin attacking this group in order to find and eliminate all of us."

"So what are we going to do?" Kara asked.

"Tonight we are going to be using the ComBots to train to fight against them," I answered. "Joseph and I have altered the NSSHS program on some of the Bots to simulate what these people seem to be capable of. So make sure you're ready for this, because you aren't children anymore; you've grown from being Disciples to being Defenders."

Everyone began double checking their suits and equipment. "Is everyone ready to get started?" I asked when they seemed finished.

"Hold on," Aaron spoke up with a mischievous grin on his face. "I think that since KT is new he needs an initiation round as a warm up; that way we can all know what he can do."

"I don't think that's necessary," KT said a bit nervously.

"Oh, it's necessary," Joseph countered; he enjoyed teasing KT almost as much as I enjoyed teasing his older brother, Silas.

With that everyone else cleared the room, leaving KT

standing alone in the center of the room as I powered up the ComBots.

"Alpaca," he muttered his euphemism under his breath and released the regulators that kept his claws from growing out of their housing within the back of his gloves.

He balled his hands up into fists as the first wave of ComBots activated and marched into the room. KT dove to his left as the first gun fired at him, the round striking the ground where he stood a moment earlier.

Coming up rolling, KT slashed at two more ComBots that were charging at him before leaping backward over another shot coming at the back of his legs.

A silent alarm went off and the supersonic vibrations disrupted the air molecules enough for me to sense it and Joseph was able to feel the vibrations even more clearly. A few of the students could have similarly heard or sensed the vibration were they not so distracted by KT's performance

"I'll look into it," I GRID messaged to Joseph before turning to head back upstairs.

There was some interdimensional technology detected somewhere right outside the house; it had to have been extremely advanced to have made it this close without tripping any of the other detectors.

I prepared myself for the possibility that I would have to call the Disciples to action against the Komplo rather than dealing with Simon myself as I molecularized myself and went through the door to investigate.

I couldn't see anyone after my first patrol so I hovered up above the house and stirred up a gentle breeze that wouldn't be noticed by whoever was lurking about. As I did I could sense the path of air was being disrupted near the back gate and as I looked closer I could see how the dust and leaves would strike against an invisible object before being blown around it.

I silently landed directly in front of the gate and used the air to outline the invisible intruder as I readied my bow, and began to feel for the body heat to help locate and identify whoever it was. It was then that I realized that it was one of the female members of the Komplo.

I fired a single arrow at the person standing there, but waited to remolecularize until after it passed through the person, causing the arrow to strike the gate behind her.

Luna activated her smokescreen and quickly relocated to a new position in the yard as she scanned around her for danger.

I could sense fear and – grief? – as I waited for her next move. She was trying to locate whoever had shot at her as she scanned the housetops in the direction of the arrow.

"What are you doing here Luna?" I called to her from where I stood.

She spun to the side and tried to locate me. "Pentecost?" She called back bewildered. "Where are you?"

I had never fully discovered the extent of the abilities granted to me by my GRID connection, nor had I revealed all that I had discovered during my journey through the realms, so my ability to turn invisible was new to her.

"Why are you here Luna?" I asked her a second time.

She began to weep, "I'm trying to save my life."

Luna and her sister were difficult to read because they were both such professional actresses as shapeshifters which also made it nearly impossible to trust what they said or how they said it. Had the Komplo truly turned on her, or was this a clever ploy of some kind to get me to reveal the location and identities of the Disciples?

"How can I trust you, Luna?" I asked remaining invisible and drawing back a second arrow. "You've turned on what your sister helped establish by joining with Simon."

She nodded at the ground as the tears continued to flow down her face. "I know I can't be trusted, but I was hoping that by some miracle you would."

I waited for some form of insight, some kind of indication of whether I should trust Luna or kill her with the arrow aimed at her heart.

Luna turned her gaze longingly toward heaven. "I know now that Jesus is Lord of all, but can He truly be my Redeemer?"

I slowly released the tension on the string and lowered my bow.

"Let's go inside," I said, giving my permission for her to move and head towards the door.

Once inside, I remolecularized only after she had disengaged her camouflage.

I tried to test the sincerity of her statement by sharing the Gospel with her. "Luna, God is willing to forgive anything that we have ever done, and Jesus endured hell so that we wouldn't have to, which means that He took on Himself the full weight of every sin that anyone has ever committed upon Himself."

Luna shook her head, her mind refusing to accept the words she was hearing as though they couldn't possibly apply to her.

"Luna, you have aided in the persecution of the Church," I said plainly and she did not deny the statement.

"That puts you in the same category as one of the greatest heroes of the Christian faith – the Apostle Paul – he declared that he was the Chief of Sinners because of what he had done and yet God still redeemed Him."

Luna's eyes widened and she said, "That's what he said."

"What who said?" I asked in confusion.

Luna was stunned, "The old man in the coffeehouse; he talked about the Chief of Sinners." She then asked with a look of hopeful desperation on her face, "Will He truly accept me?"

I nodded my head, "Jesus promised that He would never cast away anyone that comes to Him, and that means that there is hope for us all because Jesus took our death upon Himself so that we may have life."

"Just like the old man," she said quietly.

I shook my head and asked, "Who is this man you keep talking about?"

She shook her head soberly, "I wish I knew; it's only because he died that I'm alive right now to learn about the glories of God."

"Could you show me?" I said, asking her to share the memory with me.

I then watched as she entered a mainstream coffeehouse and met Pastor Juan as he tried to share the Gospel with her.

I then clearly heard the sound of a gunshot at the precise moment that Pastor Juan had shifted in his seat and could smell the distinctive scent of blood as his head fell and a bullet hole in the back of his neck began to bleed out.

I swallowed deeply as I understood what had taken

place earlier that night. "That man," I didn't share with her that I knew who he was because I didn't see how that would help, "accidently took the bullet that was meant for you, and now you have to choose how to live the rest of your life. Jesus did something far greater for you by intentionally taking the wrath of God justly meant for you because of your rebellion against Him, but you have to choose to accept that payment for yourself, Luna. Emmi's dedication won't save you."

"I know," she nodded and then turned her gaze upward once more. "Jesus forgive me; cleanse me of my sins. I give You my life, if You'll truly have me as the old man and Pentecost say. I submit wholly unto You and I confess my failure to obey Your Law."

When she finished she simply turned back to face me and said, "I want to fight alongside you and the Defenders when you go against Simon."

I shook my head, but she interrupted before I could object.

"I know all the members of the Komplo, including Simon's contact within the SOS Corps and I know everyone's abilities and their upgrades, which were provided by Virus." She drew in a deep breath and added, "And I know what Simon has had him working on the past several days."

"And what would that be?"

"Preparing the ComBots for battle against you and putting a human mind inside of one of them in order to fulfill prophecy his way."

I was instantly alarmed. "Simon has found a way to alter the ComBot programming?"

Luna nodded but then corrected, "Virus, his SOS

contact, has already made great success in weaponizing the ComBots and has begun to focus on the mental transfer."

"Mental transfer?" I asked in unbelief. "Is he insane?"

Luna nodded dismally, "I'm beginning to believe that he might be; he says that he's preparing to give life to the image."

We both stood in silence for a moment before I asked, "Tell me about these upgrades the Komplo has received."

We headed down into the compound and I updated the ComBot programming for future training based on the information she gave me.

I let Joseph and the group begin training while I began to plan out the events of the next few days differently now that I had this new information.

"I need you to share this at the SOS Corps meeting tomorrow," I said, turning to Luna.

"So I'm part of the team?" Luna asked, seeking assurance that I wouldn't discard her now that I'd gotten what I needed.

I nodded soberly, "If Virus has been as successful as you've said, then this may be our first and last mission together."

Chapter Thirty

Dovev had diligently followed the human he had been charged to watch and kept a watchful eye out for danger, if any of the other humans were able to see the way he pursued her they may have feared for her life.

The young woman he had been following was fearful, and understandably so considering the way she had made many decisions that had often put herself into danger, and lead her to such demonic places that Dovev couldn't follow after her.

There were many abnormalities when it came to the woman Dovev's charge, she had many strange abilities and even stranger associates, but perhaps strangest of all – at least to Dovev – was that his charge had lived her twenty-six years in complete rebellion to the Lord that assigned him to protect her.

Dovev noticed how the young woman was puzzled by the archaic art used for the emblem on the building as she entered the coffeehouse; she found it strange that with all the advancements this society had created, they still used some primitive images to identify themselves.

Dovev walked through the door as it closed behind his charge. None of the humans in the room took any notice of him, but there was another ministering spirit present that caught his eye.

"Kanaye, what are you doing here?" Dovev asked the other angel.

"Attempting to minister to the human under my protection, Dovev," the second towering being answered, "the Spirit wishes to use her to bring the Gospel to the human in your charge."

Dovev couldn't contain the joy that welled up within him, for after all these years perhaps tonight would be the night that his charge found salvation. "I believe that she will be open to conversation tonight, especially with what has recently transpired in her life; I think that now may be her moment."

"I am just as thrilled at the thought her redemption as you are, my friend," Kanaye answered with a smile, but with a heavy heart he added, "however, I fear that my charge may not be willing to be the herald she has been called to be."

"What do you mean?" Dovev asked, desperately hoping that Kanaye was simply attempting to make a poor jest; but Kanaye was not jesting.

"I mean that from the moment your charge walked in through the door the Spirit has been stirring within my charge to move her to share the Gospel, but the young woman doesn't wish to be a bother." Kanaye said, shaking his head in despair.

"Not wanting to be a bother? Doesn't she understand that the eternity of another being is at stake?" Dovev looked back to his charge as she received her latté and was staring blankly at the cup, her eyes moist with tears.

"I know Dovev, and I have been doing all I can to remind my charge of how a person's eternity is of much greater value than whether or not they get to enjoy their coffee, but I'm afraid that her passion for the lost has grown cold."

Just then the door opened and Avedis, another angelic being, walked in behind his charge, Pastor Juan Martinez.

"Avedis, what brings you here tonight?" Kanaye asked.

"I'm here because the Spirit wishes to use my charge to minister to both of yours." Avedis answered with a grin.

Pastor Juan stood looking at the menu that listed the various flavors and methods of preparing coffee, which was another thing that the angels couldn't understand; why did these humans spend such a great amount of time inventing new flavors and experiences to find fleeting pleasure and happiness?

As Pastor Juan looked up at the menu, Avedis tapped his shoulder and pointed at Dovev's charge. "Maybe you should talk to her; she seems troubled by something."

Pastor Juan heard the Spirit speaking and looked around the room before his eyes settled on the young, dark skinned woman sitting alone at a table; her eyes were glassy and a tear was rolling down her left cheek as she pushed a lock of her black hair behind her ear.

The elderly Pastor immediately made his way over to her table and gently asked, "Are you all right?"

The woman seemed alarmed and replied in a harsh tone, "Of course I'm fine."

But what Juan, and all the ministering spirits heard, was the deep cry of a broken heart.

You see, Dovev's charge was a shapeshifting woman named Luna Coterel, and while all the other people in the room saw a well-dressed, African-American business woman quietly enjoying her coffee, the three angels and Juan Martinez saw the real Luna – blonde, with fair skin, and while she still had the garb of a successful business woman, she was visibly broken and weeping over her guilt. They, like the Lord could see past her disguise and she found that she couldn't hide from everyone.

"Well, do you mind if I sit here?" Juan asked politely.

"Suit yourself." Came the terse reply.

"How is this going to help either of our charges?" Kanaye asked, dismally. "Luna is stonewalling Pastor Juan and my charge can't see anything but her harsh reaction to being interrupted."

"Patience my dear, Kanaye; patience." Avedis replied. "The Lord has granted Juan one final opportunity to bring healing to the broken in this world."

"Final?" Dovev asked.

Avedis nodded and motioned to the rooftop just outside the window where a fourth angel, Fidaa by name, was desperately trying to convince Catch.22 not to do this job for Simon.

"He's targeting Pastor Juan?" Kanaye asked.

"No. He's here for Luna." Avedis answered.

"Why wasn't I informed?" Dovev spoke up, a bit offended at the lack of communication.

"Because Pastor Juan is going to take her place," Avedis said cryptically.

"It's strange how often people try to hide what is truly going on inside," Pastor Juan was saying to Luna. "Look around you; this building is designed to look like an ancient Native American building on the outside, but inside it's as modern as could be. People often put on a mask to seem as though they're doing all right – that they've got it all together – even though they're broken and hurting on the inside."

Luna nodded, since she of all people knew how it was

possible to act one way despite what might be truly felt on the inside.

"But there is no masking things from God, Luna, because our actions, words, thoughts, and intentions are all open and bear before Him."

"How…?" was all she could bring herself to say, and she was visibly dumbfounded that this stranger knew her name and couldn't even attempt to hide it from anyone.

"Because the Lord revealed it to me," Pastor Juan answered simply before asking empathetically, "Guilt is a heavy load to carry isn't it?"

Again, Luna couldn't hold back the tears that overwhelmed her as Kanaye's charge noticed what was taking place from her spot in the corner.

"You can't hide from God, Luna," Juan continued, "one day you are going to stand before Him – completely exposed with nowhere to hide – and He will hold you accountable for your actions."

"My sister talked like that," Luna replied angrily though still teary-eyed, "and it got her killed. That missionary got her all worked up about following God through whatever open door was before her and she ended up walking right into her own grave."

"I can guarantee you that your sister doesn't regret her decision to follow God. Can you say the same about your choice to reject Him?" Pastor Juan asked pointedly yet compassionately.

Luna turned her head away and burned a hole into the floor with her gaze.

"Luna, Jesus came so that you might find life, so you don't have to hide yourself in your own efforts or clean yourself up before you can come to Him. If you agree with Him about what He says about sin – that He makes the rules and sets the punishment – and about redemption – that Jesus' perfect life can be traded for your sinful one, that His death cleared your account before God, and His resurrection is evidence that death has been defeated on your behalf – then you can be saved and this burden of guilt can be removed from you."

Kanaye was ministering to his charge as she rose to leave and headed out to her car, speaking to her about how receptive Luna seemed to be and how next time she could trust the Spirit's leading and receive the reward of ministering to someone instead of shrinking back in fear.

Luna turned back to Juan – whom she had never met before tonight – and she desperately hoped that he was right. But could Christ's blood be used to cover how she had tried to kill Silas in order to take revenge on Timothy? Could God forgive someone that killed His children?

"If Saul – the chief of sinners and a murderer of Christians – could be saved, then there is most certainly hope for you, Luna. Will you submit your life to Jesus as both Lord and Savior?"

As soon as Pastor Juan had finished talking, Avedis touched his lower back and caused some discomfort and Pastor Juan shifted in his chair to try and alleviate the discomfort that he felt.

Just then the window behind Pastor Juan shattered and the back of his head burst with blood he had shifted at precisely the same moment that Catch.22 had pulled his trigger and the bullet that would have entered Luna's carotid artery entered his spinal canal just at the base of his head.

Luna quickly created a smokescreen and turned herself invisible to conceal herself from whoever was shooting at her. Based on the sound of the gun and the size of the bullet wound on the back of Juan's head she had a pretty good idea who it was.

Dovev was certain as he followed his charge that the small seed of the Gospel had partially taken root and that Luna was on her way to receiving the Gospel. Catch.22's shot had prevented her from making a concrete decision and so the angelic celebration would have to wait, but Dovev was certain that he would be proclaiming the glorious news of a saved soul shortly.

Avedis on the other hand was receiving new orders from the Father as his charge was now in the presence of the Savior and would no longer need a ministering spirit to render him service.

Fidaa followed after Will Zalinsky and continued to minister to him, desperately wondering what the Lord could possibly have planned for these humans.

Chapter Thirty-One

Other supernatural forces were at work that evening. Switchblade had asked Simon about Luna's allegiance, and after consulting his spirit guides about this new development, Simon gave the order for Catch.22 to take her out; preferably before she had a chance to talk to anyone about the Komplo or its location.

Virus had also messaged him saying that he was nearly finished with the requested upgrades to the ComBot, but that there was some resistance that he couldn't overcome.

So Simon teleported himself to Virus' apartment, and mentally whispered into his ear, "What is it Rodger?"

Rodger spun around and saw Simon standing in the center of the small room behind him; too far away to have whispered in his ear and yet he didn't hear him move away.

"Well sir," the technology wizard spoke nervously, "I've managed to convince the ComBot to grant me access to its programming and I've made many of your requested changes to the code."

"Specifically?" Simon asked.

"Well, I've removed the code that limited the ComBot to using the NSSHS weapons system and replaced it with my own code that allows it to actually produce the previously simulated damage with real attacks." Rodger answered pushing his designer glasses back to their rightful position.

"And what of the mental transfer?" Simon asked, he

was working hard to hide the urgency and eagerness he felt for an affirmative answer and ignored the fact that there hadn't been a new update yet; Virus had already reported his initial success earlier that week.

"Well sir," Rodger answered nervously, "I've located the precise strand of coding that correlates to what you described as the 'soul' of the ComBots, but I've encountered a strange energy signal that I can't overcome."

"Why not?" Simon fought to remain controlled in front of this gangly, overconfident adolescent.

"Because it's not scientific or technological in nature. It's…" Rodger was at a loss for words.

"Supernatural?" Simon offered a bit perplexed at this development.

"Precisely. You've proven to me that such a thing exists beyond my field of expertise, but until now the concept of spirit guides has seemed foreign and irrelevant. However, I think that you may be the key to this scientific breakthrough and to completing my assignment for the Komplo."

"Allow me full access to your mind and I'll watch as you point out this energy to me." Simon replied motioning for Rodger to go to work on the ComBot.

"So how is this supposed to work?" Rodger asked as he followed Simon's directions.

"Simply open your mind to me as I knock," Simon answered coming up behind him and grabbing Rodger's head with both hands.

Rodger closed his eyes and mentally pictured the door to his mind, which was currently locked and bolted. There was a knock at that door and Rodger unlocked it and released the bolt for Simon to come in.

"Now access the ComBot's mind," Simon mindvoiced and although it was strange for Rodger to be hearing Simon's voice from within his own head he didn't think about that, he had a task to complete.

Rodger opened his eyes and locked them with the ComBot's and was instantly within the hard drive of the ComBot. Rodger's first attempt took days of coaxing to get the robot to accept him in and an additional six hours were needed to locate the proper coding. Later attempts to access the ComBot's programming took hours of coaxing – and that was after he had already been granted full access by the ComBot – but now with Simon's help it took mere seconds. Undoubtedly, Simon's own energy was aiding Rodger in his efforts, which was anticipated.

"Is this the coding you mentioned?" Simon asked and pointed at a particularly large memory orb stored within the hard drive. Unlike the other memories stored within the ComBot, this one radiated with a strange glow that shielded it from being tampered with; a fact that had induced several migraine headaches in Rodger of the past few days.

Simon inhaled deeply and took a moment to rummage through Rodger's mind.

"What are you looking for?" Rodger asked aloud, sensing Simon's intrusion into his personal memories.

"Silence." Simon hissed. *"I am simply seeking the orb I need to make the connection."*

Rodger assumed he meant the memory of how he had introduced himself to the ComBot – he entered in like the flu virus with full acceptance before making the changes to the cell's programming – since of course Simon would need to know how to use his power to access the ComBot's mind and reprogram it.

Rodger suddenly felt compelled to reach out and take hold of the orb, despite his knowledge of the pain that such an action would cause.

"Obey me, fool!" A thundering voice boomed from behind him.

Rodger turned to see the hulking form of a demon, an image worse than nightmares with a black mane of hair falling down over his hulking, scale covered shoulders, a large, black sickle was held tightly in a taloned fist, and great horns protruded out of his head, face, and mouth. Even more terrifying than all of that – and more suffocating than the stench of sulfur that enshrouded the figure – was the fact that he embodied evil itself and wore it as his garment. Rodger knew that he was now seeing his new master and that there would be no fighting him.

Rodger turned back to the orb that hovered in front of him and thrust both hands out and clutched it as though his life depended on it, for in his mind it undoubtedly did.

Rodger cried out in pain and physically clutched his own head and felt Simon's natural grip tighten as his own internal grip on the orb did also.

Rodger tried to release the orb but it was as though his hands had melted to the burning surface as first the light surrounding the ComBot memory orb and then the color of the orb itself were removed and cast aside.

Pure terror gripped him as he saw Simon bring another orb – this one was the deepest recesses of Rodger's mind – and handed it to the demon lord. With a cruel chuckle the demon took the orb and pushed it down into the clear shell of the ComBot's empty mind.

Slowly, Rodger began to feel himself being pulled into the glow of the orb in front of him and the nearer he got to that glow, the more his pain was absorbed by it. At the promise of relief from his pain, Rodger suppressed the urge to fight the inviting warmth of the orb and dove into it headlong and became one with it.

With the pain subsided, Rodger slowly opened his eyes, only to find himself staring into the vacant eyes of himself; Rodger was looking at his own lifeless body which was still being held up by Simon's grip on his skull.

Simon opened his eyes and smiled in triumph, despite the fact that he was breathing heavy and his own face was etched with pain as he struggled to keep himself upright.

Rodger then tried to crawl back away from the horrifying sight before him, only to find that he had backed into the wall. He then looked down at himself and saw the ghostly silverish skin of the ComBot reflecting the moonlight that shone through his window.

"What have you done to me?" Rodger yelled through the electronic voice of the ComBot.

Simon shrugged his shoulders and released his hold on Rodger's body, letting the corpse crumple into a heap on the floor. "I've simply made you as immortal as modern man can hope to be, Virus. Science has been striving for years to accomplish what you planned and I completed in a few days."

The hulking nightmare from Rodger's mind now appeared tangibly in the room next to Simon.

"What do you think master?" Simon asked without taking his eyes off of the ComBot that housed Rodger's mind.

"I think that we have given breath to the image and this process should prove to be most useful in the last hour." The demon growled approvingly in his guttural tone.

Rodger felt like such a pawn at that moment as this demon had manipulated Simon to use him as a lab rat, as some cheap and disposable experiment.

"You used me!" Rodger yelled at them both.

The demon cackled, "That's the only point in interacting with you disgusting humans at all; to use you to our advantage in our revolt."

Simon chided, "Don't get so worked up Virus for you now have simply embodied what you once worshipped; technology. You have become a god, and have greatly benefitted from the arrangement I might add."

Was Simon seriously trying to get Rodger to thank him for what had happened to him? Rodger's rage began to rise.

Simon continued to point out the 'benefits' of being bionic. "You now have the power and abilities of a ComBot, the knowledge and processing power of a supercomputer, and the immortality of technology and innovation."

"But you can't treat people like this!" Rodger pleaded.

"Why not?" The demon asked sharply. "Isn't that how you've been acting all your life? Isn't that how humanity treats its members? As pawns to be moved about and sacrificed for one's own gain?"

"Make the most of your state, or self-destruct; I care not at this point," Simon stated and turned away dismissively.

These 'people' had been treating Rodger just like the computers he had been operating on and began to take on the behaviors of; for years now Rodger had been consumed with data and began to imitate the idols he had surrounded himself with. Now he had been given an upgrade and literally became one of the computers he worshipped. So despite his original feeling of resentment towards being manipulated reason won out; that had always been Rodger's forte and emotions seemed even more out of place now than ever.

Virus looked down at the lifeless form of Rodger. "What have I gotten myself into?"

Timothy Stevens

After Luna had shared with Joseph and myself some of the upgrades that Virus had outfitted the Komplo with and I had sent the Disciples home last night she began to prepare for this morning when she would share that same information with those that assembled this early in the morning for our debriefing meeting.

Currently I was trying to prepare the Defenders to listen to and accept her as a trusted member of the team.

"What on Earth were you thinking bringing her into this base?" Matthias Archer demanded angrily.

I scanned the room with my eyes and made a mental roster of who all was present.

Marcus Williams, AKA 'Alkali', is usually a happy-go-lucky resident of the local SOS Corps and is always ready to bring joy to somebody's day as he helps supervise the youth division of the Corps. Due to an experimental excursion into the Negative Zone, Marcus' suit had absorbed a large amount of unstable energy. The suit has since been stabilized and allows Marcus to harness that unstable energy to fly, move objects at will, and fire that energy to blast his adversaries.

Titus Martinez, AKA 'Firecracker', is equally as happy-go-lucky but has an even harder time focusing than either Silas or Marcus. Having moved to help establish an SOS Base in Logan, Utah, Titus continues to train the youth in his area while moving at superhuman speeds and producing controlled explosions of various sizes and intensities under the guise of Firecracker.

These first two were part of the original Defender Corps with Silas, Joseph, and myself and would be more likely to listen to me because of our history together as friends. The other four men present however, were new additions to the Defender level heroes from the SOS Corps Council and I had much more professional relationship with them; but that was almost six years ago and I had no idea how they would respond now.

Martin Bird, AKA 'The Professor', is the elderly, SOS Corps' top research scientist and resident expert on interdimensional technology. The Professor was the man most directly responsible for the abilities and technology that powered Silas, Titus, and Marcus. Recently it seems that he has worked on some upgrades for some of my other old acquaintances from his lab in Virginia.

Anthony Vidakovic, AKA 'Fletcher', is a tall and wiry man with inner city roots and exceptional skill with a bow. In all the years since I first met him I have seen a meager handful of marksmen scattered among the realms that could come close to the shots I had seen him take, and my competing against him had helped prepare me to keep up with the rest of them. Along with his optical enhancing glasses – which could provide him with vision equal to that of peering through binoculars and also provide images with nearly every imaging system known – he now bore the works of Professor Bird in his quiver; several programmable arrows that could produce specific results. Explosive arrows, smoke screen arrows, flash arrows, flaming arrows, electric arrows, and many more were all filed and categorized in Fletcher's mind so that they could be pulled out, programmed, and fired with laser precision as he protected his native city of Los Angeles.

Mike Sanko, AKA 'Lancelot', had spent much of his early childhood in England as his father was a military officer stationed there. During his time across the pond Lancelot became an expert on all things medieval Europe, and was especially proficient on using the weaponry of that time. His highly trained skills are what helped to hone my own skill with the sword in preparing me for my journey throughout the realms. The Professor had gone to work on his weapons and had developed a giadan-cainium alloy that allowed for both extreme malleability and strength so that a particular weapon could mold and transform into a different weapon, but only at Lancelot's command. His shield and sword could be molded together to form a battle hammer, or his spear could be broken down into two arming swords. This also meant that Mike wouldn't have to pick and choose which weapons he would lug around New England with him, because he could now have any of them in his hand at a moment's notice.

Matthias Archer, AKA 'Kevlar', was so codenamed because of his high pain tolerance that made him seem almost injury-proof, and his chiseled features didn't hurt any. Raised in the harsh streets of Newark, NJ he was a man well experienced with pain and hardship, and right now his muscular bulk was tense in frustration, a fearsome sight to behold. The worst part was the fearsome African-American man was angered and frustrated at me. His upgrades only made him more intimidating as he defended the streets of his hometown; his nearly injury-proof skin had now been GRID enhanced to become nearly impervious and even bullet proof as it would increase in density upon impact.

"Because she came to me looking for help, Matthias" I started to explain.

"But how do ya know that she's not just pulling one over on you?" Anthony asked. "I mean, she was part of the Komplo because she can act and deceive. So how do ya know that she wasn't sent here to use ya to get in here?"

"You must concede to the reality of the situation, Timothy," Professor Bird added. "It is quite onerous to trust someone who can shapeshift as she does. Her entire life has been established upon on deception, so how can we be persuaded to trust her now?"

"Because Christ can redeem a life based on lies and transform it into something glorious and founded on His truth." I turned and began to appeal to my friends, "Marcus, you've always championed the idea of accepting people where they are and loving them. Well, Luna has made a confession of faith, and I have to believe it to be genuine."

Marcus nodded, "Right, and you've always talked about trying to point out to people the right way to live and how they all need to grow closer to God and become better than who they are."

"And that's what I'm trying to do; I'm accepting Luna where she's at and I'm trying to help her grow closer to the Lord. Luna desperately wants to undo the damage that she has caused."

"Can she bring my dad back?" Titus asked, anger and frustration poured out of him; I had shared with him and Marcus privately of what I had seen in Luna's memories prior to this meeting and apparently his run from Utah hadn't helped him accept the news any better. "Is that a damage that she can undo?"

I drew in a deep breath and silently prayed for wisdom. "Titus you and I both know that your father's death was out of Luna's control, but that it was fully within God's sovereignty."

I chose not to insult him by reminding him that both Marcus and I had lost someone close to us when Pastor Juan died; losing a mentor was nothing similar to the hurt felt by losing a dad.

"We've all lost someone close to us," I said instead, "and I don't know why Pastor Juan is dead – or why Silas was hospitalized by these people – but I do know that God is still seated on the throne and in complete control. We can allow these loses to cripple us, or we can use them to drive us closer to the Lord, because we choose what we do with the sufferings of life; whether we let them build us or if we wallow in self-pity."

I wasn't speaking from a position of having all of this stuff figured out and perfected. More accurately, I was speaking from the reflection of my experiences with failure and hurt; it was because I had wallowed in self-pity that I knew how detrimental it was to my life while walking with the Lord and trusting Him as He built my confidence in His sovereignty allowed me to grow beyond the hurt.

"And what about you, Timothy?" Titus continued. "How are we supposed to trust you after the way you left the Corps because of that training incident with Carlos? Are you going to abandon us again?"

So that's how Carlos explained my leaving the

teenage section of the Corps. I thought, recalling the incident where Carlos had put several of the students in what I knew to be a dangerous position that they weren't prepared to handle. I had left several months after that incident and it actually had very little to do with my resignation in comparison to the other incidents.

"There was a lot more behind why I left than that one incident, but this isn't the time to discuss that. What's more important right now is whether or not we will allow the sacrifices of those closest to us be in vain," I continued, "or are we going to make their toil and tears worth something by conquering our flesh, accepting a new sister in the faith, and putting an end to an enemy stronghold?"

The group reflected on what I had said until Anthony finally spoke up. "It sounds like we've got a new addition to the family guys; let's go welcome her."

Matthias shrugged his shoulder, "What she knows about the Komplo could be useful, I guess; if we can trust it to be true."

After the group walked out of the conference room we had been occupying and joined Luna next door, each of the guys affectionately welcomed her as a new sister; even Titus who was obviously struggling with his own loss and Matthias who had showed the greatest distrust at first. Luna was understanding and appreciative of everyone's forgiveness, to the point where she lost control of her own emotions and teared up before the group.

"I'm sorry," she said, wiping her eyes. "If you guys could all have a seat, I'll go over some of the upgrades that the Komplo has received over the past few weeks."

Luna's abrupt emotional changes were due to her

solid control over her emotions and were part of what made her excel as a shapeshifter. However, these sharp shifts in her demeanor were also part of why the rest of Defenders found it difficult to trust her for as a shapeshifter she appeared to be borderline schizophrenic, a pathological liar, or a professional actress depending on your terminology.

Luna waited until everyone had taken their seats and looked over the notes that the two of us had put together the night before. "Acedia has grown beyond the need of merely making mental suggestions to lull you to your death as the Sorcerer has enhanced her mind poison to the point where she can throw intense psychic blasts that will disorient the target, if not cause them to swoon into unconsciousness. The longer you remain motionless the greater the danger and the less likely you are to start moving again."

"What's the key to beating her?" Kevlar asked.

"Stay on your feet," I answered, "and if you get knocked down, get up as quickly as you can. Acedia's poisoning won't work unless you let it and stay down."

"Catch.22 is The Sorcerer's first Earthian addition to the Komplo." Luna continued leading the meeting forward. "Originally, his marksmanship with firearms was unparalleled and profited him well as an assassin for hire."

"And his upgrades?" The Professor asked looking up over his glasses that had assisted him in reading the notes in front of him moments before.

"Virus has modified Catch's weapons to allow him to fire various bullets; bullets that explode on impact, heat-seeking homing bullets, poisoned bullets, and more."

"Like the specialty arrows that Doc designed for me," Fletcher remarked, referring to Martin Bird.

Luna nodded. "Much of Catch's upgrades are a direct copy of The Professor's work as Virus was able to locate his designs and programs for Chopper's weapons and duplicated them."

"So this is going to be like fighting against Silas?" Marcus asked to clarify.

I nodded soberly, "Only with less machine gun fire and more sniper action, because Catch.22 is much more deliberate, calculating, and prefers to only take shots that he can't miss. Another thing we can be thankful for is that he appears to be grounded, since Virus hasn't equipped him with a jet pack or any such equipment."

"But that's all based on the last time you were there?" Anthony directed his question to Luna. He wasn't trying to be spiteful, but I could see that the reminder of Luna's original alliance pained her.

"Yes, that is correct," Luna answered with a nod. "All of this intel is based on what had taken place prior to the night I left. However, as the Professor can testify, these mindvoice codes are linked to the individual DNA of a person which limits the diversity of the mindvoice. Alter the codes now after Virus has already applied them to the Komplo would take either some extreme circumstances or an exuberant amount of time that they can't afford right now."

Professor Bird nodded, "That's part of what prevents the Komplo from simply establishing a nonpareil combatant who can independently assimilate and utilize any ability they desire. Each memory orb and GIRD modification must interact with the mind in an exceptionally precise fashion. It's similar to protein formation within cells, each definite chain of the GRID code assembles a specific structure within the orb and that explicit configuration regulates the function of the orb. Major strands of the GRID coding that dictates the GRID function is the DNA and brainwave pattern of the individual, thus there will invariably be an idiosyncratic nature to the resulting abilities."

"Meaning what in English?" Matthias asked, a bit annoyed at the Professor's technical ramble.

"It means that GRID codes are about as unique as our DNA and are fundamentally attached to it as well." I clarified.

"So it's unlikely that there will be any further upgrades or drastic changes because they must be based on the current skillset and mindvoice capabilities." Luna continued.

Together, Luna and I continued to outline the different abilities we would have to combat against.

Abafando, an older man that had interacted rather disagreeably with Joseph in Arenea, had received an upgrade to his mindsong. Before he was limited to muting or suppressing a single person's gift, but now he could produce a blanket mind-fog that would cloud the abilities of everyone it came in contact with. And despite his age and elderly appearance, Abafando was a decently skilled hand-to-hand combatant and shouldn't be underestimated.

Luna described a second Earthian recruit codenamed 'Switchblade' because of his lethal proficiency with any bladed weapon. Both he and Catch.22 were mercenary-assassins that had more or less been hired on by Simon, and Virus had copied the upgrades given to Lancelot's weapons and had equipped Switchblade with metal armguards that would house the extra metal before it was forged into a weapon.

Virus had put together a couple of Sangátian memory orbs for The Widow that heightened her proficiency as a shrinking assassin; increased senses of balance, strength, endurance, reflexes, sight, hearing, and speed would cause her to be more of a challenge than when Joseph first encountered her in Osria.

The Panther had learned an Arenean mindsong – producing the sound of either a deep growl or an overbearing roar – which could produce fear and terror in its hearers and the roar could also reach sound blast levels and throw back his adversaries along with a Myathian ability to blend almost completely into the shadows and becoming nearly invisible in the dark.

Simon the Sorcerer had excelled and grown his knowledge and skill in the dark art of magic as well as honed his original combat technique to near perfection and needed no upgrades from Virus.

"So seven Komplo members and seven Defenders. I say we still have the advantage." Anthony remarked cheerfully, "They need at least a dozen or so more to even make this interesting."

"Oh, it'll be interesting enough," Luna informed him soberly. "I don't know how successful Virus has been in accomplishing Simon's desire to achieve a mental transfer, but he has proven quite successful at editing the ComBots to make them battle worthy."

"How have they done that exactly?" Marcus asked, concerned.

"According to these notes," The Professor was scanning the files in front of him, "Virus has removed part of the primary coding and inserted his own in its place. Specifically, he removed the inhibitors that restricted the ComBots from using anything other than the NSSHS program for simulating battles and incorporated the ability to inflict genuine damage to the target. However, this has come with the loss of information pertaining to certain attack simulations and the ComBots appear to be moderately restricted as a result."

"'Somewhat restricted'?" Titus asked. "What exactly does that mean?"

"Virus' program is fairly unstable," the Professor answered without looking up from his notes, "which causes the effects to be imperfect and inconsistent, meaning that each ComBot may very well mutate disparately due of this program. Furthermore, there is the probability that an abundant amount of these Bots will be rendered dysfunctional in some way or even self-destruct."

"That's good. That'll make less robots to have to dismantle ourselves." Anthony remarked.

Now the Professor looked up from his files and over the frames of his glasses, "Unfortunately, each self-destruction sequence includes the explosion of the ComBots and whoever is in the vicinity, effectively causing the bots to become walking bombs."

"That's bad," Anthony quipped again, though with a bit less joy.

"How many of these modified ComBots does the Komplo have?" Marcus asked.

"Enough," Luna answered simply. "The Sorcerer has had a MAPT device running nonstop for the past week producing them."

"That would put the number well over two thousand ComBots, producing a ratio of over two hundred and eighty-five to one," The Professor remarked, dismally. "I don't know if you will be able to take on that many ComBots in addition to the Komplo."

"What if it was only a ninety to one ratio?" Luna asked, causing me to wince as she did. Because the night before, we had talked about whether or not to involve the Disciples in the attack against the Komplo. I was against it, because I feared that their four year training period against smaller, 'natural', threats would have left ill prepared to go against such a dangerous force and I didn't want them jeopardized. However, we both acknowledged that there seemed to be very few options left open to us and it was quite likely that the Disciples would be needed if we stood a chance at being victorious against Simon's forces.

"What do you mean?" Titus asked her.

I drew in a deep breath and answered for her. "She means that I have a way to add to our numbers."

The group turned and look at me inquiringly.

I placed my hands on the table and braced myself for what had already been set in motion. "I have been preparing a group of young teenagers to become future Defenders; or at the very least equip them to be able to defend themselves and their families when times became darker and more dangerous. Because I've been designing the tech and discipling them spiritually I've only had four years to train them physically and none of them have any real combat experience, but there are a total of fourteen committed students in their late teens and early twenties that I have been intensively training as Defenders."

"Now even if these kids can handle themselves and hold up under these circumstances, that's still nearly a hundred to one odds." Mike interjected holding a hand out over the table, his English accent carried a concerned tone. "Are you sure you even want to involve them in this?"

I shook my head, "I'm sure that I don't want them to get hurt because of their involvement. But I also know that because of the training that God has used me to provide for them, it's only a matter of time before He uses them in a way that will cause pain, stretching, and growth for each of them as well as for myself."

"So you'll have them fight with us?" Matthias asked.

I shook my head, "I'll present the opportunity to them and see who God calls to join us, but I cannot make this decision for them; Each of them must follow God's individual leading for their days just as we do."

Professor Bird then spoke up with the next course of action for the group, "Then it would prove advantageous for Anthony and I to escort Luna down to the Lab. From there we can endeavor to pinpoint the whereabouts of the Komplo while also attempting to impart to her some ameliorations of her own whilst the rest of you get suited up."

The Professor and I had used a cutting edge Myathian innovation of the OLED technology to allow a set of battle clothing to become concealed as everyday clothing and revert its appearance at a moment's notice and I – along with every other Defender in the room – was currently wearing one of these suits These camouflaged uniforms are what would allow me, the Defenders, and the Disciples to engage in surprise attacks as quickly as possible and were thus perfect for casual, everyday use. However, the OLED technology caused all of the equipment to become weaker over time and was really only suitable for emergency situations. The Professor was sending us to change into one of the several sets of uniforms that each of us had that were intended solely for intense battle and training.

After exchanging glances and nods with everyone, the Professor continued, "Timothy, you and Titus can suit up in your old quarters – Marcus and I have maintained everything just as you left them – then you, Marcus, and Titus can formulate the battle arrangements and team configurations for the assault upon the Komplo prior to contacting your students for group orientation."

"Sounds good," I replied with a nod.

"After you get situated in one of the guest quarters; Mike, Matthias, would you two mind preparing the training level for a massive sparring session with sufficient space for the twenty-two combatants that will need to be orienting themselves?"

"Not a problem, Professor," Matthias replied. "Excellent, then we shall converge there with the Disciples in two hours," Professor Bird concluded with a nod of affirmation, and with that the group disbanded.

Chapter Thirty-Three

When I arrived at my old prep room I found it exactly like Professor Bird had said it would be; unchanged from the orderly and sparsely filled room I had left behind as I had only stored the basic necessities here when I was an active member of the SOS Corps because I still lived and operated from home. There was only a small palate to sleep on should an overnight stay prove to be necessary, a desk that doubled as a dresser holding a few changes of battle clothes neatly arranged inside a couple of the drawers, a Bible, a lamp, and a few other favorite books sat atop of the desk, a small chair sat in front of the desk, and a large mirror hanging above it. Otherwise the room was basically empty, which meant that I had left the room almost the same way that I first found it.

I closed the door behind me and rematerialized the sword, bow, and quiver from the atmosphere in order to toss them on the pallet while I went over to the desk drawer, pulled out a battle uniform, and mentally disengaged the camouflage on the clothes I was currently wearing before removing them and tossing them into the laundry basket in the corner; the clothes would eventually be cleaned in a specially designed Myathian washer that also repair some of the wear and tear in the OLED technology.

I quickly pulled on a new pair of my shear-resistant buckskin pants before wrestling on a new set of boots, and after I had once again forced my feet into submissive positions within the confines of the boots, I looked up into the mirror and became distracted by what I saw.

I sat there for several moments and traced the lines of several scars that covered my chest and torso; each one had a story and a memory attached to it – some good and some not so good – and I was at once surprised and discouraged at the clarity in which some of those memories came back.

The most prominent one was of a large cross that Simon had personally and publically branded into the center of my chest as a demonstration of both of our loyalties. I had sworn my allegiance unto the One that had died for me upon the cross and Simon's sided against me and joined forces with the demonic forces as he pressed the firebrand into my flesh. This was a scar that I was 'proud' of because it served as a continual reminder of the good that God had done in my life. As far as I can remember, that was the last time heat or fire had ever hurt me and marked the day that I answered the call and became Pentecost.

But there were other scars – like the grizzly one that ran diagonally across my entire torso – that I was deeply ashamed of because they were the results of my own sin and arrogance. Most of these scars were evidences of my own failure to remain focused on the Lord and swallow my pride as I had put myself in many positions that I wasn't ready for or had no business being in. While the Lord had healed and redeemed me from all of them there were still some permanent consequences.

I had several other scars across my back that I couldn't see that were due to the lashes of the whip as well as from the literal backstabbing of one I had considered a friend.

I began to reflect on the spiritual scars that I had received, some of which ran deeper and were exceedingly more painful than many of the physical ones my body bore.

Scars that were earned because of my devotion to the Lord and others that I had brought upon myself. Scars that were taken to save a friend, and others that were given to me by close friends. I realized at that moment that every scar – emotional or physical – were testimonies of where we have been and what God has brought us through. As shameful or triumphant as some of the stories might be, it is all by the grace and sovereignty of God that they have occurred, and I wouldn't be the man I had become without them.

The door behind me opened with a knock as Marcus walked in. When he noticed the scars on my back he said, with just a hint of sarcasm mixed with his disbelief, "I always thought that you couldn't be hurt by anything."

I grabbed the leather breastplate from the desk and wrapped it around my back before turning to face Marcus as I fastened the straps.

"I never meant to appear invincible, Marcus," I said gently. "I'm human – just like the next guy – and I have faults and struggles too. God has just allowed me to heal quickly and grow beyond some of them."

Marcus nodded, but didn't seem completely sure of what to say or do next.

I swallowed hard, "I've been meaning to apologize for what took place during our battles against the Pantheon; I was trying to help and I never intended to drive you away. It's one of my deepest prayers that we would be able to take steps toward restoring the friendship that was lost."

Marcus nodded and spoke up finally, "I know that you weren't trying to give that impression. I was just…going through some other stuff and I took that out on you. I know that I was one of your closest friends and I'd like to get that back too. Especially now, considering what happened to Silas."

I winced internally but tried to remain focused on amending the relationship in front of me rather than being distracted by what was in God's hands. "Life is certainly too short to allow bitterness to grow between friends. I'm sorry for not talking to you about this sooner, but I was afraid that I could somehow make things worse."

Marcus chuckled, "I don't see how things could have gotten too much worse; we've been practically avoiding each other since the incident."

I chuckled as well, "I guess you're right, but I still have a problem with getting past that fear."

"Hey, I totally get it man. I can remember the time when–" Marcus was interrupted by a large blast that caused the compound around us to tremble and threw us to the ground.

"Please tell me that was just Titus letting off a bit too much steam over in the training room?" I asked, picking myself up off the ground.

"I wish I could, man," Marcus replied, getting up and heading out the door. "We both know that Titus doesn't have that much firepower in him to have caused that blast and that the training room he would be using is in the opposite direction of the blast."

I quickly retrieved my weapons from the palate and followed after him. "You weren't supposed to tell me that."

Marcus began to glow as he generated enough energy to levitate, "It looks like that Komplo couldn't wait and brought the fight to us." He said before flying down the hallway in the direction of the blast.

I ran behind him to keep up and called out, "Just like old times."

He turned back and said with a smile, "Yeah, just like it was in Versonnex."

I was pleased that my friendship with Marcus was on its way to being restored; I only prayed that we would both live long enough to gain some ground in getting back to where we were before.

As Pentecost ran down the hall after Alkali, he began to sense a strange stirring in the air, and after retrieving his bow and an arrow from his quiver he called to his friend, "You may want to land and walk it for a bit."

"Why? What for?" Alkali asked looking back and moments later he fell to the ground and tumbled down the hallway a bit before coming to a stop.

"Look there," Pentecost motioned with his bow towards the gray haze began to thicken and swirl down the hall towards them, "That must be Abafando's mind-fog; while surrounded in this stuff we'll have to focus harder on performing our abilities, and the thicker the fog the harder that will be."

Alkali strained for a moment to test how much effort it would take to sustain levitation and flight in order to gage how to perform the rest of his abilities.

"This is going to be interesting," he said once he had finished his test.

"There's someone here," Pentecost said turning around and drawing the string back on his bow.

"Who? Where?" Alkali asked turning the opposite direction with his fists radiating with his blue energy blasts.

Pentecost scanned the hallway with his eyes, "I can't tell; this fog is muddling my ability to sense their body temperatures, but I can still pick up the presence of two people."

"Two?" Alkali asked.

Pentecost nodded, "Hm-hmm, one in each direction."

Alkali thought for a moment, "Since we can't see them, I'd guess that we must be dealing with the Widow, Panther, or the Sorcerer." He then turned and added over his shoulder, "Unless Lunulata turned out to be against us."

"I'm as sure of her allegiance as I am of yours," Pentecost called back, his eyes still scanning the hallway. "Simon has long since found a way to mask his own thermal output to prevent me from detecting him, so we should be dealing with the Panther and Widow."

An image flashed in Pentecost's mind and he saw the Widow slowly climbing down a web inches above Alkali's head.

He quickly pivoted at the hip and released the arrow that he had drawn. The arrow shot high and broke the line that the Widow had been climbing down, yanking her off target and sent her falling down to the ground. Widow quickly fired a second strand off to the side which connected to the wall and with a hard yank on the web-line she was able to pull herself to the wall within a few seconds of her first line being broken.

By this time Timothy had retrieved an additional arrow and fired it at her location along the wall.

The Widow leapt up towards Pentecost, shot a web-line at the arrow as it approached and pulled it upward towards herself. She was able to use the contrary motion of the arrow to increase her own velocity as she flew towards Pentecost. When she neared him, she extended her leg out and grew to full size just as her foot reached his jaw.

Pentecost careened backward and hit the ground a few feet back with a thud.

Alkali fired a concentrated energy blast at the Widow

as she landed. However, she was able to sense the incoming blast and shrunk to avoid it, appearing a few moments later directly in front of Alkali in order to jab her knee into his torso.

That energy blast fired by Alkali flew down the hallway and exploded when it reached the end, causing a shadowy figure to leap out from the mindfog and bound off the wall before charging forward on all fours toward the ruckus; the Panther had been crouching in the shadows of the fog and had been forced to expose himself by Alkali's energy blast.

Pentecost emerged from the mindfog and drew his sword as the Panther arrived at his location and the Panther rose to stand on two legs and slashed at Pentecost with his left hand. Pentecost avoided the cut and brought the hilt of his blade down hard across Panther's face.

Panther's face suddenly shattered and revealed the robotic skull of a ComBot beneath the Giadan skin.

After the Widow had resized herself to attack Alkali she shrunk back down and reappeared behind him, and after looping a strand of webbing under his right arm and back over his left shoulder, she pivoted her body with a hard yank on the cord which flipped Alkali over onto the ground behind her.

Alkali tumbled but had enough momentum to quickly rise to his feet before Widow had enough time to attack.

"They're just ComBots, Alkali; don't hold back." Pentecost yelled out to Alkali as he brought his blade back diagonally up across Panther's torso and sliced the robotic frame open and turned around to see how his friend was fairing.

"Well, in that case," Alkali answered as he focused through the mindfog around him to use his energy manipulation to grab hold of the Widow-Bot and hold her fast. With a motion of his hand he threw her against the wall to his left, then across the hall to the right; each time the giadan lined skin of the ComBot cracked and broke.

Pentecost then held his sword out to the side with both hands and called out to get Alkali's attention.

Alkali then threw the ComBot back and impaled it on the blade.

"What's going on?" Alkali asked as Pentecost lowered the angle of his blade to allow the ComBot to slide off.

"It would appear as though the Komplo is testing out their army," Pentecost replied, carefully inspecting the edge of his blade for any damage.

"So why did they shatter like that?"

Pentecost shrugged his shoulder and looked at his friend, "My best guess is that these Bots were designed to mimic the Komplo members with such extreme accuracy that it weakened the giadan alloy and caused a more brittle physical structure."

"So this is one example of what the ComBot mutations are like?" Alkali asked.

Pentecost nodded. "Let's just hope that the other mutated forms are this easy to deal with."

The Professor, Lunulata, and Fletcher were also thrown to the ground by the initial blast that had rocked Alkali and Pentecost and smoke filled the room as Lunulata cloaked herself in a panic.

"Luna? Lunulata?" The Professor called out.

"Forget it Doc," Fletcher told him as he retrieved his bow and arrow, "she's gone."

The two of them began to cautiously make their way to the door; the mindfog began to swirl its way into the room just as they reached the door.

"What's that?" Fletcher asked motioning to the fog.

"That must be Abafando's mindfog, and considering the density of the fog, I'd venture say that he must be at a very close proximity."

"Listen, Doc," Fletcher said, peeking out around the doorway. "I need you to start accessing the computer systems and see what's going on – how many hostiles are we dealing with and their locations are first on the list – you know the drill."

"I'm on it," The Professor answered and scurried over to the nearest computer still remaining upright and usable.

Fletcher double-checked the hallway in both directions outside the door and moved in the direction that the mindfog was coming from.

As Fletcher progressed down the hallway the fog began to become denser and he began to feel as though he were walking through molasses. With the aid of his glasses he was able to pick up the thermal image of a man standing in the densest portion of the mindfog.

"Gotcha Abafando," Fletcher whispered as he strained to draw back the arrow that he had been resting on his string.

Suddenly it was as though the fog had entered Fletcher's bloodstream and frozen it solid and the mist around him seemed to have developed icy talons that now held him in place; Fletcher couldn't even bring himself to move his hand enough to release the string he now held taught. The fog and clamped down around him and wouldn't allow him to move and Fletcher was now trapped within his own body and sheer terror threatened to overwhelm him as his breathing became heavy and his heartrate increased with his growing anxiety.

Slowly, the thermal image of Abafando moved closer to Fletcher and the mindfog increased its intensity and strengthened its icy grip around Fletcher.

"Well, now," Abafando said as he approached Fletcher's frozen form; his accent was thick and sounded to Fletcher to be very similar to Russian. "Virus' upgrades seem to be paying off don't they?"

Fletcher's eyes blinked; it was the only movement that he could perform because it was involuntary.

"Ah, yes," Abafando remarked, noticing the movement. "Let's see just how much focus is required to shut down your body completely. Shall we?"

Abafando's eyes glossed over in a gray sea as he focused the mindfog's intensity on Fletcher's mind. Fletcher began to gasp and wheeze as the fog began to interfere with his brainstem's ability to give directions to his lungs and his heart began to behave erratically – going from beating at breakneck speeds to nearly stopping within his chest – as the communication between his mind and his body continued to break down.

Just as his vision began to darken, there was a small explosion and a bright flash directly in between Fletcher and Abafando as Firecracker had ran up behind them and tossed a small explosive to distract the villain and caused him to lose his focus. Fletcher was once again able to move and breathe and gasped deeply while releasing the arrow and falling forward to the ground.

The arrow struck Abafando squarely in the chest and he went down in a heap. As the mindfog cleared Firecracker rushed over to Fletcher as he coughed and struggled to convince his lungs to take in air once again.

"Sorry, I didn't get here sooner," Firecracker apologized doubled over, "but this fog slowed me down from being able to outrun a train to barely being able to beat an Olympic sprinter. You okay?"

"Peachy," Fletcher coughed.

"All right then, we need to get moving," Firecracker said as he rightened himself and glanced over to where Abafando lay. "Hey, Fletcher, check this out."

"What now?" He asked picking himself up and following Firecracker's gaze.

That's when he noticed that the skin around the arrow had cracked and shattered like glass, and that a strange smoke began to hiss and spray out from the wound.

"That must be one of the ComBots," Firecracker said finally.

Fletcher toggled through some of the scanners on his lenses, "The smoke seems to be a much weaker form of the mindfog, which means we should see a major improvement in our abilities pretty soon."

Firecracker rubbed his head and a pained expression spread across his face.

"You okay?" Fletcher asked.

Firecracker shook his head to clear it and shrugged his shoulder, "Yeah, I think I might be coming down with the flu or something; I've been a bit off since last week."

"Hey man, we don't need you acting as a biological weapon right now; we've got enough to deal with this Komplo attack." Fletcher rebuked, only half-jokingly.

"I hear you. Let's go check on the others," Firecracker replied with a brief chuckle.

Fletcher nodded, "You go and locate as many as you can, I'll head back and double-check on the Professor."

"Sounds good. We'll meet you back at the Welcome Center," Firecracker said before disappearing in a blur.

The Professor had still been running several scans on the SOS Security systems when he heard the door behind him open. He turned expecting to see Fletcher, but was startled to find that Acedia had entered the room instead.

Before he could react in any way, Acedia threw a psychic blast that sent the Professor careening back into the desk and onto the floor.

Suddenly, Lunulata appeared and swung down from her place of hiding on the ceiling to the front and just right of Acedia. As she came down, Lunulata wrapped her right leg around Acedia's neck and locked her ankle behind her left knee as her leg went over Acedia's shoulder and wrapped behind her back. Lunulata quickly shifted her weight and flipped Acedia unto the ground before twisting sharply at the waist and breaking her neck.

Lunulata and the Professor both rose shakily from the ground and began to notice signs of Acedia being a ComBot; the area around her neck had cracked open and the impact of hitting the ground had also caused some shattering to the brittle giadan.

"Are you all right, Professor?" Lunulata asked the shaky Professor as he rubbed his temple.

"I'm experiencing a great deal of pain, but I am alive and I believe that I will recover shortly. Thank you, Lunulata." The Professor then turned back to the monitor and again searched for the hostiles that were present within the SOS Headquarters.

"I'm sure that the pain will subside shortly, Professor," Lunulata said as she walked up behind him.

The Professor then spun around as he heard the sound of a scuffle behind him as a second Lunulata had appeared and the two were now combating each other.

Just then Fletcher walked in and upon seeing the commotion readied his bow with an arrow. Unfortunately, he couldn't determine which Lunulata was an ally and which was the foe.

"Fletcher, use this," The Professor had picked up an arrow with a flattened head from the desk and tossed it to the archer after he had replaced the other arrow into his quiver.

"Which one do I fire at?" Fletcher asked readying the arrow but still uncertain at who was the hostile here.

"Pick one," the Professor replied. "Aim near their heads and the arrow will do the rest. After you fire ready yourself a second arrow, for if the first has no effect on the one you chose, you must quickly fire upon the other."

Fletcher drew back his string, hesitated for just a moment to decide which Lunulata to fire at before finally trusting the Professor knew what he was talking about, and fired the arrow.

When the arrow struck the head of the Lunulata it held fast and the ComBot began to seize up and convulse before collapsing to the ground.

"What kind of an arrow was that, Doc?" Fletcher asked a bit bewildered as he relaxed his pull on the string; he had been ready in the event that he had picked the wrong Lunulata.

"Essentially the arrow caused a localized EMP that fried the circuitry of the ComBot. It clung to its head because of the magnetic attraction to the giadan and would have had no effect upon Lunulata."

"So why didn't that ComBot version of me shatter on impact like the Acedia one did?" Lunulata asked the Professor as he once again turned to the monitor and his scanning of the headquarters.

"I would assume that it is because the ComBot had to mimic your shapeshifting abilities and therefore had to retain a strong giadan alloy, thus the mutation had to have produced a different weakness. In this case that weakness allowed the electromagnetic arrow to cling to the otherwise poorly magnetic giadan surface of the ComBot."

"So how many ComBots are still lurking about, Doc?" Fletcher asked, moving up beside the Professor at his computer.

"It appears as though Pentecost and Alkali have dealt with a couple imitating the Panther and Widow. Abafando, Acedia, and Lunulata are down. Which would logically leave Switchblade, Catch.22, and the Sorcerer. However, I've only been able to detect two other hostiles, both of which appear to be engaged with Lancelot and Kevlar."

"Those would be Switchblade and Catch.22," Fletcher deduced, "Simon's abilities would keep the Bot from being detected."

"Actually, a ComBot wouldn't be able to mimic his abilities at all." Lunulata interjected.

"Why not?" Fletcher sought an explanation.

"Because they're not natural abilities that can be produced by a GRID code," she replied with a shrug of her shoulder. "Simon is called the Sorcerer because he draws his power from the supernatural and that kind of power can't be replicated by science and technology."

"She's right," the Professor affirmed. "The Sorcerer's power is demonic rather than scientific and therefore could not be replicated by the ComBots themselves. However, the demonic forces that Simon has aligned himself with can manipulate those portions of the natural realm that God grants them access to, which could very likely include the ComBots."

"So just because a ComBot can't mimic the Sorcerer doesn't mean that there isn't ComBot running around with some sort of spell, or hex, or whatever or that a demon isn't empowering it, right?" Fletcher asked.

"Precisely," the Professor affirmed, "and there is no guarantee that there is only one of each Komplo member represented here or that there aren't more ComBots that have yet to be activated either."

"Let's just go and meet up with the others at the Welcome Center and figure this out together." Fletcher concluded, moving towards the door with his arrow still on the string.

Kevlar and Lancelot had begun to run towards the Welcoming Center after they had recovered from the blast, until a bullet caught Kevlar in the chest and caused him to stagger back a few steps.

Lancelot readied his shield and drew his arming sword from its scabbard as he progressed forward to locate Catch.22 among the mindfog.

Due to the mindfog's effects Kevlar would end up with a bruise in the next few minutes but was no worse for wear; a bullet of a higher caliber than a .223 and it might have been a slightly different story.

Kevlar gently rubbed the place where the bullet had struck him as he moved to catch up with Lancelot until a door to his left opened up and Switchblade stepped out swinging a blade at Kevlar's chest.

The blade thumped on Kevlar's burly form without inflicting any damage, but Switchblade had positioned his foot behind Kevlar's legs and had enough push in his swing to shove Kevlar off-balance and send him crashing to the ground.

Switchblade followed up by using both hands to swing his blade down at Kevlar with all his might in hopes that he might inflict some kind of damage. Kevlar shifted his head to avoid the headache of having the sword's edge club him and bounce his head against the ground and Switchblade allowed the blade to rest there against Kevlar's shoulder and produced a knife in his right hand as he dropped his knee down into Kevlar's solar plexus; the knife was then thrust in vain at Kevlar's ribs and the blade snapped in two.

At this point Kevlar thrust his right hand up and clutched Switchblade around the neck and pounded his head against the wall, an act which sent giadan shards flying as the ComBot's skin and parts of its skull shattered.

Lancelot had carefully progressed down the hall until

he could make out the form of Catch.22 and while crouching low behind his shield, Lancelot sheathed his sword and grabbed his knife from his boot.

Upon reforming the knife into a small boomerang, Lancelot remarked, "'Tis not exactly a medieval weapon from across the pond," he played with the weight of it in his hand for a moment, "but 'twill get the job done."

Catch.22 fired again and a split second after the bullet ricocheted off of Lancelot's shield the boomerang was released and came flying at the sniper.

Because of the mindfog that had filled the area, Catch.22 didn't realize the danger until he had been struck in the head by the massive force of the boomerang. The ComBot then collapsed to the ground with the metal boomerang protruding out of its shattered skull.

Kevlar had heaved himself off of the ground and made his way to Lancelot's side at this point. "Nice hit," he remarked.

"Thanks," Lancelot said, turning to his companion and noticed that Kevlar's shoulder was bleeding. "Are you all right?"

Kevlar shrugged and rotated his bleeding shoulder, "Yeah, I'm fine. It's just a scratch really. That punk back there decided to rest his blade on my shoulder and the lack of pressure on that sharp blade made my skin bleed."

It was a strange thing for Lancelot to see Kevlar hurt at all – even if it was a mere scratch as he claimed — but before he could comment on it Firecracker raced into the area

"Hey guys. It looks like you've got things handled here and I've already checked in with Pentecost and Alkali, so I'll see you at the Welcome Center." He said hastily before taking off.

A moment later he rushed back and asked Kevlar in disbelief "Are you bleeding? Whoa! I didn't know that could happen to you. You better get that taken care of, 'cuz this is probably just the beginning." And with that Firecracker took off again and helped round up the others.

"I surely hope that our friend is wrong about this event being the start of our troubles," Lancelot remarked, his English accent carried a much more somber and despondent tone then it usually did.

"Yeah, well, we both know that he's probably right," Kevlar replied touching the wound on his shoulder and rubbing the blood between his fingers. Satisfied that the blood was thickening and the wound would be closed up soon, Kevlar suggested that they make their way to the Welcome Center.

† † † † † † †

Later in the Welcome Center...

Firecracker raced down the hall toward the Welcome Center and saw a lone figure standing in the center of the room. The man had a dark black hood pulled low over his face and the train of his cloak swirled in the mindfog that had largely dissipated though still lingered. His hands were formed in a triangle with his fingertips pointing downward and there was no mistaking him as anyone but the Sorcerer.

As he entered the Welcome Center, Firecracker used both hands to scatter three explosives within the room – right, left, right – and timed them with a purposefully scattered placement so that if the Sorcerer should dodge one he would have to move into one of the others.

The Sorcerer simply looked up and turned his head to face the hallway that Firecracker had just entered through. A split-second later he pivoted at the waist to face him and moved his arms and hands in a circular, sweeping motion and the three explosives arched and were swept along with his motioning and positioned themselves above and around the Sorcerer to form a triangle with the point nearly touching the ceiling and the bottom corners were the same distance off the ground. Firecracker screeched to a halt and saw an eye form within the triangle, blink once, and then disappear.

Moments later the three explosives fired off in different direction and targeted three specific points: one that flew directly behind the Sorcerer and blew through the wall that contained some specialized ComBots that were intended to be a last resort security measure, the second went to his right and blasted through the cainium-lined wall that covered the electrical wires that connected the computer system for the headquarters, and the third, which went forward and to the left with a much more intense explosion than the previous two, struck a place along the wall took out a hidden access panel that granted the SOS Corps members and the Defenders access to work with the security systems.

Each explosion had increased in intensity beyond what Firecracker had originally thrown and exploded precisely as the other Defenders entered the Welcome Center and those entering nearest to the blasts were thrown to the ground or against the hallway wall if they managed to remain upright.

"Sorcerer," Pentecost called out a bit angrily after he had righted himself, "what scheme has caused you to attack us here?"

The Sorcerer replied with a tone of arrogance marking his near-German accent and a smug expression upon his face, "Why, Timothy, is that anyway to greet an old friend? After all that we went through together in Kalmar I expected a bit less formality from you."

"I'm not the one that ended the friendship, Simon," Pentecost countered, controlled but still obviously angered. "You brought an end to any claim to my trust and cordiality when you betrayed us in favor of Satan."

"My, my," the Sorcerer answered, shaking his head and clicking his tongue, "such hostility and vengefulness from one that once welcomed me as a comrade."

"He talks too much Pent," Fletcher stated drawing an arrow on his string. "Why don't we just finish this?"

"Careful," Firecracker cautioned while readying himself along with the others, "I've already tried that and it didn't turn out as I planned."

"Indeed," the Sorcerer turned to face him, as a renewed tone of arrogance laced his voice. "I recommend exercising restraint, as would your leader if he knew my plan. Young Timothy and I know full well that one cannot fight against prophecy."

"So you claim to fight on the side of prophecy now?" Pentecost challenged, his sword clenched in his right hand.

"What twisted translation are you trying to fulfill anyway?" Alkali asked, his fist glowing bright blue with his energy charge.

The Sorcerer turned again and narrowed his eyes, "One that shall usher in the New World as prophesied."

"I'm afraid that your Komplo doesn't contain the

proper number of members to fulfill the prophecy concerning that order, Sorcerer," the Professor remarked. "By my count, you only have seven fighting members and ten sources of power are required."

The Sorcerer turned full circle to face the Professor's remark head-on. "'Tis true that my original intent was to use that particular prophecy to my own advantage, and I would have had nine fighting members at this point had they all proven trustworthy," at this the Sorcerer cast a despising glance at Lunulata.

To her credit, she didn't back down or avoid his glare but replied with a hint of vengeance and mockery in her voice, "I suppose that no one takes pleasure in a traitor. Do they Simon?"

The Sorcerer seemed to ignore her attempt at baiting him with his past and continued, "However at this point I have changed the focus of my endeavors and I assure you all that you will utterly fail in your attempts to thwart my scheme."

"Fletcher's right," Kevlar commented, rolling his wounded but healing shoulder, "you talk too much."

The Sorcerer mockingly took a bow, "Very well, kind sir. I shall cease with the pleasantness of our delightful conversation and move on to a more fortuitous topic. Virus?" He called out turning to the section of exposed wires and cables as they sparked.

A moment later the humanoid form of Virus appeared in the room, for he had concealed himself as he worked at tapping into the computer system through the exposed wires.

"All finished, sir," he replied and turned to walk towards the Sorcerer.

"Rodger?" Lancelot asked bewildered. "Good heavens man, what has happened to you?"

Indeed, Rodger had changed drastically; so much so that even Alkali – who had trained with the young man until recently – had assumed the man before him to be an older relative of some sort rather than being Rodger himself. Virus had chosen a human form that was similar in appearance to Rodger, however a good head taller while lacking the glasses and having a much stronger build.

"I've undergone an extensive upgrade since you last saw me, Lancelot." Virus answered flatly. "Rodger is no longer in existence or of any concern of yours, for the Virus has arrived."

"Simon, what have you done?" Pentecost asked, dumfounded that the Sorcerer would have gone to such measures with human life.

"You trapped Rodger inside of that thing?" Firecracker asked in bewilderment.

"Don't worry son," the Professor tried to console the young man inside the machine, "I'm sure that we can help you in some way and reverse what this monster has done to you."

"Help me? Reverse it?" Virus asked without emotion. "And turn me back into the weak, cast-off known as Rodger? My dear Professor, I now have a position of power, prestige, and belonging along with the immortality of technology. Why would I go back now?"

"Rodger," Pentecost spoke softly as one would a wounded animal to calm them from their aggression, "Simon once faced a decision much the same as the one you have now; he wanted power and chose to pursue that power into the dark realm of witchcraft. The Professor was right in referring to Simon as a monster, for we all become like what we worship and serve. Simon chose to intentionally serve the darkest monsters of hell, and if you continue to serve him you will slowly become like him yourself."

"Who said that I was serving him?" Virus countered, his near stoic countenance and tone only now began to show trace signs of anger.

"Virus is his own free agent, my dear Timothy," Simon clarified, his voice was smooth as honey and dripping with deceit. "He has chosen to assist the Komplo in ridding ourselves of you and your band here before he returns to fulfilling his own desires of greatness."

"And how does he plan on doing that?" Fletcher asked.

The Sorcerer shrugged a shoulder nonchalantly, "By sealing you within your compound; this headquarters of yours will become your tomb."

The ComBots began to boot up and whir to life one by one and as they moved about the large room they began to fire upon the Defenders and the lights above them began to flash with an ominous red warning.

"Farewell my dear, Timothy" the Sorcerer called out above the cacophony. "Perhaps we shall meet again in eternity when I am lord of a portion of Lucifer's kingdom."

Pentecost turned from impaling a ComBot and saw both the Sorcerer and Virus disappear in a cloud of green smoke.

"Gentlemen, the self-destruct sequence has been activated." The Professor called out in reference to the red warning lights.

"That gives us only a couple minutes to figure out how to survive the explosion that brings down the compound and the building upstairs upon us all." Firecracker called out as he crashed into a ComBot and skidded to a stop before racing around the room again.

"With that access panel taken out there's no way for us to cancel the explosion or call off the ComBots." Lancelot said as he shielded the Professor from a wild swing of a ComBot that had formed its arm into a battle hammer; moments later the attacking ComBot was cut in two by Lancelot's sharp blade.

"Yeah, and these ComBots don't shatter like the others," Kevlar remarked as he put a deep dent into a ComBots face; the Bot collapsed with its body convulsing for a moment before all movement stopped.

"Professor, any idea what kind of disadvantage they might have?" Pentecost asked as he removed the robotic head from a ComBot.

"They're on autopilot and have access to a limited attack pattern and strategy capability; meaning that while they are physically more stable than the others these will have a much worse technique."

"All right then," Fletcher fired an explosive arrow that lodged itself in the right shoulder of a ComBot before detonating and taking out two others. "Strong body, but weak brains."

"Indeed," Lancelot replied. "However, the manner by which we plan on escaping our own fortress eludes me, brothers."

"Alkali," Pentecost called out while quickly slicing through a pair of attacking ComBots, "Could you sustain an energy field to protect us from the debris of the explosion?"

Alkali had taken to the air and was blasting at the ComBots from above. He had just taken one out from the ground and another as it flew towards him to tackle him out of the air before responding, "I can, but only for a few moments and only if I charge up for a bit and it won't keep us from being barbequed by the heat from the blast." Another ComBot leapt from the ground behind him and he spun around to blast it back down just before it reached him.

"All right guys, I need a perimeter," Pentecost called out to the group. "Firecracker, Fletcher you're our offensive attackers; try and keep the ComBots at a distance."

"Got it," Firecracker replied, he was breathing a bit more laboriously than was normal for him but he was still able to increase his speed to keep the ComBots busy and blast those that got to close while Fletcher positioned himself more strategically to cover the opposite side of the room from Firecracker.

"Kevlar, Lunulata, and Lancelot, you're our defensive line; keep the Professor, Fletcher, Alkali, and myself from getting taken out so Alkali can charge up and protect us from the debris and I can take care of the heat from the blast."

The Professor and Fletcher moved closer to Pentecost while Alkali flew down nearby and Kevlar and Lancelot took positions on opposite sides of the group. Lancelot formed his sword into a second shield for Kevlar to use against the energy blasts from the ComBots and withdrew the knife from his boot and lengthened it so that it would be more beneficial in battle.

The Professor then held up a hand and said, "Pentecost, I do believe that Lunulata would be of better service if she assisted you and Alkali."

"How so Professor?" Pentecost asked as the rest of the team was engaging the ComBots.

"One of the GRID updates I was able to perform prior to the blast will allow her to absorb part the GRID lag that would adversely affect the two of you and disperse it at an accelerated rate into the atmosphere."

Pentecost nodded his approval. "I'd love a more detailed explanation of that later, Professor."

"I'd be more than happy to oblige you, should we both survive long enough for that to transpire."

Pentecost nodded again and began to circulate the air in the room in preparation for having to ward off and disperse the extreme temperatures that would be generated by the destruction of the headquarters.

At this point, Alkali had charged sufficiently to cause a hazy blue dome to form around the Defenders.

"Everybody needs to stay inside the circle," Pentecost called out. "Keep the ComBots out if you can, but be sure that you don't stray out from the protection of the field."

Firecracker adjusted his circuit so that he could continue running around the other Defenders and also stay with the blue energy generated by Alkali.

Lunulata had moved to the side of Pentecost and Alkali as they stood back to back and placed a hand on each of their heads. As their focus increased so did the strained look on her face as she took on herself some of the mental pressure as an octopus could absorb water or oxygen into its body. Her efforts, though necessary to prevent the two men from collapsing, did not completely remove the burden from them and they too began to groan and grimace as they sought to protect their team.

Pentecost continued to circulate the air up and down the halls and around the room at increasing speeds to keep them from being incinerated while Alkali increased the strength of his energy field that would prevent the shrapnel and falling debris from crushing them as each member of the Defenders did their part to ensure that they were successful; Fletcher and Firecracker preventing the ComBots from entering the force field, Lancelot and Kevlar taking out those that managed to escape the onslaught of arrows and explosions and make it within the field while also deflecting and absorbing the different ranged attacks from the ComBots, Lunulata struggling to take on as much of the GRID lag from Pentecost and Alkali as she could without causing herself to blackout, and the Professor praying earnestly that it would all be enough to deliver them from the Sorcerer's attack against them.

Joseph Stevens

The team was going through some training drills against some ComBots mimicking the Komplo when I began to sense the alarm go off in the base.

"Everybody hold up," I lifted a hand and signaled for the ComBots and Disciples to disengage.

"What's up, Joe?" Mark asked removing his Maestro mask and walking up behind me.

"Everybody listen," I called everybody over.

We had been trying to add basic fighting skills to everyone's GRID abilities to make them more combat ready.

"What's that ringing?" KT asked putting a hand to his ear and rubbing it.

"I don't hear anything," Adam said.

"Yeah, I hear it too," Beth added with a nod. "Almost like a smoke alarm. Only quieter."

I turned and looked at Mary and Mark, "Can you guys hear or feel the vibrations?"

They both nodded.

"That's the alarm indicating that the SOS Corps HQ has been attacked."

"Should we go help them?" Adam asked, eager for a real fight.

"Why bother?" Mark chuckled, "The Defenders can handle a skirmish on their home turf, can't they?"

"Let's hope so. For now we should get to the monitor

room and make sure." I began to quickly lead the group out of the training room and down the hall to the video conference room that contained numerous large holo-screens connected to INS and also the security system shared by all the underground bases. I quickly flipped on a monitor, used the holographic controls to pan through to find the camera pointed directly at the SOS Corps from across the street, and commanded the other cameras in the area to reposition themselves to focus on the same spot. The building above the underground HQ was already in flames and a news van for the local outlet of a liberal national news organization was prepping their equipment; the cameraman was getting shots of the blaze to air on the news and the reporter was creating and rehearsing various lines.

It seemed unusual that the national news media would have happened to be on sight and ready to record the instant that a house fire erupted; and the fact that that house happened to hide the location of the SOS Corps secret base was beyond a coincidence. The alarm told me that someone was attacking the base, but the flames signaled to me that the self-destruct sequence had already begun for the HQ and there would only be a few more moments for the Defenders to stop whatever was going on underground before the base exploded; the building above would collapse at the same moment to bury the sound of the explosion and the HQ beneath the wreckage.

"So much for the Defenders being able to handle things themselves," Beth commented.

"Should we go help them now?" Mary asked concerned.

Suddenly, the building behind her collapsed, signaling

the destruction of the HQ underground – this was last-ditch effort in place in all the bases to stop whoever might overrun the defenses from being able to use any of the weapons and technology inside them – and I could only watch as the flames consumed the building and pray that my brother made it out of there before the explosion took place.

"It's too late," I replied to Mary soberly.

"What do you mean?" Aaron asked alarmed.

I shook my head, "When the house collapsed, so did the HQ underneath."

No one said or asked what we knew that meant; anyone inside of that compound was most likely crushed by the rubble if they hadn't already been killed by the Komplo attack.

I was already a bit ticked off at Timothy for mentioning the possibility that something would happen to him that would need me to take over both the Bible study and the Disciple's Program. I had done a lot of growing over the last two years and while I was more willing to lead the group in his absence I wasn't at all eager for him to pass on his mantle; especially if it meant that something happened to him. He might be ornery and a bit of a jerk at times, but he was still the only older brother I had, and I didn't want to struggle with trying to replace him in my life.

The reporter made a comment about the collapse of the building to her cameraman and wrote something down in a small notebook in her hand.

"So how did the media happen to show up at the SOS HQ at the precise moment that it bursts into flames due to a Komplo attack?" Mark was the first one to speak after the collapse of the building.

"Someone must have tipped them off," I answered as I began to flip through some options in my mind. "Simon must have wanted an audience for the defeat of the Defenders."

I watched the monitor and began to notice that some of the debris began to shift as the flames and even some of the ash from the building began to stir abnormally. Moments later the wreckage erupted and a heat wave spiraled upward as a large blue ball broke up from the ground containing the weary Defenders.

"They're alive!" Mary exclaimed as the blue ball landed and disappeared.

The reporter quickly called for her cameraman to follow her across the street. I spotted Timothy on the screen as he, Marcus, and Luna were kneeling on the ground; she was resting her hands on each of their heads and the three were breathing heavy. With each breath she painfully took in the other two seemed to gain strength while she recovered only once she exhaled and by the time the reporter and her cameraman had crossed the street the three had gained enough strength to rise to their feet.

"Here we go," Mark commented as the reporter shoved her microphone at the nearest standing Defender, which was Mike at the time. The reporter quickly stated her name and the name of the news group she represented and 'politely' asked if she could ask a few questions.

I noticed that Titus was still doubled-over and breathing heavy. Luna noticed it too and quietly walked over to where he was at. When she asked if he was all right, he smiled and stood upright claiming to be fine but, "just out of shape". Luna didn't seem convinced but didn't push the issue.

Even though it wasn't live the reporter did her best to position herself and phrase her questions for the TV audience later that evening.

"Gentlemen that was quite a display back there. I still can't believe what just happened and I was here to witness it myself. Can you answer the question that I'm sure a lot of people out there are asking right now, and tell us who you are?"

Mike cleared his throat and prepared to answer her question. He had already sheathed his blade in the scabbard at his side, the blade fit loosely as the sheath was made for a larger blade, and took his second shield from Matthias and strapped it over his shoulders while she had made her advance across the street. I figured it was a smart move for him to not reform any of his weapons on camera.

"Well, madam," he said as his English accent suddenly became more pronounced with both nervousness and distinction, "I suppose first I shall state plainly for all to be assured that we are only mortal human beings; there is nothing extraordinary concerning our lineage."

She pulled the mic away from Mike and spoke into it herself, only half-joking, "So you're not aliens?" She moved over to allow Anthony to confirm.

He shook his head and chuckled, "Heck no. I ain't no little green guy from space, I'm just a guy with a bow and arrow from the hood."

"I see," she reclaimed her mic and hesitated to ask her next question. She was trying to pick her next victim in order to find the best interviewee for the news; she would want to keep things looking spontaneous without seeming too chaotic. "So what do you gentlemen call yourselves?" This question was directed to Matthias as the group had huddled in a semi-circle in front of her.

Matthias shrugged his shoulder and he uncrossed one arm to point as he made some brief introductions, "I'm Kevlar, he's Fletcher, that's Alkali, Pentecost, the guy with the shields is Lancelot, over there's the Professor, her name's Lunulata, and he's Firecracker."

"Okay," she was a bit taken back by his straightforward nature; definitely not a good 'on the air' personality. At least she was asking info questions about their names, something that would be scrolling on a banner or read by the anchor rather than shown on a video anyway. She allowed Matthias to answer her next question. "And do you have a team name?"

"We call ourselves the Defender Corps, it helps us remember what our job is all about." Matthias nodded, his eyes obstructed by the dark sunglasses he wore and his arms were still crossed. He definitely looked more like a gruff bouncer for a rowdy nightclub than a noble Defender of the weak.

"I see. And would you consider this 'Defender Corps' to be a paramilitary or militia group?" Her questions were obviously getting more pointed; she was done being polite, now she wanted dirt.

The Professor was given this question and he pushed his glasses to their proper place on his nose as he answered, "Well, considering that the true definition of 'militia' includes any military force that is raised from the civil population to supplement a regular army in an emergency and a 'paramilitary group' is any unofficial force organized similarly to a military force, any paramilitary group ought to be considered a militia. However, in direct answer to your question, I believe that the Defender Corps would be rightly classified under the heading of a militia in the original sense of the word."

The reporter was a bit confused by the 'answer' to her question, and I doubted that she would be asking the Professor any more questions. "I'm not sure if that was a 'yes' or a 'no', Professor, but thank you."

She cleared her throat and consulted her notes to try and refocus. After a moment she directed a second question at Anthony, "Should the American government feel threatened by your group?"

So far I was happy that she hadn't found anything damaging to the Defender Corps, other than perhaps their poor interviewee personalities. Though all of the Defenders were usually careful about what they said and how they said it, Anthony, Titus, and Marcus all had attention issues that could end up ruining the group if the liberal media found something to twist in their rash statements. I was also worried with how Luna would handle herself if faced with a difficult question as she was new to the faith. Currently, I was thankful that these three hadn't said anything that could be twisted or received much air time yet and I continued to pray that the reporter would ignore them and that God would give everyone the right words to say.

Anthony shrugged his shoulder, "I don't see why the government should be worrying about a handful of people trying to help others and keep the nation safe. Does the government have a problem with a neighborhood watch association group? Or whatever they're called."

She pointed the mic at Titus after asking, "So why the masks? Do you have something to hide?"

"Not at all," Titus shook his head, "I'm just trying to protect those I care about from being targeted by those seeking revenge."

"Is that what happened here today?" The reporter asked. "Was someone targeting you? Why were you all inside of that home?"

"Well, uh…" Titus was a bit unsure of how to answer that. "We had a base of operations within that building, and we were attacked inside there, yes."

"Don't you think you're gambling a little freely with the wellbeing of others? How should the other individuals living in this neighborhood respond to the threat of their safety?" It was Marcus' turn up to bat.

"Well, our goal was to be in the midst of the people so we would be nearby to help when something goes wrong; like the fire stations, hospitals, and police departments. And we knew that people would target us eventually – like some target the police officers – but we hoped that we would be concealed enough to keep those people from finding us."

"Well, apparently your ruse didn't work, Defenders." She then fixed her gaze upon Timothy, "And what about you? Why aren't you wearing a mask?"

"Simply put, because I've never felt led to. Alkali needs his visor to help control his abilities, the glasses that Kevlar and Fletcher wear also aid them in the use of their talents – as do Lunulata's goggles – but I myself have no need for eyewear and I feel as though God wants me to serve the people without a mask."

"So you're religious? Do all the members of your

group believe as you?" The reporter had found the goods that she was looking for and she was going to keep digging.

Timothy answered carefully, knowing what she was looking for and not wanting to give it to her. "Each of us made the individual decision to follow Jesus as the risen Lord that we know Him to be and have entered into a relationship with Him. However, I wouldn't classify any of us as being 'religious', at least not in the modern sense of the word."

"I see. So is the Defender Corps and religiously exclusive group? Do you exclude the admittance of people of other faiths or people of no religious creed?"

Timothy swallowed and I knew that he prayed a silent prayer for help in that brief moment. "As Christians we believe it is important to reach out to everyone and accept all people so that they may come to the knowledge that Jesus has died to grant them refuge from wrath and is alive today as evidence of that fact. As Defenders, we acknowledge the fact that people who agree upon this fundamental principle of reality will agree on most other things and will work out their differences civilly as brothers. And thus far, the group has not received any applicants – Christian or otherwise – for us to accept or turn down on any basis and its members have been established and ordained by God."

"So can people of differing opinions or minority groups expect equal treatment and protection?" A sly grin spread across her face and a devious tone tainted her voice slightly; she was going for the kill. "Can the homosexual and Muslim communities anticipate your assistance?"

Timothy smiled and lowered his head for a moment before speaking into the mic, "I hope you do not find it rude if I ask you some questions prior to answering yours."

The reporter nodded, she wasn't going anywhere until she got what she came for and would offer anything to get it. I had to wonder how she seemed to stay so calm and cool under the hot Arizona sun with a blazing bonfire just a few yards away.

"Why do you ask questions while anticipating the most damaging answer? Do you already have your story written and only need us to put our own necks in the noose for the sake of the camera? Why do you ask a question in order to attack us?"

The reporter was unchanged by my brother's questions, though the cameraman seemed to be bothered by something; maybe it was only the heat of summer as he carried the weight of the camera on his shoulder.

Timothy drew in a deep breath and continued, "I know that you don't have to answer my questions and none of that will be on the news later. So to answer your question: never in the past have any of us interviewed those in danger before we helped them, nor do we plan on starting such a practice in the future. When we save someone's life we pray that they would use that as a second chance from God to draw closer to Him; for the believer that means serving Him faithfully with their whole being and for the non-believer that means seriously considering what truly lies beyond the doors of death and where they truly stand before God."

"Thank you Pentecost, and thank you Defender Corps; I only have one more question for you before you go. Considering the way that you have endangered the people already, how can you honestly expect them to trust you now?"

The microphone came to rest in front of Luna and I knew that this question held many layers of unknown pain and guilt for her since she had endangered many more people than just those living in the neighborhood surrounding the SOS HQ.

Luna remained in control of her emotions and maintained a professional appearance, "I can only testify from personal experience about the greatness of God's transforming work of grace in my life. I don't know if people can forgive me or trust me again, I simply know that God already has and that is enough for me."

I don't know if it was what the reporter was looking for, but I liked the way Luna answered her question.

"Let's rest up a bit before they get here," I told the group and shut off the monitors. "I think that things are going to get even more intense when they arrive."

Timothy Stevens

We eventually made our way stealthily back to my home base and sat in the video conference room, the smoldering remains of the SOS and Defender Corps base was staring back at us from one of the holographic-screens and the others showed various maps of the US.

"Well guys," Anthony said looking at the smoke rising from the timbers of what was once their home, "let's start by listing the good things…The sky is blue…That's about all I got guys." Anthony couldn't even muster more than a half-hearted chuckle at his own joke.

I struggled to find some words that could bring these guys together again and follow God's call for us. "Listen guys, I know that we've had some setbacks a—"

"Setbacks?" Titus interjected. "Was my father's death a setback?"

"Some setbacks and tragedies," I continued trying to sooth his anger without taking it personally. "I understand the dismal feeling that things are hopeless. However, we must rely on what we know to be true in moments like this. What anchor can we rely on in this storm? God's Word tells us plainly that He remains sovereign and in control regardless as to what takes place here on Earth, and I know that you guys already know this. So are we going to focus on that truth and fight with purpose or are we going to be dashed on the rocks because we floundered and drifted aimlessly in our despair?"

"Well, if we're going to do this we need to have a plan." Mike commented. "How exactly do you propose we defeat Simon within his fortress when we couldn't accomplish it within our own?"

"Let's start with the 'where' and then work our way forward," Luna replied and began to manipulate the controls to pull up an image of a mountain range that was located in southern New Mexico. "Simon has established his base of operations here, in the Black Mountain Range in New Mexico. The Mimbres River located nearby is purified to supply the Komplo with fresh water."

"Did they have any kind of defensive strategy in place in case we attacked them?" Marcus asked.

"Only a rough idea was laid out for us," Luna pivoted in her seat to face Marcus as he sat to her right down the length of the rectangular table we occupied, "however there are some obvious benefits to certain members holding their positions in specific locations."

"Right," Anthony began to point at the holo-image before us from his seat directly across from me, "the leeward side of this mountain range would give Catch.22 a perfect sniper's position for anyone trying to climb up the mountainside."

"The treed side of those mountains would give the Panther plenty of space to hide out," Matthias stated from his right, his arms still crossed and his left hand tenderly rubbed a thinning scar on his right shoulder.

"As well as for the Widow," Luna added to my right, "since the tree coverage would give her something to attach her webbing to."

Professor Bird began to share his silent ponderings

with the group from his seat next to Matthias, "And I believe it to be most advantageous for Abafando and Acedia to be located near the pinnacle of the mountains, as his dense mindfog would be able to drift down the mountains to affect all of you and Acedia would be offered a more beneficial vantage point as well."

"I'd say that Switchblade's weapons seem to require a more limited range in order to be effective," Mike's English accent spoke up from my left. "He would need the advantage of the trees concealing his position while also having open shots; I'd say that he would be positioned where the tree line thins between the windward and leeward side of the mountains."

"Simon would need to be near the peak of Mount McKnight as well," I added stroking my chin. "He needs the lofty height and the idea that we are working our way up to his position to stroke his ego. Virus would be effective just about anywhere and will probably be filling in some of the gaps on the leeward side."

"And what about our attack?" Titus asked from Anthony's left. "What would be the best way to spread ourselves out?"

"With our numbers we can spread ourselves out into seven teams of three," Anthony said after quickly counting up and dividing the number of warriors that we had at our disposal. "I wouldn't want a group to be smaller than that."

Mike added. "So who shall we group together to form these three-stranded cords?"

"Before we discuss that," I interjected, "I believe that it would be important to notify the prayer warriors."

The others stared back blankly.

"You do have trusted prayer warriors to notify? People who know some of the purposes and missions of the SOS and Defenders Corps in order to cover us with prayer? We had at least a half-a-dozen when I left years ago."

Marcus shrugged a shoulder, "Nearly all of them moved or have died so we don't have any assigned prayer warriors to call anymore."

I sighed heavily. No wonder the local SOS branch had lost their vision. "I'll take care of notifying the prayer warriors then. I know of several who have been covering me and my team every day, even before we became a combative force. We need to have spiritual backup, especially when going against Simon."

I'd have to remember to give Grandma and Grandpa a message after this meeting along with my wife, my parents, and younger brothers as they were the key prayer warriors in my life and knew about the SOS Corps, the Defenders, and the Disciples. There were also a few older men and women at Church that had been praying for us; most didn't know the full story about what we did – or even that any of these organizations existed – but I had been able to let them know when something big was happening and to be in prayer for us and that was what I'd have to do after this meeting.

The Professor cleared his throat and resumed control of the holo-screens, in order to display the seven Defenders and fourteen Disciples to bring us back to the practical elements of the evening. "The abilities that Timothy described his Disciples as having would indeed produce some extremely desirable combinations, countermeasures, and preferred assignments."

"Some obvious positions are to have Oceanica and

Luna near Mimbres River, and Carpenter should take up a position in the woods." I commented and dragged those members to the preferred locations where the theorized Komplo members would most likely be waiting.

"I'd say that Marcus should take Plasma and Arcade and focus on Virus once we figure out where he's at." Anthony said and moved those three to a position above the mountain range where the holographic Virus also floated aimlessly. "Plasma's energy blasts and absorption would work great against the robot and Arcade's abilities should keep him guessing for a bit."

"Titus needs to lead the attack against Abafando," Matthias added and manipulated the holo-images. "His speed oughta keep Abafando frustrated enough."

"Songbird should join him," I added and repositioned her smaller image, "her energetic, vivacious personality would also prove equally challenging for Abafando to keep down."

"I do believe that I shall like to have Maestro assist me in my advance against Switchblade," Mike motioned and moved Maestro and his own image to the location where Switchblade would most likely be waiting. "I'd appreciate his abilities to alter the trajectory of physical objects."

"Man," Marcus sighed, disappointed, "here I was hoping to have Mar—I mean, Maestro and NightOwl fight with me since we've already worked together before."

"Sorry, Marcus," Anthony shrugged his shoulder, "you can't have your cake and eat it too."

"Or in other words," Matthias added, "you can't fight with your favorite Disciples and win the battle."

"I do believe that Jade would be most advantageous

to you as well, Mike." Professor Bird remarked, bringing us back to practical discussion after we enjoyed a momentary chuckle. "And I think that Safeguard would make things most difficult for Carch.22."

"I think that we need either Catamount or Swift against Panther in the woods and the other in the desert on Catch.22," Titus said. "We need someone to track the Black Cat in the shadows and those two would be hard for the sniper to spot against the desert background."

I shrugged my shoulder, "Swift operates better in the desert; so let's place Catamount in the woods." I had wanted KT to join me and Joseph against Simon, but I would let things develop as God directed.

"I think that Matthias should take care of Catch.22," Marcus added, "his bulletproof skin should give him a huge advantage against the sniper.

Matthias nodded and moved his and Anthony's holographic form into position, "And Fletcher can go bow hunting in order to take care of the Panther with Catamount and Carpenter. But where do we put the others?"

"Atomizer and Oceanica work well together," I paused and considered the layout of the land a moment before adding, "and I think that he might be helpful against the Widow as she would likely position herself near the river."

"Why's that?" Titus asked.

"Because she'd expect me to be there," Luna answered. "I'm not only a traitor to her, but as an intelligent woman I've found the foolishness of God to be true. The only people alive today that she would hate more than me are Pentecost and Reverb."

"I supposed that you'll be taking Reverb with you to face off with Simon?" Marcus asked and began to move the two of us into position at the pinnacle of the mountain.

I nodded, "And since it'd be better to pair NightOwl and SongBird together, I'll take Clay with us."

"I'll remain aboard the jet to monitor the enemy's movement and prevent any ComBots from escaping from the mountain range." The Professor concluded.

"Well, we don't got a lot of time everyone, so we better get moving," Titus said and raced for the door in a blur. "Let's make this quick, 'cuz I got a date tomorrow night," he added before opening the door and disappearing down the hall.

The rest of the team made their way to the training room, which was being modified to mimic portions of the Black Mountain Range that we would be fighting on. There would be no way to simulate the entire battlefield or predict the manner of mutations that the ComBots would come against us with or the strategy of the enemy so this would simply be a set of warm up exercises for the seven 'cords' that would be fighting the Komplo.

I was concerned that this could be the first and last stand that these Disciples would be able to make in defense of the Church, but we didn't have any other option. The Defenders needed to entrust their legacy, their call, to the next generation, and the Disciples needed to inherit the call of the Defender Corps and carry it on in God's grace. The experience of the older generation needed to be passed down to the passion of younger; no matter what the price. And the passion of the youthful generation needed to be directed by their elder's legacy; no matter what the situation.

I could only pray that God would somehow see them through the ordeal of the next few days.

Chapter Thirty-Seven

"Due to a blunder on the part of our dear friend, Catch.22," Simon had begun his meeting, "Lunulata has transferred her alliance to the enemy."

"For a man with perfect aim, you surely do miss your target quite a bit, Catch." Panther remarked with a grin, clearly enjoying himself.

"Hey, I can't be held responsible for fluke movements of people in the line of fire." Catch.22 moved to the edge of his seat and spoke defensively.

"And what of Virus' inability to track down either Pentecost or Reverb?" Acedia asked. "It appears that we have more than one imbecile as a member of this Komplo."

"This is not a matter of my incompetence, " Virus countered stoically. "I have searched every database in existence for the names 'Timothy' and 'Joseph Stevens' based on what the two of you have told me," Virus referenced to Simon and Widow, "and they have all come up empty. The only facial recognition that I have been able to achieve have been of sightings of Pentecost or Reverb; their alternate identities are concealed by something other than technology."

"He's right," Simon spoke up. "There is a spiritual barrier guarding any information concerning the Stevens brothers."

"Isn't that supposed to be your forte?" Widow asked pointedly at Simon.

Simon kept his cool and ignored her accusational

tone. "I have been looking into the matter, however my spirit guides have been unable as of yet to penetrate the veil shrouding our enemies."

Catch.22 shuddered at the remembrance of his encounter with Simon's 'spirit guides', as Virus would have done if his physical form would respond to emotions such as fear. Both knew that a more proper label for them would be what the Defenders undoubtedly referred to them as: demons.

Widow disliked his constant reference to these spiritual entities, it reminded her of the way those ignorant Christians and primitive peoples of her land doted on about their gods. She reasoned that these guides were either Simon's intelligent way of appearing mysterious, or that more advanced and intelligent beings with gifts – telepathy, perhaps? – were the true source of his abilities.

"Regardless, we must anticipate that the enemy will be seeking to attack us in retaliation for our rehearsal at their base." Simon continued with an air of authority in his Germanic voice that few would question.

"Agreed," Panther growled, "the Defenders are wounded and humiliated and will be seeking a swift revenge."

"But an enraged enemy is harder to restrain," Abafando commented and took a drink. "I doubt that they will accept a second defeat easily.""

"I agree with you both," Simon continued, "However, I believe that we shall be better off if we maintain our position here rather than relocating our castle."

"I agree," Switchblade began to add, "After all, this position was chosen because of how easy it is to defend."

"I suggest that we encircle the base in anticipation of

an attempt to surround us." Abafando advised, his Russian accent greatly contrasted with Switchblade's. "The ComBots need a human to take orders from and if we assume a single front then the Defenders could surprise us from a different side, we may find ourselves overrun before we can correct the situation."

"I'll take the leeward side of the mountain," Catch.22 staked his claim on his position first. "The foliage is less dense and I'll have an open range on any target that might show up."

"I'll monitor the Mimbres River," Widow spoke up. "I'll take pleasure in executing the wench for betraying us."

Acedia and Abafando both took up positions near the top of the mountain, Switchblade along the tree line to the north, and Panther took the larger portion of woods to the south.

"I'll remain within the base and consult the spirits as the battle progresses," Simon concluded.

"Speaking of which," Panther spoke up with a finger raised, "how are those spirits coming with my upgrade?"

Simon reached into his cloak and pulled out a small syringe with a deep violet liquid. "Here you are my friend. They have finished the Nephilim-serum; I call it the 'Nepherum'." Simon caused the syringe to levitate across the room to Panther.

"And this will do all that you promised?" Panther asked grasping the syringe and admiring the light as it passed through the dark liquid.

"Yes. Superhuman strength, speed, stamina, instincts, and abilities consistent with your panther persona; you will rival the gods for a period of time after injecting yourself with this. The spirits have worked very hard to produce the Nepherum and your DNA is one of few that will accept their creation as each formula is as unique as a mindvoice."

Panther continued to admire the syringe and Simon cautioned, "I must remind you that this will likely inhibit your rational mind, nearly entirely. In many respects your body will be raised to the level of deity while your mind is debased to that of an animal."

"Don't worry, Sorcerer," Panther grinned and slipped that syringe into a small pocket in his left glove, "I can handle it."

"I'm sure you can," Simon replied, "but I must caution us all to be prepared; Timothy is no fool and neither is his Master. Lunulata has undoubtedly informed him of our ComBot army and they will not recklessly invade our castle without a plan in place by which they might conquer us."

"But the odds are against them in every way," Switchblade countered, "I don't see why –"

"Yes, Switchblade. You don't see." Simon interrupted. "But I do, for I have seen what these people – these Christians – are capable of with the aid of their Master. There are many levels of the spirit world that you cannot appreciate. I assure you, they do have an advantage, but their victory is not as certain as they would hope."

The two teams of Defenders had united into one and divided themselves into their seven smaller cords and boarded the Air Defender Jet, taking off in the direction of the Black Mountains. As they approached early in the afternoon, the Professor began to make a wide circle around the Mountain that would allow each cord to bail out and engage the enemy in their assigned locations.

In order to get them to the ground safely, the Professor had prepared a couple of hydro-electric, hover-technology equipped jet-skis for Lunulata and Oceanica and colored them to reflect their individual personas; Lunulata's displayed a large blue-ringed octopus swimming quickly through clear blue water, the long tentacles streaming back from the front of the jet ski, while Oceanica's displayed waves and jet bubbles rushing back as she flew forward. The Atomizer would be able to ride along or fly down by himself in order for all members of Cord 6 to reach the ground.

To get Cord 7 to the ground, Carpenter would flatten out his CW block into a large enough hang-glider so he could carry Catamount and Fletcher down in harnesses.

Cord 5 had determined that Jade would form a large giadan disk that she and Maestro would work together to keep steady and lower it safely to the ground with the two of them and Lancelot onboard.

Cord 2, which was composed of Alkali, Arcade, and Plasma who could all fly, were set to engage whenever Virus spotted them.

Cord 3 contained Firecracker – who was completely

capable of scaling the mountain long before the others even reached it – SongBird, and NightOwl, both of which could fly down to the mountain to engage with Abafando and Acedia. Cord 4 would touch down by having Safeguard create a force field to contain herself, Kevlar, and Swift as they dropped down to the ground like a giant, invisible bomb.

Within Cord 1, Pentecost himself could fly and both Reverb and Clay could absorb the impact of hitting the ground without being any worse for wear; though it had been discussed that Clay could also form himself into a parachute and lower the two of them down, they decided against the parachute idea because they would have to move as quickly as possible to breach the base while the others distracted the ComBots.

Pentecost and the Professor had already briefed the cords concerning the physical design of the ComBots and explained that Virus' program would mutate them with specific abilities and weakness – with the possibility that each ComBot could have a unique mutated ability set independent from the others – so that they would all know how to take them down. Each ComBot was designed to run as closely to the human body as possible – in the event that one of them would have to be put down – with the main processing unit contained within the cranial cavity, air needing to be taken into the body via the mouth and nose and stored in two 'lungs' in order for the proper nuclear reaction to take place within the liquid-electrium 'bloodstream' that flowed out from the generator 'heart' along artery pipes and back through the veins before being expelled again while communication throughout the body occurred via hardwire 'nerves', both of which followed the basic pattern of the human body as far as their general location were concerned, and a giadan skeletal structure was moved by a system of giadan 'muscles' that would contract when stimulated by the 'nervous system'.

It was decided that the Air Defender would fly directly to Mount McKnight and draw Virus' attention with his largest force for Cord 2 to fly out and meet after which the jet would bank hard to the north to drop off Cords 6 and 7 – with Carpenter guiding Cord 7 to their proper destination – before circling the mountain and allowing Cords 5, 4, and 3 to each take their turns to bail out; SongBird and NightOwl would leave the jet just before Cord 1 in order to meet up with Firecracker and distract Abafando and Acedia guarding the bases entrance.

The entire mission was designed to give each team the proper amount of time to reach the ground and begin engaging with the enemy, though no one had any way of knowing how the ComBot forces would be divided up, or what would happen if the Sorcerer or any of the others spotted them prior to them being able to position themselves; they didn't have time for such concerns because the fate of Earth rested on stopping the Sorcerer from being able to take over the planet with these ComBots.

As they approached the mountain they momentarily landed the jet to allow Firecracker to leave the plane and wait some distance off while the others were dropped off in the air; that way Firecracker could race up the mountain while the other members of his cord flew down and met him in time to engage the enemy together.

When the hatch opened Pentecost caught a glimpse out the door and the light pouring in the door seemed to trigger a vision. He could see angelic forces battling all around the mountain as angels and demons invisibly struggled for the upper hand while the Defenders fought against the Komplo.

The vision faded and Pentecost called out to all on the plane, "Take courage everyone; the Lord is fighting for us this day," he then gave a silent prayer of thanks unto the Lord for the faithful saints that were covering him and his team with their prayers.

The Sorcerer struggled to make contact with his demonic spirit guides, however they all seemed to be otherwise preoccupied and gave him no council and limited power could be drawn from the various incantations, charms, and idols that were at his disposal.

"Something is wrong," he muttered returning from his trance. He then solemnly messaged his team, *"There's change in the wind; everyone be ready."*

But there was no response, for no one heard him as the angels of heaven intercepted the demonic messages.

"We've been spotted," Fletcher called, looking up from the monitors in front of him. "We've got a group of ComBots coming to welcome us, Virus seems to be leading them."

"Cord 2, you're up," Pentecost called out and the three members moved to the back of the jet and flew out the door.

The Professor quickly turned the plane after the team had cleared themselves out of the flight path as Plasma, Alkali, and Arcade spread themselves out and charged through the ranks of ComBots, firing energy blasts as often as they could while avoiding the lasers that shot out from the eyes and palms of various ComBots surrounding them. They flew in semicircular patterns that crossed at specific intervals so they could take out the ComBots from each other's tails. They knew early on that they would be bearing the brunt of the battle as the ComBots would be stronger and more controlled being near to Virus.

The ComBots didn't alter their appearance in any way, and their abilities were generally limited to lasers. Those that projected from the eyes were more focused with a better aim while the blasts from the hands contained a higher energy level with greater consequences if the team were to be hit.

Alkali barrel-rolled to avoid a blast and grabbed the attacking ComBot, tore it in half with his energy field, and threw the pieces into another pair of ComBots which exploded and took out the others nearby.

Plasma maneuvered around the shattered remains of the ComBots and threw several large electrium blasts to detonate before finding it necessary to form a dechomain shield to absorb an unavoidable laser blast.

Arcade had quickly scanned the attacking horde with his helmet and figured out the weaknesses of the ComBots. Along with the lasers a few of the ComBots were moldable like clay and would form their bodies into weapons upon gaining a close proximity to the heroes. Arcade quickly activated the fire-mode and began to target the ComBots with this particular malleability as they had comparatively lower melting points and were weak against the heat generated by the suit; His plan was to exploit the various weaknesses found in the ComBot armies in order to thin out the numbers that came against them.

"Most of the ComBots have a basic mutation that lets them be perfectly balanced between movement speed, defense, attack speed, strength, and difficultly level," Arcade informed the rest of the members of his cord while dodging a blast and retaliating with a fiery stream that melted the ComBot before him.

"So they're decent at everything without any real flaws or strengths?" Plasma asked as she absorbed the laser blast from one ComBots eyes and used that energy to intensify her retaliatory electrium attack.

"The Professor said that the basic drawback would be that these guys would be limited in the attacks that they could use," Alkali replied using his energy to crush one ComBot and throw the crumpled form into another. "Lasers, electricity, and physical attacks with some limited shape shifting."

"So there's a lot of energy for me to absorb?" Plasma asked, throwing three energy blasts down at the three ComBots trailing behind Arcade.

"Oh, yeah," Arcade replied and threw a fireball at a ComBot approaching Alkali from the side, "and I'll filter through and take out the special ComBots."

"Sounds good, we have to make sure that the Air Defender and the other Cords make it to their locations without being overtaken by the ComBots," Alkali commented as he covered Plasma with a force field, causing a rapidly approaching ComBot to slam into the side and fall down to the Earth.

"Everyone keep doing what you're doing and watch

each other's backs and we'll all make it through this together." Alkali said, as he and his Cord followed behind the Air Defender to encourage the ComBots to keep their distance.

During this time Cord 7 had bailed out of the jet and Carpenter was gliding the troop southward down the mountainside as quickly as they could to regain their defenses. Until then, the primary focus of Cord 2 was to keep the ComBots from taking down the glider.

The three landed and – after disconnecting the harnesses and reforming the Cainium-Wood – began to listen for signs of the Panther. Cord 2 was now able to be less protective of the group and moved to help cover the decent of Cords 6 and 5.

"We've got company," Fletcher said pointing upward as several ComBots located them and began to swoop down through the tree branches.

Catamount pointed to the woods to the right, "And that's not all." The bushes and trees came to life all around them with ComBots.

"Carpenter!" Fletcher called out and began to fire his arrows upward.

"I'm on it." Carpenter replied and motioned with his hands as several trees from nearby began to move and groan as their branches and roots began to puncture the abdomens of several ComBots, crush a few more, and strangle others within their reach while sweeping back and forth in search for more.

Catamount began to engage with those on the ground that escaped the trees and were approaching and Fletcher picked off those that were still in the air.

"Any idea what kind of mutation these ComBots have?" Catamount ducked and dove to avoid a wild swing followed by a laser blast before slicing the neck of one ComBot and stabbing deep into the back of another.

"Not yet," Fletcher used an explosive arrow to blast the head off of one ComBot and blocked the arm of another – its hand had transformed into a large club – with his bow before stabbing an electrically charged arrow into the torso of the Bot.

"I've got something," Carpenter spoke up as he formed a large battle hammer from his Cainium-Wood and swept three ComBots to the side with one swing. "The ComBots are really aggressive, actually a bit too aggressive. Their attacks are forced and almost desperate which leaves some major openings for counterattacks."

"So these brutes are going to take us out at any cost to themselves?" Fletcher asked as he broke off the weaponized arm of a ComBot with his bow and threw the spear-like shaft at another before shooting another exploding arrow at a cluster of others.

"That only goes for those on the ground. Look up there," Catamount said, directing the Cord's attention upward.

There were more circling above them out of range and firing down at them and Fletcher turned his attention to removing this new group from the skies above them.

A tree from behind him crashed down upon a crouching ComBot nearby. Catamount moved to try and cover both Fletcher and Carpenter as needed.

Catamount sniffed the air and told Carpenter, "I've

found the Panther."

"Where?" turning to face her and bashing his Cainium staff into a nearby ComBot's head and motioning for a tree to strangle a more distant one.

"He's running deeper into the woods; farther up the mountain. He's going to warn the others." Catamount sliced into the ComBot in front of her and began to run after the fleeting sounds of Panther's retreat.

"Catamount!" Carpenter called out.

Fletcher turned and realized that she was missing. "Where'd she go?"

Carpenter motioned in the direction she left in. "After Panther," was all he had time to say in between attacks.

"Can you hold them here?" Fletcher asked, in desperation.

Carpenter nodded, he was visibly tired and sweat poured down his face. "Go get her."

Fletcher nodded and took off to provide Catamount some back up as Carpenter continued to manipulate the trees as giant claws to take down the ComBots.

A few ComBots trailed the Air Defender as it circled its way around the mountain and Cord 6 disembarked with Lunulata and Oceanica aboard their jet-skis and headed for the river while Atomizer flew through the cainium skulls of the seven ComBots before landing gently on the edge of Oceanica's jet-ski. Moments later those seven ComBots that had been trailing the Air Defender plummeted to the ground with electricity sparking out of the miniature holes in their heads.

More ComBots peeled off from engaging with Cord 2

in order attack this new group of heroes.

Oceanica and Lunulata landed on a deep, slow moving section of the river and swam to shore to allow their suits to absorb some additional water for the coming battle as the ComBots closed in from above and landed on the shore. Atomizer ran atop the surface of the water and skidded to a stop on the soft silt just as the girls also reached the water's edge.

"What's the plan?" he asked, growing to full size.

"You take out the Bots in the air and keep an eye out for the Widow but do not engage her so we can focus on the ground troops," Lunulata answered him. "Oceanica it'll be important for you to stay hydrated from the river and I'll be needing you to keep an eye on me and give me a splash here or there so it'll be best to keep the fight close to the river. We'll just have to figure out the ComBot's mutations as we go."

"Got it," the two siblings answered with a nod and began to engage with their assignments.

After Atomizer took out several unsuspecting ComBots in his miniature size, several more shrunk down to the locate him and began to behave like several mentally unstable, animatronic versions of the Hornet from Osria. The swarm began to move towards Oceanica, with high-powered electric 'stings' at the ready once they were within range.

Atomizer intercepted them and shouted "Berühren Sie nicht meine Schwester!" Which is translated *"Don't touch my sister!"* He kicked one in the stomach and bounced off of it, flying directly into another with his fist striking into the face of another. He had to keep moving and bouncing to keep them from swarming him, but the rapid movement was beginning to drain his suit since he wasn't enduring a hard enough impact to power it up.

Lunulata vanished in a puff of smoke and moved over next to the nearest ComBot, grabbing its head and twisting sharply before jumping upon the next ComBot and twisting hard to bring it to the ground. "The ComBots have a heavy armor which slows there movement; the slower they move the harder you'll need to hit them." She called out to Oceanica as she continued to invisibly move to the next ComBot.

"I've got this," Oceanica said, covering Lunulata's advance by spraying an approaching ComBot with a firehouse-type blast and crushed it against a tree. She did her best to keep a foot in the river to maintain a full tank for her suit and to prevent a ComBot from approaching from behind.

Several more focused blasts and more ComBots fell to the ground with limbs, heads, or torsos sliced open by her waterjets.

Meanwhile, the jet had dropped off Cord 5 and Lancelot was able to use a sharpened boomerang to decapitate many of the approaching ComBots as Jade left commandeering the giadan disk to Maestro so she could help ward off the ComBots as they descended. Maestro was able to slow down their fall to prevent any injury, but the weight of three people atop of the disk made a frighteningly quick drop down to the Earth unavoidable.

As soon as they landed, the three of them faced outward in a triangle and prepared for a fight.

Lancelot began giving some quick instructions to the group, "Maestro, I'll need you to redirect any energy based attacks from Jade's section as she won't be able to deflect them herself."

"Got it," he replied readying his baton.

"I'll do my utmost to prevent any of the ComBots from getting too near. Jade, I would be most appreciative if you would be so kind as to assist me in holding off the enemy forces."

"It'll be my pleasure," Jade said, forming a jade-green giadan shaft in her right hand and a smaller knife sized object in her left.

Maestro began to gently wave his baton to have a gentle song flowing in the clearing they stood in when a ComBot fired an electrical blast at the group. Maestro raised his left hand and halted the blast, then waved it off to the side in beat with the song he was performing; it blindside another ComBot and fried the unsuspecting machine's circuitry. After which a nearby ComBot began to fire some giadan bullets out from a small hole on the top of its wrist and although Maestro was able to redirect much of the stream back at the mechanical horde, there were still some of the small bullets that were moving too rapidly to heed his commands.

Jade formed a large giadan shield that deflected the remaining bullets before motioning with her hands for that covering to branch off into three sections which flew forward and through several of the ComBots on the front line before circling back around and dealing with some others that had charged forward in the meantime.

Lancelot threw his boomerang just before rapidly drawing his sword and slicing a limb off of the closest ComBot, the boomerang decapitated a ComBot before returning to be caught just as Lancelot impaled a ComBot and he quickly threw the boomerang again before pulling his sword from the fallen Bot. Lancelot used his shield to absorb a laser blast from the left and cut down the ComBot to his right before needing to stab his sword into another Bot to his left and caught his boomerang with his now free right hand then he threw it again, ducked under the clubbed hand of a ComBot, bashed his head in with the edge of his shield, and retrieved his sword in time to block the sword-turned arm of a ComBot.

The boomerang returned and sliced off the head of the ComBot, but froze just before it also removed Lancelot's.

"I hope you don't mind if I borrow this," Maestro commented as he directed the boomerang to fly in a large circle around the group and leave several ComBots headless.

"Be my guest," Lancelot grunted as he continued to mow down the nearby ComBots.

Maestro continued to flail his arms around in a rhythmic fashion as the boomerang and several other rapidly moving objects from the ComBots swirled around them in time with the motioning of his hand to the song that he heard. If an energy blast was fired it received his immediate attention and was quickly absorbed by the nearest ComBot while any physical attack moving slowly enough to listen was caught up in the song and became part of the circulating tornado of weapons until they became too deeply lodged within a ComBot to respond any longer.

Jade continued to manipulate her giadan formations to crush, impale, or otherwise subdue the ComBots as her original giadan platform and shield were now morphing constructs that continued to dismember the ComBot army as it advanced.

"I'd say that we're dealing with a company of ComBots affected by Virus' basic mutational program," Lancelot said after observing the tactics and abilities of the ComBots. He then shifted left to finish off a ComBot when he noticed the glint of metal flying through the air towards Jade, pivoting to the right and barely managing to deflect a small throwing knife with his sword to prevent it from lodging itself inter her back.

"Everyone look sharp," Lancelot called and motioned with his sword in the direction the blade had come from, "our host has arrived."

Switchblade bowed dramatically and began to circle the group as they were preoccupied with the ComBots until he reached the side between Maestro and Jade where he threw out a handful of ninja stars in hopes that – at the very least – Lancelot would catch one of them in the back.

Maestro held up his left hand and the scattered stars froze in the air, "Sorry, that's in the wrong key for my song," he quipped as he began to pick a target for each blade, looked directly at an individual weapon, and then motioned with his eyes and hand to bury the star deep within the head or chest of a ComBot.

Switchblade realized he would have to change his approach as no one in the Komplo had anticipated these new warriors nor did they have any knowledge of their abilities, but there was something nagging at him that he would have to take care of before finishing off this bunch. He smiled methodically as he observed Lancelot battling the ComBots; studying each slice and cut, observing each combination, and appreciating every parry and thrust.

"This should be a very interesting game," he said to

himself as he continued to circle the trio and throw various sharpened objects at them; they were purely distractionary attacks as the main event of the battle was yet to come.

There was no need for Cord 2 to cover Cord 4, for no one could see Kevlar, Swift, or Safeguard as they plummeted invisibly within the force field produced by Safeguard. Prior to this attack, Safeguard had discovered that she had limited control over the movement of the force fields she created and she worked at maneuvering the invisible ball into clusters of ComBots and sent them careening downward in crushed forms. Safeguard strained to maintain the force field as they struck the mountain and formed a large crater on the surface.

"Can you hold it a bit longer?" Kevlar asked concerned.

"Yeah, it was just the landing," she replied weakly as she struggled to stay conscious, "I'll be fine."

"Ok," Kevlar looked up and down the mountainside from where they were at. Several ComBots came out of hiding all around them and began scanning the area for what had caused the disturbance with several staring directly at the crater that the invisible heroes stood within.

"We need to cut down on some of these numbers and get a better position before we start a fight," Swift began to push on the edge of the force field in order to edge it down the mountain.

Kevlar caught on and turned to Safeguard before helping, "Steer us over to the ComBots keep an eye on how fast we're moving, and slow us down when we need it."

Safeguard nodded and began to float within the force field as the two guys began to push the edge of the ball and sent it rolling down the mountain, running to keep up like they were in a giant hamster ball.

Safeguard controlled the direction and speed of the field with *Natsar* and plowed over several unsuspecting ComBots, crushing them into the rocky ground beneath. A few of them had used some kind of infrared detection method and sensed the presence of the force field while others could sense the body heat inside. Some narrowly escaped being crushed because of this knowledge while others began to fire lasers or electrical blasts that were deflected by the force field, frying or incinerating sections of the mountainside and several of their robotic comrades.

After they reached beyond the lowest ComBot sentry Safeguard deactivated the force field and returned everyone into the visible spectrum.

"They still have the high ground," Kevlar commented, "but there's less of them now we aren't surrounded any more. Did anyone see Catch.22 as we rolled down the mountain?"

Safeguard began, "No I –"

"Get down!" Swift yelled ducking down and motivating Safeguard to form a force field around herself as a bullet ricocheted off a rock behind Kevlar. Swift had been listening intently as the ComBots rushed down the mountain towards them and had heard Catch.22 readying his aim and move his finger to the trigger of his rifle.

"There," he said pointing upward for Kevlar to see, "right up there behind that large boulder; directly behind that patch of prickly pear cactus.

"I see him," Kevlar said drawing an arrow from his quiver. "Safeguard, Swift, do your best to not get shot while I try and get up to take that sniper down."

"You got it," Swift said and caused his four metal claws to protrude out from his gloves.

Kevlar swung his arm into the neck of a ComBot in front of him and removed its head and tried to climb farther up the mountain side; until another used its whip-like arm to wrap around his ankles and pull him back down to where he started. After freeing himself and regaining his footing, Kevlar ducked under the whip-like arm of a ComBot and tackled the ComBot before putting a deep dent into its face.

Swift had been busy slicing through the ComBots, removing heads and limbs while also gutting several of the robotics assailants. Swift kicked with his leg at the knee of a Bot, dove to avoid a bullet coming from Catch.22 , stabbed his claws into the torso of another ComBot and slashed diagonally upward and exited near the shoulder. "These ComBots get high marks for style, but there isn't a whole lot of power behind their attacks," He heard motion behind him so he ducked and spun around, cutting an approaching ComBot in two at the waist.

"Yeah, they seem to be going with the 'death by a thousand cuts' method of killing us." Kevlar drove his elbow back behind him and broke the ribs of an approaching ComBot before grabbing it by the neck and throwing it over his shoulder into another one standing a few feet in front of him.

"So we can't afford to get worn out or distracted," Safeguard said as she began to fling *Natsar* out and shoot force fields out, smashing them into the ComBots as though they were bowling pins. She lifted *Natsar* to block the hammer-turned fist of a ComBot moments before its head exploded due to an expanding force field from inside it. She then turned invisible and moved behind another ComBot before stabbing the sharp point of *Natsar* into the neck of the robot and the group continued to battle against the others.

"Swift, do you think you can make your way quickly and quietly to Catch.22's location?" Kevlar called out as he threw a ComBot up the mountain to preoccupy the sniper.

"Only if these ComBots get off my back," he said slicing through the face of a ComBot and ducking under an electrical attack while sweeping the legs out from under yet another Bot behind him.

"Safeguard?" Kevlar asked turning to look her direction and his fist went deep into the chest of a Bot that had moved behind him with his axe-hand ready to pound into his skull.

"I can only cover him for a few seconds," she rammed *Natsar* into the face of a ComBot and it crumpled to the ground, she stomped on its head for good measure before turning her attention to throwing several more force fields out to bash into more of the mechanical attackers, "I can't keep my focus for longer than that with all this carnage going on around me."

"I'll keep you covered," Kevlar assured her. "Swift, you've got maybe twenty seconds to find some cover before we have to refocus our attacks. Ready?" he asked them both before shouting to Swift moments later, "Go!"

Safeguard turned to render Swift invisible and he quickly cut off his claws to prevent them from getting in the way as he rushed over to some nearby desert brush to conceal himself. He quickly and quietly began to move from hiding place to hiding place behind the rocks, bushes, and cacti up the mountain to try and reach Catch.22 as quickly as possible.

Safeguard was able to keep Swift invisible for a bit longer than she originally thought and he used that to his advantage. Eventually, she had to stop in order to shield herself from an electrical blast and Kevlar continued to keep pounding through the ComBots.

Catch.22 was frustrated, but was developing the sense that he was going to have to change his technique. Instead of his normal routine of carefully watching in order to tactfully take a shot he was going to have to take on a more rapid fire approach and he was actually going to have to use some of Virus' modified bullets to get a clean shot as the African-American man seemed to be bulletproof and the redheaded girl kept disappearing. And the other guy kept moving and dodging his shots as though he knew they were coming; and where was that dude anyway?

He peeked his head up above the rocks he was hiding behind, ducked back down, and then fired three explosive bullets down in the direction of the young redhead below him. The three bullets exploded against a circular dome that formed around her as she blocked an attack from one of the ComBots.

"Blast it, Simon," he yelled. "What have you gotten us into?"

SongBird and NightOwl flew out from the Air Defender and dove down to the top of the mountain. SongBird had been singing a song of encouragement for all the Cords to hear the entire time she was aboard the jet and since the Professor had informed her that the ComBots would be immune to her emotion affecting songs – but their auditory sensors would still be just as sensitive to her mindsong scream – she wouldn't be singing very many other songs today. A cluster of ComBots diverted from attacking Cord 2 to try and intercept the two girls and SongBird unleashed a loud scream that sent several of them crashing into each other or plummeting to the ground before they rightened themselves, however a few of them were sensitive to the supersonic vibrations and the giadan within their skin and skeleton system shattered.

"Okay, now that was just amazing," NightOwl encouraged her friend and gracefully maneuvered around several of the attacking ComBots. As she phased her way through one and grabbed its 'heart' she pulled it out and caused the Bot to plummet to the ground as she grabbed the head of another and removed it from the robotic body.

The two girls continued their decent, with SongBird taking advantage of her smaller size and sparrow wings to dodge and weave around all the ComBots and causing several of them to fire upon their comrades, NightOwl was continuing to feel the similarities between her own aerial flight and the dance lessons she had been taking for years.

The two reached the foggy surface of the mountain top as Firecracker raced through and cut a trail in the fog.

"Okay, girls," he said coming to a stop in front of them, "here's the plan: keep moving so that Abafando can't trap you with the mindfog and Acedia can't blast your mind with her sorcery. We gotta clear the doorway for Cord 1 to get through to the Sorcerer. Just do your thing and we'll be home in time for dinner. Any questions? Good." He said racing off to begin crashing into and through the nearest

ComBots.

NightOwl grabbed SongBird's shoulders and phased them both as a laser fired through them and melted a hole through a ComBot behind them.

"He doesn't stick around very long, does he?" SongBird asked before screaming toward the laser firing ComBot in front of her; the scream threw the ComBot back into the tree and caused it to become impaled on a branch.

"I guess not," NightOwl replied as they both readied their wings and took off to take care of the surrounding ComBots.

SongBird flew forward towards a group of three ComBots standing in a close triangle with two standing off to the side while one stood in between them a bit farther back. She quickly flew between the first two ComBots and kicked her legs forward, planting them squarely into the chest of the other ComBot and pushed off of that ComBot with her feet and flapped her wings to propel her in the other direction with a mighty spin, which caused the tip of her wings to barely touch the ground as she knocked the other two ComBots aside.

When she looked back she noticed that the first ComBot had crumpled under the force of her kick, literally as its chest was dented inward and it lay on the ground laboriously taking in air. The other two ComBots fared similarly and were struggling with broken limbs and sever injuries.

"Hey guys, take a look at this," she called to the rest of her cord as she flew off to take down some more robots.

NightOwl looked down from where she flew, "It looks like they don't have a very high physical defense, must be because of the mindfog surrounding them." She phased through a ComBot just as another one behind her fired a laser and incinerated its partner.

"Yeah, and that's why the ComBots following from above won't fly down here," Firecracker threw an explosive upward into the air then crashed through a ComBot on the ground as he ran; the explosion took out three flying ComBots and Firecracker continued to race by and crash into the ground based ComBots. "Their programing would get fried if they came down here, but their bodies would be fine. You girls focus on getting rid of those up there and I'll make quick work of the ones on the ground."

"You got it man," NightOwl called back as she silently arched upward and flew through ComBot after ComBot and pulled out important hardware as she did. She open her wings like a canvas and spun, kicking her legs out and gripping a ComBot's head with her ankles and sent it spiraling out of control as she continued her spin and began to fly in the opposite direction.

SongBird continued to do her best to take out the ComBots as she sang a song of encouragement to her teammates, which was pretty easy considering how well things were going at the moment. She let out a mighty scream that caused the auditory sensors in the ComBots directly ahead of her to explode within their heads and their hands went up and clutched the sides of their heads in pain.

After all the other Cords began to divert the attention of the ComBots, Cord 1 began to descend down toward the peak of the mountain.

As they made the drop down to the mountain, the

Professor still struggled to out maneuver the ComBots that trailed him aboard the Air Defender and flipped several switches and pushed many buttons to activate some of the temporarily automated defensive maneuvers of the jet in order to allow him to move over to the weapons station and activate the offensive systems to target the ComBots in time for him to make it back to the pilot's controls and avoid having a ComBot laser blast through the jet's side.

Pentecost dropped the fastest as he was able to aid his decent with a torrent of wind flying behind him, though Reverb was close behind because he was able to similarly propel himself with sound blasts. Just before landing, Pentecost pulled up and hovered as Reverb slammed into the ground moments later with a large crater forming around him and a local tremor sent the ground around them rippling outward and several ComBots were thrown upward by the blast.

Firecracker had to leap over the rippling terrain and skidded to a halt. "Easy man, we don't need to take the whole mountain down," he wheezed. Pentecost began to grow concerned about the stamina of all the team members as Firecracker disappeared again to finish routing out the ComBots within the mindfog.

Moments later, Clay reached the ground having flattened himself out moments before landing to allow him a quicker advance towards the Komplo's base along with the others.

As the three ran into the headquarters, they immediately found themselves entering the Komplo's own version of a Welcome Center with several ComBot sentries rapidly firing laser blasts from their eyes and hands along with several other electrical blasts streaming towards the main entrance. It was so intense that the three had to back up in order to avoid being blasted.

Pentecost turned to his brother. "Reverb," he began.

"I'm on it," Reverb replied as the two of them would often know what the other was thinking without using words or communication with a GRID connection.

Reverb knelt down and began to send out a rhythmic pulse through the ground that vibrated down the hall to the ComBots and caused a minor earthquake to shake up the Welcome Center. Pentecost then grabbed both Clay and Reverb by their arms and flew down the hallway in a molecular state.

When they entered the Welcome Center again, several of the ComBots were sprawled on the floor due to the tremors, and their disorientation was combined with the surprise of suddenly having three men appear throughout the room who began taking them out.

Clay had stretched his hand forward to wrap around the neck of a ComBot and constricted his grip as he pulled backward on the Bot and slammed him into two others before throwing it against the wall.

"This doesn't seem like a very big defense force," he said as he used that momentum to throw his right leg out in an elongated, roundhouse kick into the head of another ComBot that was readying its laser eyes. Clay ducked to the ground to avoid an electrical blast and stretched his leg out again to not only sweep but wrap around and grip the ankle of the ComBot and throw it against the same wall as his previous, robotic companion.

Reverb ducked underneath a swing from the ComBot

directly in front of him as he moved forward and jammed his elbow into its back before throwing his hands forward and sending three ComBots flying back into the walls behind them with a sound blast.

"The Sorcerer would have most of his forces outside with the others," he commented as he swung his arm to the left and into the face of a ComBot before diving to the right to avoid being hit by the deadly laser of another Bot.

"I don't think he was expecting us to make it this far," Reverb added as he came up rolling and threw his fisted hand forward and moments later the ComBot's head exploded from being hit by an intense sound blast as Reverb rose up and jammed his knee into a close standing ComBot's torso and brought both his hands down on its back.

Pentecost had drawn his sword and slashed open the chest of one ComBot when another fired a laser from its hand at him. He deflected the laser into another ComBot with his sword as he continued his advance toward the one that had fired the laser. Another threw an electrical blast that was absorbed by the sword moments before the heated blade removed the head off of the laser blasting Bot.

Pentecost then pivoted around and blocked the sword-turned-forearm of a ComBot – his blade already began to radiate heat and partially melted the ComBot's weapon – and positioned himself to avoid being electrically blasted as he bore down under the pressure being exerted upon his blade. He kicked at the knee of the robot and sent it kneeling to the ground moments before its head was removed and Pentecost then cut to his right to bring his sword into the chest of a ComBot while also swatting away another electrical blast. He then molecularized and moved to eliminate the final ComBot more efficiently; moments later the electricity firing ComBot fell to the ground, limbless and with a stab wound through its robotic heart.

It was then, after all the ComBot sentries had been defeated, that Pentecost and Reverb were able to hear the sound of Catamount calling for help and several oaths from the realms milled about in their minds.

"Perhaps Simon was expecting us, and had these ComBots here only to slow us down," Pentecost looked to the two young men in the room with him, "He knew that we wouldn't make it past this point anyway."

† † † † † † †

Panther could hear the jet approaching before the attack started, but he assumed that it was a typical jet because neither the Sorcerer nor Virus had alerted the Komplo of any danger. When the sounds of explosions could be heard in the skies above him he knew that they were under attack and he could see the Air Defender rapidly approaching.

As he gazed upward, Panther could see that there were three figures flying about and destroying much of their ComBot army as Virus led the charge against the Defenders; Virus had chosen to appear just as the other ComBots under his command during the battle, only larger and more foreboding. Panther braced himself when he saw a large glider descend out from the plane and move in his direction with two individuals dangling from harnesses.

Once the trio landed he observed the way they combated the ComBot for a few moments and began to realize that this was what the Sorcerer had meant when he said that Pentecost would not be so foolish to commit suicide, but would instead come prepared in expectation of victory.

He was the first to spot them and began to quickly and quietly make his way back to the side entrance of the Komplo base, and when he heard the sound of someone following him he halted to listen intently as he crouched down low to the ground. It had to have been the girl, for the others would certainly cause too much noise for either of them to be moving this quickly and silently.

Panther then removed the syringe that the Sorcerer had provided him with and gazed at the light shining through it for a moment before stabbing the needle into his thigh and injecting himself with the liquid.

He could immediately feel the burning effects of the potion and inhaled sharply, his eyes darkening as his pupils widened. His eye teeth became elongated fangs and his muscles expanded, pulling his suit tight over his body and tearing at some of the seams. Meanwhile his mind had also been effected and became quite brutish and debased itself to the level of an animal; he began to perceive the world as a panther would as he sniffed the air looking for his prey.

He snapped his head around quickly as he heard the sound of Catamount coming upon him in the forest. In his demented state, he saw a potential mate rather than prey. "Hey there, pretty kitty," he purred to entice her, "want to have some fun?"

Catamount was taken back by this and was unsure as how to respond.

"Oh, come on," Panther said gently as he moved towards her, still remaining close to the ground and moving on all fours, "I'm not so bad, and I know I can convince you to enjoy it."

Panther then leapt forward at Catamount and she dove to the side to avoid his grasp, each of them coming up rolling.

"Come on now, Pretty-Kitty" Panther chided mockingly, "we don't have time to 'play cat & mouse'." Panther licked his lips in anticipation and delight.

Again, Panther jumped for Catamount to tackle her and pin her to the ground. However this time she dove underneath him and rolled, swinging her legs upward and kicking him in the stomach as she went. Panther buckled and rolled but was no worse for wear and quickly charged toward Catamount when he heard the sound of an arrow whistling through the woods. Panther then vanished into the shadows of the forest moments before an arrow struck the truck of a nearby tree and Fletcher marched up to Catamount through the trees.

"We've got to stay and work together Catamount," he scolded, moving under the shadow of a tree. "This isn't a training session, girl. We can't afford to go and do our own thing here in the real world because there will be real stuff happening that won't just go away when the simulation ends."

Fletcher slowly began to struggle and his words became more labored as he spoke until he coughed and spat out blood. Then the shadow above him shifted and solidified into the form of Panther perched atop of Fletcher's shoulder with his clawed fingers still protruding out from his chest, for in his shadowed form Panther had been able to slowly insert his clawed hand into Fletcher's windpipe and the arteries in his neck.

"Well, now Pretty-Kitty," Panther sneered, "we can return to our game."

Fletcher fell forward and Panther leaped from his shoulders toward Catamount, who was paralyzed at the sight of Fletcher's death.

The two rolled and struggled on the ground for a brief moment before Panther quickly pinned Catamount's hands to the ground above her head and he sat atop of her.

"I promise to make this pleasurable my dear," he whispered, "and afterward we may feast on our intruder" he added referring to Fletcher's fallen form.

Catamount attempted to throw him off but the potion had increased his strength beyond what she was able to fight against.

Just as Panther threw his head forward towards Catamount, roots from the soil beneath her shot upward out of the ground and pulled him back and off of her, wrapping tightly around his chest, arms, and neck. Panther attempted to unleash a roar through his constricted throat as he fought against the massive roots before a Cainium-Wood spear penetrated his twisted mind.

Catamount turned and saw the fatigued form of Carpenter make his way towards her. "Thanks," she whispered.

Carpenter only nodded but didn't answer until after he pulled his Cainium-Wood out from the side of Panther's head and extended his hand to Catamount. "Do you think we can work together now?" he asked her pulling her up from the ground.

Just then another troop of ComBots emerged from behind the trees and surrounded the two heroes.

"Can't you take them out with the trees?" Catamount asked as the two stood back to back.

Carpenter shook his head, "I'm too worn out from holding the others off for so long. We'll have to go with my usual strategy."

"Which is what exactly?" Catamount asked readying her claws.

Carpenter glanced over his shoulder. "Run fast and scream a lot."

"What?" Catamount asked in disbelief.

"It's just a joke, okay?" Carpenter chuckled and then added, "But seriously though, the battle cry does help you attack and startle the bad guys."

When the ComBots had closed in enough, Carpenter let out a yell as he split his Cainium-Wood into two sections and formed the one piece in his right hand into a large shield and a sword formed from the other piece in his left hand.

A laser charred the shield as he moved forward and stabbed his sword into the chest of the ComBot and followed by slamming the shield into another. Carpenter then ducked under an attack and thrust his sword upward through the ComBot's torso and commanded the wood to grow outward and branch off to impale three others behind the first before it all shrunk back down and returned to its original sword formation.

Catamount shrugged her shoulder and charged forward, slashing off limbs and cutting open torsos as she moved through the ComBots. Eventually, Catamount brought herself to unleash a battle cry, which erupted from her throat as a mighty roar that threw several ComBots back into the trees and several others clutched the sides of their heads while others stumbled in bewilderment.

"Now that's what I'm talking about!" Carpenter called out as he blocked the battle-axe turned hand of a ComBot and removed it with his sword before also removing its head.

Catamount then signaled to the other Cords, *"Hey guys, we've got some problems. Panther is down, but so is Fletcher and Carpenter is limited in his abilities. We need some back up. Fast!"*

Pentecost's first solution was to send Firecracker to quickly get Fletcher out and help Carpenter and Catamount. However, he quickly found out that wasn't truly an option.

Firecracker had been plowing through the ComBots left and right and throwing explosives to take out clusters, but he knew that something wasn't right because he was breathing heavy and sweating profusely which wasn't normal for him. He slowed down and leaned against a tree to try and hold back a wave of nausea that threatened to overtake him.

Then he looked up and saw Kaleigh Thomas, his wife who he had met back before moving to Utah she worked together with him for the past several years in the SOS Corps.

"Titus," she said sweetly, "when are you going to stop this nonsense?"

Firecracker shook his head and tried to focus as his mind became clouded and the ground seemed to shift beneath him.

"What about the life we were going to live together?" Kaleigh asked earnestly. "This life as Defender will kill you, and then what will become of me? You spend so much time trying to save the world, but what about me? What about us?"

Firecracker was so tired, he knew that if he sat down and rested for a moment he could sort through what was happening and what Kaleigh was saying so he slowly lowered himself down even though there was a nagging feeling that he desperately needed to stay standing.

"That's it," she said soothingly, "just rest now. There are many others that can help, so you don't have to fight this battle."

SongBird had been circling the area and several ComBots had plummeted to the ground due to the fierceness of her scream and her tenacious combat style when she first caught sight of Acedia and Abafando through the mindfog.

"I've found them!" she called out to the rest of her cord and saw Firecracker sitting directly in front of Acedia, a violet cloud swirled about his head as she swirled her hands out in front of her.

SongBird called out to Firecracker with a gripping song of battle and perseverance as she tried to urge him to his feet, "Get up Firecracker. You've got to stand up!" But he couldn't hear her through the mindfog and Acedia's mind poisoning.

SongBird flew lower and ComBots began to leap up to snatch her from the air and other tried to shoot her down as well, but she would not be deterred. She inhaled deeply as she flew towards Acedia and let out a loud scream and while the mindfog muted the sound enough to prevent Acedia from going deaf, it was still painfully loud. Acedia dropped to her knees and covered her ears as the violet cloud around Firecracker dissipated.

Abafando moaned, he had been struggling with

holding back Firecracker and the other heroes as best as he could, but his age had limited his abilities and he had been overexerting himself for most of the battle. SongBird's final scream was simply too much for him and as he struggled to muffle the sound and protect Acedia a major blood vessel in his brain ruptured and he began to experience the horror of having his own body refuse commands as he had a stroke and his brain stem was slowly crushed by the pressure of the blood filling his cranium.

When Acedia lost her focus and her allusion faded, Firecracker was able to see her standing where Kaleigh had once been and he stood to his feet. The trees around him began to spin and he heard Acedia hiss, "You fool. I would have given you a blissful death, but now you shall suffer under the Widow's venom."

It was then that Catamount had called out to everyone within hearing and Pentecost messaged in response, *"Hang on guys, help is on the way. Firecracker, do you think that you can get Fletcher out and help Cord 7 for a bit?"*

Firecracker smiled weakly as he struggled to remain upright, *"I'd love to man…but…I'm gonna need…someone to…carry me outta here…"* his voice trailed off and he collapsed to the ground.

"Firecracker!" SongBird cried out and swooped down, plowing her wings into several structurally weakened ComBots in the process.

NightOwl moved to her side and urged her to stay calm, "If you panic, than anyone hearing your song will start to panic."

"So what are we going to do?" SongBird asked as she struggled to compose herself.

"We refocus," NightOwl explained. "We've taken out the ComBots circling us above, so now we move to the ground troops and hope that they're still weakened once the mindfog clears."

"Where'd Acedia go?" SongBird asked, looking around.

"I don't know," NightOwl shook her head, "she ran under the tree cover and I lost sight of her after that; we have to keep this doorway clear for the others to get out."

"Okay," SongBird answered as the ComBots began to circle around them and close in. "How are we going to do that exactly?"

Kevlar and Safeguard struggled to keep the ComBots and Catch.22 busy in the hopes that no one would notice that Swift had disappeared and begin searching the area for him. One ComBot began to look up the mountain side but his search was cut short by a force field crushing his cainium skull.

Kevlar ran at another ComBot, kicked his knee up into its stomach and brought his hands down hard unto its neck when it doubled over. Kevlar took a step forward and felt a laser blast enter his thigh – his skin was impact-proof but not energy-proof – and he dropped to the ground and rolled to his knee.

Safeguard saw him fall and moved to his side and created a force field around the two of them and asked urgently, "Are you all right?

"I'll be fine," he lied. He knew that it was only a matter of time before the femoral artery that had ruptured in his leg bled out and he died.

Kevlar looked up at Catch.22, "We need to buy Swift some time, and with us both here in this bubble the ComBots have plenty of time to realize he's missing."

"Well, what do you suggest?"

Kevlar thought for a brief moment before answering, "Do you think that you could launch us all the way to Catch. 22's location?"

Safeguard looked up the mountain, "I think so."

"All right. When we get up there I want you to release the force field as soon as I say so and duck behind your shield. Hit the ground rolling and be ready to fight off some ComBots."

Safeguard nodded, aimed upward towards Catch.22's location and the force field flew forward as Safeguard swung *Natsar*. "Now Safeguard," Kevlar called out as they approached and the force field disappeared as Safeguard tucked up behind *Natsar*. She narrowly missed hitting Catch. 22's head as he ducked to avoid being hit; Kevlar also flew over the sniper and both heroes hit the ground rolling moments later.

Catch.22 had dove to the side to gain some distance between himself and the oncoming heroes and as he came up rolling he found himself staring into the face of Swift through the bushes.

Swift threw an uppercut towards Catch.22's gut and the sniper moved his rifle to block the swing. Swift diverted his swing slightly and activated his claws a second time as he brought his right hand – claws also extended – down at Catch.22's side as Swift's left four claws cut through the action of his rifle and those on his right hand cleanly removed his sidearm from his hip without damaging him.

A ComBot suddenly flew over and tackled Swift before any further attacks against the sniper could be taken. Swift squirmed in the ComBot's grasp until he could plunge his metal claws into its torso and the ComBot and Swift crashed into the ground and he came up rolling from the wreckage.

Kevlar was fading and he knew it, he could just barely stay on one knee and defend against the nearby ComBots to try and aid the two young heroes.

Unarmed, Catch.22 moved over behind Kevlar and pushed him to the ground and placed a foot on his chest.

"You can't escape it Catch," Kevlar stated breathing heavy.

Catch.22 huffed mockingly, "Escape what? You are the one in danger."

Kevlar shook his head, "You think you're in control, but you're the one in a catch-22 problem; 'cuz the darkness threatens to consume you as you flee the very One that desires to save you. You can't escape it without Him, and there is no outrunning Him."

With that Kevlar fell asleep and awoke in the presence of his Lord. Catch.22 turned and ran off weaponless through the Komplo base, and abandoned the battle.

It wasn't until a bit later that Swift realized that Catch.22 had disappeared and messaged Pentecost about it and Kevlar's death as he and Safeguard continued their struggle for survival against the ComBot army.

Alkali rapidly fired three energy blasts at three different ComBots as he flew through the air and followed by shooting a stream out towards a lone ComBot in the fray; the force of the blast halted his movement and even pushed himself backward, but the ComBot didn't fall as the others had.

"What?" Virus' mechanical voice boomed across the sky, "You thought that software was the only thing I could upgrade? I don't need to shapeshift as much as these pawns so I was able to replace much of my original giadan structure with cainium. It makes for a more durable armor," Virus flexed his arm as a fire ball struck him from behind.

"Less talking, more fighting," Arcade quipped as he flew by. He quickly transformed his suit to ice mode and began to skate around on newly formed ice paths and made his way around the sky freezing the ComBots that had lower body temperatures and couldn't break free as easily; the ComBots were either shut down by the solidifying of their liquid electrium bloodstream, or plummeted to the ground trapped in a giant ice cube.

Arcade glitched to avoid a retaliatory laser blast from Virus and found himself off his path and dropping towards the ground. He quickly switched over to his standard suit as his quick scan of the battlefield declared that most of the ComBots with special mutations had already been taken out and the standard suit would work best against the average mutation of the ComBots.

Plasma used a dechomain field to absorb Virus' optical laser blast aimed for Arcade and used the added energy to intensify an electrium explosion that took out a large contingent of ComBots behind Alkali.

Alkali dismantled one ComBot and blasted a second with an energy blast before flying through the sky to keep his eye on Virus.

Pentecost messaged asking if there was an opening for one of them to assist with some evacuations of fallen members. *"I know that you guys are dealing with the largest force; I'm just trying to feel out my options here."*

"Sorry, man," Alkali replied just prior to being tackled by a ComBot and the two struggled for dominance, *"we've got our hands full up here."*

Lunulata had been making her way through the ComBots, surprising the moderately armored robots and putting them out of commission while Oceanica continued to blast and slice the more heavily armored and lumbering ones and Atomizer continued to bounce around like a miniature pinball.

"Hey, Lunulata?" Atomizer called out, "I found that crazy lady with the spider-webs."

"Where is she? Do not engage her Atomizer," Lunulata warned him a second time.

"Yeah, I heard you the first time, but she didn't." Atomizer called back as he narrowly avoided being snared by her webbing and crashed into a heavily armored ComBot mimicking the Scorpion.

Atomizer jumped back to avoid being crushed by his powerful hands and dove to the side to avoid the painful electrical energy blast that he fired from his wrist. He turned in time to see the Widow leaping towards him and quickly put his hands out to catch her wrists and extended his legs out as he dropped to the ground, catapulting her into the air.

The Widow flew through the air and fired a web-line to tether herself to a tree and swung out towards the camouflaged Lunulata, growing to full size and dropping down on top of her.

The two women tumbled and each one came up rolling away from each other. Lunulata vanished in a puff of smoke and began to approach Widow from behind, but the Widow was able to feel her footsteps and hear her approach and spun around swinging her knee towards the invisible Lunulata.

Lunulata caught the knee moments before it hit her and saw that Widow had drawn her two poisoned daggers and was about to aggressively stab them into her chest. Lunulata reacted by throwing Widow's leg away from herself. Widow was momentarily surprised by this move and was thrown off-balance but managed to catch herself before falling to the ground.

"So you want to play with venom, Widow?" Lunulata asked threateningly as she readied the incurable toxins stored in her gloves and her hands began to glow iridescent blue.

With Lunulata preoccupied with the Widow, Oceanica and Atomizer had to work harder to keep the ComBots at bay.

The Scorpion-Bot fired his short-distance electrical blast to try and corral Atomizer. Atomizer's suit, which had not endured a hit in a while, had used up a great deal of its stored energy and he was essentially grounded in his miniaturized state until he could endure a controlled impact to recharge it.

The next time the Scorpion fired an energy blast, Atomizer didn't attempt to avoid it and – while his suit was recharged by taking on a large portion of the effects – the pain was excruciating and the shock of the blast through him back several inches – a great distance remembering that they were only a few centimeters tall – and he struggled to regain his bearings. Atomizer had a high pain tolerance level beyond the absorption granted by the suit, but everyone has their limits and Atomizer was nearing his.

The ComBot sought to capitalize on its fallen prey and moved to grasp Atomizer in its iron grip. However, Atomizer was able to recover enough to launch himself forward and tackle the ComBot, completely removing the upper portion of the robot's body as he continued to fly beyond it.

He then bounced off of a tree branch and landed on the ground, growing to full size behind a ComBot and flipping it over his back in order to slam his fist into its head before shrinking back down and flying towards another; he had a lot of energy from that electrical blast and it had to be released rather quickly to avoid an overload. To bring his power levels back down to normal levels, Atomizer began to spray small bursts of his shrink ray at the ComBots. Several of them had their limbs or heads shrink and tear off of their bodies.

Meanwhile Oceanica was beginning to lag, she threw one ComBot back with a highly pressurized stream of water and had to throw her knee into a ComBot at close quarters and quickly removed its head with a waterjet. When she looked down she realized that the water level of the small pool had lowered and was farther away now. She looked up and pushed back another ComBot as she stepped backward to move closer to the water's edge and stumbled over a stone.

As Oceanica struggled to regain her balance a ComBot dove for her and tackled her into the water and as her suit quickly rehydrated she increased the water pressure to crush the head of the ComBot holding her under and launched herself upward out of the water as though she were standing upon a geyser, with water spraying up from the pool like a fountain. From this height she began to circle around and continued to pin the ComBots down with her torrents of water.

One such outpouring swept through the area were Lunulata and Widow stood and had both a rejuvenating effect on Lunulata and a draining effect on Widow's suit.

Lunulata grabbed Widow's wrist when she came charging forward with her daggers and quickly swung her legs up and twisted at the waist to lock her feet over the shoulders of Widow before using her momentum to drop to the ground and flip the Widow over herself; the two landed with Lunulata still holding the hands of the shrinking assassin and her ankles were now wrapped tightly around Widow's neck as well.

Lunulata pleaded with Widow to stop fighting and surrender, but she only continued to struggle and strain against Lunulata's grasp on her, so Lunulata was forced to maintain her tight hold until Widow stopped moving for a lack of air.

Once Lunulata was convinced that the Widow would not rise, she messaged the rest of the Defenders, *"Widow is down."*

She quickly made her way to the nearest ComBot and continued her fight against the army when Pentecost replied, *"Can you spare Atomizer for a rescue mission?"*

Lunulata looked around at how many ComBot were in the area, those that had fallen along with those still standing, and the thought of losing a Cord member wasn't pleasant considering how many there were left to fight.

The ComBot Lunulata had targeted was now on the ground with its neck broken and she picked another target, "Atomizer? How's the battle against the shrunken ComBots going?"

"There's still a ton of them left out here," Atomizer coughed as he grew to break free of a chokehold from a Mantis-type ComBot; the ComBots arms had been ripped off in the process. Atomizer stood bent over for a moment before a ComBot mimicking the fighting style of Ant grew and flipped backward to throw its knee into Atomizer's head.

Atomizer fell back to the ground, jumped back up, grabbed the ComBot's right wrist with his left hand, and threw his fist into the ComBot's chest; the ComBot's arm was removed at the shoulder as the ComBot itself flew backward into a nearby tree.

"We've got a bunch of INSECT enabled ComBots, and we can't lose the only Defender we have that can combat them." Lunulata messaged apologetically as another ComBot fell before her.

Switchblade had made his way around Cord 5 a second time and was now directly in front of Lancelot when he commanded the ComBots to pull away from him and focus on the other two.

"You carry a sword," Switchblade called to him forming a blade in his right hand, "are you any good with it?"

Lancelot stepped forward and the other two repositioned themselves to cover each other, "Wielding a blade does not lead a boy to become a man, but true submission to the Creator of men allows us to be deemed worthy of manhood."

"Spare me the speech, drongo," Switchblade replied dismissively, cutting left, then right as Lancelot approached.

Lancelot blocked the first strike with his shield and the second with his own blade. At this point, he was at a decisive disadvantage as Switchblade had been studying his fighting style and undoubtedly had discovered various weaknesses or flaws to capitalize upon. Even though Lancelot currently had the advantage in weapons as he carried both a shield and sword, he knew nothing of Switchblade's abilities or style and would have to spend a great deal of time attempting to feel him out even though he'd already been worn out from the war with the ComBots while Switchblade was still fresh.

Switchblade switched to a left handed grip to try and limit Lancelot's ability to block with his shield. Lancelot cut from his right to draw Switchblade's blade away and drove the edge of his shield forward towards his face.

Switchblade drew some metal away from the blade in his left hand – which shortened the sword considerably – and formed a Sai in his right hand to catch the shield between the prongs; the two continued to struggle for control in a battle for dominance.

"You're not bad, for a tired drongo," Switchblade said through clenched teeth. "I would have enjoyed finishing this dual of ours," he added, almost regretfully and apologetically. Lancelot inhaled sharply as Switchblade recalled his scattered weaponry from around the forest and it stabbed through the Defender on its way to Switchblade's gauntlets.

"We've got a problem," Jade said, looking over to the side as Lancelot fell at Switchblade's feet.

"It's worse than that," Maestro replied after a moment

of contacting the group and informing them of Lancelot's defeat, "Pentecost says that it'll be a while before we get any help."

"So what do we do?" Jade formed a giadan shield to block a large rock tree that had been thrown by a ComBot.

Maestro thought for a moment when an idea occurred to him. "Can you make me a giadan shaft about two feet long and keep me covered for a while?"

Jade fashioned the giadan pole and held it up for him, "Sure. What are you going to do?"

Maestro nodded to the giadan and the shaft began to levitate, "I'm going to keep that assassin distracted so long as you keep me alive, but I'm going to need your help in a minute or two."

"Okay," she replied and the two shifted their focus.

Maestro commanded the shaft to fly directly at Switchblade as several stones and dead trees begin to swirl around the assassin. Switchblade deflected the giadan projectile and worked at swatting away the stones and other objects with his two, newly fashioned, swords.

A ComBot fired an electrical blast at Maestro and Jade had to form a giadan disk underneath him and shift him to the side. Maestro struggled to remain standing atop of the giadan disk like a novice surfer. Several objects swirling around Switchblade – that followed the lurching motion of their conductor – haphazardly careened into the swordsman; several stones struck him in the back and a large, dead tree branch nearly clubbed him in the face.

"Jade," Maestro called out as he increased the tempo and the objects began to swirl around Switchblade at an increased speed, "do you see it?"

Jade looked behind her and saw the giadan shaft she had made stabbed deeply into a live tree directly behind Switchblade. "Switch!" she called out as she dropped control of the giadan disk holding Maestro aloft and spun around to face Switchblade.

Maestro resumed controlling his hover craft and moved out of Jade's way and began to cover her from the various ComBot attacks, as much of the debris swirling around Switchblade was now diverted and flying full force in this new direction a large branch had nearly knocked his sword out of his left hand and several stones pelted him from behind.

Meanwhile Jade threw another giadan disk toward Switchblade while simultaneously commanding the shaft to remove itself from the tree and move up behind him. Switchblade swatted away the projectile in front of him, but didn't know about the one behind him until it crashed into his head and knocked him unconscious.

"It worked," she said, returning to directing her giadan weapons into the surrounding ComBots.

"Hey Pentecost, Switchblade is knocked out, but it'd be really cool to get some help down here ASAP." Maestro messaged as the two surviving members of Cord 5 struggled to keep themselves as such.

"What are we going to do now?" Clay asked as Pentecost continued to mentally flip through his options.

Pentecost silently prayed over what to do before sharing his plan via the GRID with Reverb. After a moment of prayer – followed by a brief moment of protest and correction of the idea – Reverb gave an affirming nod and

Pentecost then verbally shared the plan with Clay.

"We're going to have to split up. Clay, go back outside and make sure that this exit point is secure for me to make it back out while Reverb helps Cord 7. Once you're finished Clay, send SongBird to help Cord 4 and Reverb will send Carpenter over to help Cord 5 before moving to help cover the other Cords. Once the tunnel is secure enough for you to maintain it alone, send NightOwl to pick up and relocate some of the other Defenders before heading up to help Cord 2 in the air."

"And what about you?" Clay asked as Reverb began to run down the hall to help his friends.

"I'm going to go deal with Simon; he chose to place more ComBots on the outside because he's overconfident and because he knew that I wouldn't underestimate him and take you guys in there. Now get out there, we don't have much time."

Clay picked up on his urgency and ran out after Reverb.

Pentecost turned around and began to move deeper into the Sorcerer's dark lair, his sword now glowing brightly because of the heat of battle.

Reverb ran out of the tunnel door and powerfully leapt in the direction of Cord 7, the mountainside rushing beneath him as he descended.

"Get ready to jump!" he messaged what was left of the cord as he approached.

They glanced up in his direction as he shouted, "NOW!"

They jumped just as he slammed into the ground and sent a shockwave out from the place of impact that through several of the ComBots backward and jarred several of their wire connections loose; the ground again rippled outward and threw many more ComBots down and injured them.

"Boy am I glad to see you," Carpenter said, wiping his forehead; he had several cuts along his arms and a few other injuries but looked like he would survive the day.

"Help has arrived," Reverb said, "But I need to send you over to help Maestro and Jade before the ComBots start attacking us again."

"Okay," Carpenter nodded and asked, "How are we going to do that?"

"Take Your Cainium-Wood and wrap yourself up in it like a mummy," Reverb replied. "Just make sure that there are two handles – one at your shoulders and the other at your knees – for me to grab onto."

"Okay. How's that supposed to help?" Catamount asked, looking up from examining a laser burn on her left calf that was still healing.

"It'll keep him from getting whiplash when I throw him." Reverb answered.

"What the heck?" Carpenter asked alarmed, his body was already held immobile by his Cainium-Wood incasing.

"I'm going to throw you up in the direction of Cord 5, and when you start dropping reform the Cainium-Wood into a glider so you can make it to them."

"You're serious about this?" Catamount asked rising to her feet and moving towards them.

"Oh yeah. Now take a step back, and be ready to finish up with these ComBots until NightOwl comes to pick you up."

Catamount stepped back as Reverb grabbed the two

handles on Carpenter's back.

"You ready, bro?" Reverb asked balancing Carpenter in his arms.

"Let's do this!" Carpenter replied, trying to seem more confident than we really was as he dangled in Reverb's firm grip.

Reverb readied himself and spun around several times before releasing Carpenter like a rocket up the mountain.

"That was totally awesome, bro!" Carpenter yelled down as he formed his Cainium-Wood wings and began his descent.

Reverb turned to Catamount as several of the ComBots began to stir and reinforcements arrived from the air. "I know you're tired," he said to motivate her, "but we need to hold them off and keep fighting together."

Catamount nodded and readied her claws for battle.

When Clay made it out of the tunnel, he saw a ComBot trailing behind SongBird and threw his hand forward to snatch it from the air and yank it into the ground below and lassoed another ComBot that was preparing to fire a laser blast at NightOwl and broke its neck against a tree.

"What's going on?" SongBird asked as she neared her brother.

"We're going to take out these ComBots while you go help Cord 4. Go!" Clay motioned to his sister to take off.

SongBird nodded and took off as NightOwl got closer.

"Go ahead and check in with the other Cords and relocate some of the Defenders," Clay called up to her, "and then go help Cord 2 in the air. I've got things covered here."

"You're sure you got this, man?" NightOwl asked phasing to allow an electrical blast to pass through her.

"Yeah, I'm sure," Clay replied grabbing the ComBot's head and slamming it into the ground. "Just get going. If any Cord can spare a member carry them to a group that needs them. Check with Reverb if you need to communicate with all the groups."

NightOwl nodded and flew off in the direction of Reverb while Clay continued to take hold of the various ComBots in the area to cover her movement and secure the exit for Pentecost.

Meanwhile Pentecost had made his way to the center of the Komplo base, a large pentagram had been carved perfectly within the center of a large circle and several other pagan symbols and markings covered the floor and walls of the five sided room. The strange symbols would have almost had their own appearance of beauty in their symmetric arrangement and positioning had they not also had a dark and sinister presence about them.

Pentecost readied his sword in front of him and proceeded cautiously and a large gargoylic mask along the wall to his right came to life and flew towards him with its fangs ready to bite down on him. Pentecost swung his sword to meet the mask and it sliced cleanly in two, the edges seared from the heat of Pentecost's blade and the smell of burning flesh filled the room.

An ornate hexagram shifted on the wall to his left and the room began to lurch and shift; a large block came out from the wall behind him and he had to jump to avoid being tripped up by it as more protrusions began to move about the room and the room itself began to flip around him. As Pentecost struggled to maintain his bearings, a tile from the floor – which was now just to his right – shot outward and knocked the sword from his hands.

Pentecost outstretched his hand and used the air in the room to pull his sword back to his hand before stabbing the heated blade into the ground as it rotated back beneath his feet and the room steadied itself and the various protrusions slowly returned to their proper places.

"Enough of these games, Simon," Pentecost called out into the shadows. "I doubt you traveled all the way from Kalmar for this."

"Why, Timothy," the Sorcerer called back as he entered the room behind Pentecost, "I had the earnest expectation that you would enjoy my warm welcome. It was the least I could do for an old friend, especially after the manner in which you and your companions welcomed me into your charming headquarters."

Pentecost turned and looked into the face of the Sorcerer, his face grinning with a mocking expression of glee. The Sorcerer carried the large double-edged spear of Nimrod and his black robes flurried around him.

"Do you recognize this Timothy?" the Sorcerer taunted as he twirled the spear before him. "I went through a great deal of pain and coin to acquire this beautiful weapon.

Pentecost's sword, now hot from the previous skirmishes and its temperature steadily rising, burst into flames.

The Sorcerer's smile darkened with twisted pleasure, "I was planning on restraining myself, but since you seem eager to end your life..." the Sorcerer twirled the spear around and an eerie green glow surrounded the weapon, "I shall be most pleased to oblige your desire; for old time's sake."

Pentecost moved forward and cut downward at the Sorcerer and wrapped his blade around to the right after Simon had moved the spear above his head with both hands to block the blade. The Sorcerer released the spear with his right hand and moved it around to block Pentecost's attack.

"I was most impressed at the manner in which you retrieved your weapon, Timothy," the Sorcerer commented after he pushed Pentecost back away from himself. "Might it be that you have increased in the knowledge of your abilities?"

The Sorcerer shifted his grip to hold the shaft as though it were a longsword and struck out at Pentecost, the two weapons met with another volley of cuts and parries.

"You're not the only one full of surprises, Sorcerer." Pentecost replied flatly as they locked in a power struggle.

"Why, Timothy?" The Sorcerer chided, "Again with such formality? Whatever happened to our friendship?"

The two pushed away from each other and Pentecost parried a thrust and countered with a diagonal cut down from the Sorcerer's right shoulder. The Sorcerer met the cut and scrambled to defend against Pentecost's continued attacks.

"You ended our friendship when you sided with the occult and turned your back on the Way." Pentecost said without a break in his attacks. "I still pray for Simon to embrace the Light of God, but I have no trust in or concern for the Sorcerer as he lurks in the darkness."

"You're not still sore about that whole branding incident are you?" The Sorcerer asked in order to turn the conversation in a manner that would hopefully infuriate his opponent; and draw the attention away from himself.

"You taught me to be discerning concerning human nature and how to handle betrayal," Pentecost answered without taking the bait and nearly sent the Sorcerer's spear clattering out of his hands with a powerful slice.

The Sorcerer's mood darkened as up until this point he had managed to hold his ground against Pentecost, but now he was pushed into a steady retreat. Pentecost had been pushing him back against the wall and now he had nowhere to move.

The Sorcerer then struck the ground with his spear and the green cloud surrounding it enveloped him and he disappeared. Pentecost readied himself as he waited for the strike that he knew was moments away.

It was as though someone tapped him on the shoulder and signaled him, but Pentecost knew exactly when and where the Sorcerer appeared and spun around wildly, kicking his leg out and striking the Sorcerer's knuckles hard, knocking the spear far out of his hands and pounding the hilt of his blade into his tormentor's face sending the Sorcerer careening backward to the ground and slumped against the side of the room.

With a chuckle the Sorcerer rubbed the place where Pentecost had struck him, "Well now that was intriguing, wasn't it? But what is of greater interest to me is what you now propose to do with me? I find it hard to believe that you would execute me now that I'm unarmed, Timothy. Or does your hatred for me run deeper than you admit?"

Pentecost hesitated for a moment and knew that the Sorcerer was trying to goad him into arguing with him and considering the statement. In order to verbally argue with him, Pentecost would have to consider the words of his enemy along his own emotions and would be giving the Sorcerer a foothold in his mind, so instead of answering Pentecost extinguished the flames surrounding his sword and stabbed the still hot blade into the Sorcerer's thigh.

The Sorcerer screamed in agony and groaned a second time as Pentecost removed the blade. "I know that your demon friends will keep you alive as long as they feel they have need of you," Pentecost said as he used the heat from the blade to sear the wound shut, "but they won't be able to remove this scar or restore the full use of your leg. God is giving you a warning, Simon; you cannot defeat Him, and you will lose much more than your leg if you continue to try."

"And you'll lose your family for this!" The Sorcerer spat clutching his leg as it continued to agonize him. "I'll find them, the brothers you spoke of and that woman of promise you married. I'll destroy them all, Timothy. By the powers of Satan, I swear it!"

Pentecost ignored him and turned to face what else he knew was in the room, for he had sensed from the air currents that there was more to be seen. In his pain, the Sorcerer had lost control over the illusion that he had formed to conceal what was truly in the room and Pentecost saw the massive, spiraling tower of machinery that filled the center of the room and the large monitor that revealed the locations of all the viral ComBots the Komplo had in its command. What caught Pentecost's attention was that there were six orbiting the Earth above the United States; four were distributed over the continent while the remaining two hovered over Hawaii and Alaska.

"Enjoying the view?" The Sorcerer groaned. "Those ComBots were mutated to contain enough unstable electrium to be the nuclear trigger for a massive EMP strike against America. In a day your nation will fall; commercial Babylon will fall and the pillaging lead by the Islamic Syrians will ravage your land. I learned long ago that it's quite difficult to fight against prophecy; 'tis interesting to now be fighting *with* it against you."

Pentecost continued to examine the machine and noticed an energy gauge that was monitoring the rising power level of a large laser at the top of the tower.

"There's a laser focused on each of your precious Defenders, Timothy," the Sorcerer said, still clutching his wounded leg with his hands. "The ComBots have been studying their abilities and analyzing them for weaknesses and have sent that information to me."

The Sorcerer waved with his hand and Pentecost's mind was flooded with images of each of his students being struck by the laser from this device.

"None of them will survive, Timothy. That is my farewell gift to you." The Sorcerer chuckled, "You've been fighting to your own demise."

Pentecost realized that once the device was fully charged it would send out a laser so strong that it would burn through the Cainium-Wood and giadan abilities of Carpenter and Jade, would overload the dechomain field of Plasma, and would be sustained long enough to wear out Safeguard and cause her to faint so that none of the heroes would be able to survive the attack and there would be no outrunning or outmaneuvering it.

Pentecost flew to the top of the tower and continued to pray over his options. The Sorcerer scoffed, "Be reasonable, Timothy. Everyone has their limits, even you. There's no possible way that you could absorb that much thermal energy."

Pentecost was shown a solution and knew what he had to do. He started by informing the others that things were about to get messy. "Guys, we've got less than a minute before an EMP takes out all electrical technology in America. Professor, you need to get out of the Air Defender, now. And Clay, make your way down and help one of the other Cords; I'm not going to be needing that exit anymore."

"Professor," Alkali called through the radio system, "You've got to get out of that jet before it crashes."

"I conquer, Alkali," he replied as he continued to maneuver the Air Defender to avoid being taken over by the ComBots. "However, if this jet is overrun by the ComBots then we will be in a most dire situation. Also, if this jet begins to plummet without an alteration in its course it will destroy several cities below us or even land atop of the Defenders."

The Professor continued to avoid the ComBots while trying to gain distance from the mountain and choosing as best he could a path away from the towns and cities.

Alkali noticed that NightOwl had joined them in the air at this point and called out, "Arcade, Plasma, I'm pulling out; NightOwl will take my place."

"Where are you going?" NightOwl called out as she removed the head from a ComBot.

"I've got to make sure the Air Defender doesn't destroy some city down there," he said taking off after the jet and blasting away the various ComBots trailing it.

"What are you going to do?" she called back through the communication link.

"I might need to hold up the jet so the Professor can glide over the buildings."

"Alkali, that is a dangerous move on your part," the Professor replied and the jet spun to avoid a laser blast, "we don't know what that amount of energy produced by your suit will do to you. Your suit is highly unstable and it could

_"

"It could kill me or send me back into the Negative – I get it Doc – but if I don't try hundreds of people will be killed. If I've got to lay down my life for them to live, then that's what I'm going to do. Besides, if I was able to escape the Negative once, I should be able to manage it again."

"Alkali, don't do this," NightOwl pleaded, "I'm the only one allowed to kill my SOS trainer, which means that you're not allowed to overcharge your suit and kill yourself."

"Sorry, Beth," he replied without slowing down or altering his course, "this is part of what I do as a Defender, and I can't hold back now."

Pentecost inserted his blade into the opening that served as the barrel for the laser gun.

The Sorcerer struggled to rise to his feet as his leg continued to throb, "You insult me by assuming that I wouldn't have prepared for something as simple as you hacking into my machine to destroy it? Even your *lahat* blade cannot pierce the hex I have placed on that device."

Pentecost didn't bother correcting him and informing him that his blade was really a *mal'ak* blade and superior to the *lahat* because he couldn't cut through the protective hex anyway. "I already told you once Simon," Pentecost replied instead, looking up from the laser gun and through the heat already rising from it, "you're not the only one that's full of surprises."

Pentecost grabbed the hilt with his right hand and laid on top of it to cover as much of the laser cannon as he could with his body and could feel the rising temperature within the cannon and the heating up of his own blade as he readied himself; any moment now and the laser would be ready to fire.

Above ground the Defenders continued to struggle against the ComBots and several of them were nearly overrun when the EMP strike planned by the Sorcerer took place and all round America technology ceased to exist; cars ceased to function, planes began to fall from the sky, and patients on life support began to die as the hospitals lost power and all electronic components – including backup generators – were rendered useless by the EMP.

The only blessing was that the ComBots were also affected as the giadan cover didn't protect the circuitry in their computer brains and their generator hearts. Arcade's suit even seemed to be adversely affected but he managed to remain in the air and slowly descend to the ground as the ComBots continued to collapse and Virus himself began to convulse as his body refused to cooperate before he too fell to the ground in defeat.

The Professor fought to try and steer the Air Defender as Alkali positioned himself underneath it; Silver City was within sight and – according to Alkali's best guess – was directly in the path of this collapsing jet. Alkali pushed upward and tried to give the Air Defender as much lift as he could to help it glide over the rapidly approaching city while the Professor pulled hard on the controls to help maneuver the plane away from the city.

The laser fired beneath Pentecost and the intense heat generated began to be absorbed by him and his sword until they both began to glow and radiate with the intense heat.

Pentecost yelled under the strain being put upon him as he focused all his attention on the laser cannon beneath him and the Sorcerer could only watch in disbelief as the hero attempted to accomplish the impossible.

Alkali cried out and pushed upward against the massive jet above him and managed to lift it a few feet and as he kept straining and pushing upward his suit began to glow brighter and brighter, increasing in temperate and brilliance as the energy pulsating through it continued to intensify. Suddenly, there was a brilliant flash of bright blue light and the heat pushed the Air Defender upward into the air so that it would continue to glide over the city, but when the light dimmed Alkali was nowhere to be found.

Pentecost finally achieved what he had been striving for and had managed to molecularize himself and the laser cannon that would have incinerated his teammates and students.

The Sorcerer stared on in disbelief when the cannon perched atop of his towering machinery – along with Pentecost draped over it – suddenly vanished and seconds later he was thrown backward as heated molecules of Pentecost and the laser rapidly expanded after such an excessive amount of thermal energy was instantaneously molecularized.

A green cloud enveloped the Sorcerer to protect him from the blast as a portal was opened by the exuberant amount of thermal energy that was condensed to molecules. A handful of dinosaurs from Kalmar marched through the portal before it closed second later with an equally aggressive explosion as when it opened.

The battle had ended, but the war had just begun. The Sorcerer would not rest until this planet was under his control and Yahweh was defeated to the glory of Satan.

† † † † † † †

Our Discipled Defenders regrouped after the battle and carefully carried their fallen comrades home for proper burial. All except for Pentecost and Firecracker who were both declared missing in action, Alkali who was trapped in the Negative Zone, and the Professor who had been consumed in the wreckage of the Air Defender.

The Sorcerer had sealed himself within his séance room and concealed it with a spell so that none of the Defenders would discover him as they searched the base in hopes that they would find Pentecost, Alkali, or Firecracker somewhere inside and they destroyed any weapons that they found during their search.

Once they returned to their headquarters, SongBird asked the question that they were all feeling: "What are we going to do now?"
Reverb looked up and answered, "After we rest ourselves, we work at the ministry that God has called us to and help save as many lives as we can. Everyone go home to your families and make sure that they're safe and meet back here as soon as you can; we have a call to inherit."

Epilogue

London, England   Monday, September 16, 2044

"News reports from around the world are flooding in concerning the fall of America," a British news anchor reported to his television audience, "as a massive EMP strike occurred earlier this morning for the Americans and has decimated the nation."

The video feed then switched over to a female news reporter working the story as it developed, "Massive ocean liners float off of the American coastlines as they narrowly missed being caught up in the strike against America and being rendered immobile by the EMP as they approach to deliver their cargo. Many manufacturing corporations around the world are now suffering as their largest customer – the American people – are now no longer able to buy their goods."

The video switched over to showcase the economic collapse that was occurring worldwide as businesses found that they no longer had anyone to sell to.

"Satellite and drone images reveal that absolute terror has taken over the American people as massive riots now fill city streets, along with countless attacks from seemingly Islamic militia groups; the carnage is devastating. What's worse is that there are enhanced humans rising from the ashes that seem bent on adding to the destruction."

Overhead images of the Widow and Switchblade together with another villain moving through a large crowd that had gathered at a large church appeared on the screen as they continued to attack and murder several people; the new recruit was wearing the black garb of a ninja has he moved towards the crowd while swinging his swords as Switchblade threw various blades and Widow used her webbing to capture several members of the crowd before moving into the fray.

The video cut away just after the first sign of blood and switched over to show Virus – who had used his mindvoice to link into the computers inside the Komplo base and make himself a new robotic body – moving through a large city, firing lasers at the towers that remained alongside as two cybernetic twins moved around and added to the chaos; the younger sister had robotic legs that moved about at high speeds as she crashed through small buildings and vehicles to terrorize the people while her older brother was able to lift and throw vehicles with his metallic arms.

Again, before things got too graphic, the image cut away and showed the Sorcerer and Acedia moving through another once bustling city with two unknown companions, unleashing their mystical powers to create further destruction. The man with them wore a red karate uniform with golden straps and accents while the woman was adorned with several crystals dangling from her earrings, necklace, and bracelets and had a bright pink top with flowing sleeves along with lavender leggings and magenta boots.

The red ninja swirled his hands in a circle and pulled back his right fist as his hands began to glow and after a moment he threw his right arm forward and opened his palm as a golden ball of energy flew forward and struck a parked automobile as Acedia walked through the streets and threw painful psychic blasts at the people, the Sorcerer limped along and used various incantations to move objects or destroy them and the other woman moved forward to another parked car as the crystal around her neck glowed brightly imbuing her with enough strength to lift the vehicle and throw it into a nearby building; a man from inside the building retaliated by firing several shots out at her, but the crystal glowed again and a protective barrier formed around her until the man's gun was emptied and she slowly approached the window where the man stood and he backed away inside the building as a bright light shone from both the crystal and within the window.

The camera cut back to the female reporter and she shared with her audience, "We do not know where these individuals came from, what the nature of their abilities are, or what their purposes are. We do know that there does also seem to be a group of enhanced individuals who stand opposed to this destruction and have been fighting against the militias and the villainous enhanced. However, whether these 'Defenders' will prove to be worse for the world than those they fight against is yet to be determined."

The camera again switched over to the news anchor for his closing remarks, "As we close off this report I can only say that I myself am horrified at what is taking place and that immediate action must be taken to stabilize the world economy and bring some measure of security to the people of the global community. From Phillip Reynolds, good night and God help us all."

Glossary

Arenea was the first realm explored by Joseph Stevens. The inhabitants of this realm are skilled at using the GRID to produce a mindsong. The realm was originally discovered by Kinnowr, one of Jubal's sons.

Cainium is a metal discovered in the realm of Myathis that is several times denser than titanium.

Cainium-Wood is named after the element cainium and is several times denser than ironwood.

A **Komplo** is the name for a group of warriors that position themselves against the Church and the Defender Corps. In general terms, each realm will always have its own Komplo to deal with.

A **ComBot** is a specially programed, biological robot designed for extensive combative training. Timothy and Joseph Stevens have programed them and installed several interdimensional components to ensure their security and effectiveness.

Dechomain is a Myathian artificially manufactured non-metal that absorbs nuclear and electro-magnetic energy.

The **Defender Corps** was started under the supervision of Rick Stevens and Charlie Maxwell and was intended to be a means by which the SOS Corps could enhance its effectiveness by training and equipping its soldiers to be Defenders. Timothy and Joseph Stevens were the first to be trained and equipped as Defenders.

The **Defender Discipleship Program** was started in faith by Timothy and Joseph Stevens in order to train younger men and women to be diligent students of God and to equip them to be capable Defenders of the Church.

A **Doorway** is an opening or a portal between realms. The opening of a Doorway will emit extremely high amounts of GRID Signal.

The **Earth Moving Ants** Devices (EMA) were invented by the Osrian scientists Dr. Antoine Tumin and - Petric . The device communicates with the local ants to construct massive underground structures.

Earthian is the interdimensional term used to describe people and things that have their direct origin in the realm of Earth.

Electrium is an extremely reactive alkaloid element that has been synthetically produced by Myathian chemists.

Giadan is an extremely malleable and conductive metal produced in the laboratories of Myathis.

The **God Revealing Internal Dialect (GRID)** is a mental communication link that God had established to allow an individual to become a conduit of God's power in a unique way, revealing and proclaiming His power, as He directs, to the world; also known as a mindvoice.

GRID Aware is one of the terms used to describe someone that can make a GRID Connection, accessing the abilities God designed specifically for them.

A **GRID Code** is a mental 'program' that is used to produce a specific effect based on the GRID Code installed.

GRID lag is the fatigue produced by excessive use of one's GRID Connection.

GRID Signal is the traceable energy put off by the use of a GRID Connection. The strength of the GRID Signal indicates the strength of the Voicer, or the size of the task completed via the GRID.

The **Information Network Scanner (INS)** is a filtering program used to gather, analyze, filter, and present the most current news locally, nationally, and globally.

Instant Nuclear Size External Combat Technology (INSECT) is an Osrian invention that allows the instantaneous alteration of the Planck length of the atoms in a given subject, effectively altering the size of the subject.

The **Inter-Dimensional Communications System (IDC)** is a compilation of technology from the seven realms created by Joseph and Timothy Stevens to establish the means for reliably-consistent interdimensional communication.

Ishshah is the name of the *mal'ak* sword possessed by Rykard Sevecian and Pentecost

The **Isle of Stability** is a stable extension of the periodic table that is only theorized as a possibility on earth, but has been discovered and heavily utilized in the realm of Myathis.

Kalmar is the original homeland of Rick and Grace Stevens; the realm specializes in using the GRID to write a special code that can be programmed to stable rocks or metals and have a variety of effects. The realm was discovered by Lahat, one of the sons of Adam.

A *lahat* is a type of weapon that has been programed with a GRID Code allowing it to perform various effects.

Maglevium is an extremely rare superconductive metal made by chemists in the realm of Myathis that allows for instant levitation.

A *mal'ak* is a type of weapon that has been forged by angels and given to choice humans to allow them to take part in the supernatural battle.

The **Myathian Automated Production Tech (MAPT) Device** is a machine that produces and programs the parts for various technology and equipment used by the SOS Corps, the Defender Corps, and the Defender Discipleship Program.

A **memory orb** is a mental data package that allow the complete transfer of a person's selected memory via the GRID.

A **mindsong** is a mental song that produces various effects by stimulating the emotions of its hearer or by orchestrating the movement of specific objects. The emotion stimulated as well as the size and density of the objects effected are determined by the type of mindsong.

Mindvoice is a popular interdimensional name for a GRID, especially among the non-Earthian population.

Myathis is a realm of scientific and technological achievements. The Myathian scientists specialize in nanotechnology and chemistry. However, the advancements made with the discovery of the 'Isle of Stability' have come with a high price. The realm of Myathis was discovered by Choresh, the son of Tubal-Cain.

Mygas is a realm that was discovered by Tanneph, one of the sons of Adam. Here the people have discovered a way to create biotech wings that are surgically attached to the spinal cord at infancy and allow the individual to operate the wings upon adulthood via the GRID. Certain Mygan countries have developed technology that enables them to instantly filter oxygen from water allowing for individuals to readily explore the ocean.

Natsar is the *lahat* shield possessed by Safeguard that allows her to create cainium strength energy fields and render objects invisible.

The **Negative Zone** is a place between realms. This false reality is a place of endless possibilities of one's own creation. In the Negative, the deepest desires of man's heart can instantly become all too real in various manifestations.

The **Nervous System Stimulation for Hostile Suppression** (NSSHS) program is a Myathian peacekeeping weapon designed to stimulate the nerves of the victim in such a way as to produce the programed sensation and intensity of pain without inflicting the necessary bodily harm to be for such a feeling to occur

Osria is a realm discovered by Rehmes, another of the sons of Adam. Rehmes is also the original inspiration for the invention of the Osrian INSECT suits.

Organic Light Emitting Device (OLED) is an organic nanotechnology perfected long ago by Myathian scientists but also experimented with by Earthian scientists. OLEDs are basically flexible, high-definition, organic, electronic screens that have a wide variety of potential uses.

The **Personal Apartment Network Intelligence Computer** (PANIC) is the personal computer network designed and utilized by Rodger Jones.

Sahar is the *mal'ak* bow owned by Grace Sevecian and Pentecost.

Sangáti is a relatively small and isolated realm discovered by Miqneh, the son of Jabal. Sangáti warriors utilize the GRID to enhance their senses and reflexes. Sangátian weapons and abilities mimic that of land animals.

The **Special Ops S.H.E.E.P. Corps** (SOS Corps) is the Earthian organization that is responsible for the establishment of the Defender Corps. The title is intended to remind its members of its humble goal and complete dependence upon God. The acronym S.H.E.E.P. itself stands for the Savior's Heavenly Empowered Extraction Personnel and this too is designed to remind agents of their life's mission.

The **Welcome Center** is the codename for the main entrance point into the SOS Headquarters and is specifically designed as a strategic defense location to cause for an easy warding off any kind of invasion or attack from the outside.

A **Voicer** is one that is capable of using a Mindvoice or is GRID aware.

Xenon is one of the noble gases and glows bright violet when ionized

Lightning Source UK Ltd.
Milton Keynes UK
UKHW042100300519
343406UK00003B/28/P